Liberty Bell Center

LEV. XXV V X. PROCLAIM
N PHILADA BY ORDER
PASS AND STOW
PHILADA
MDCCLIII

LIBERTY BELL CENTER

BOHLIN CYWINSKI JACKSON

edited by rodolphe el-khoury

foreword by mary bomar

essays by rodolphe el-khoury, richard sommer,
laurie olin, and bernard cywinski

BUILDING MONOGRAPH
series directed & designed by oscar riera ojeda

ORO *editions*

Contents

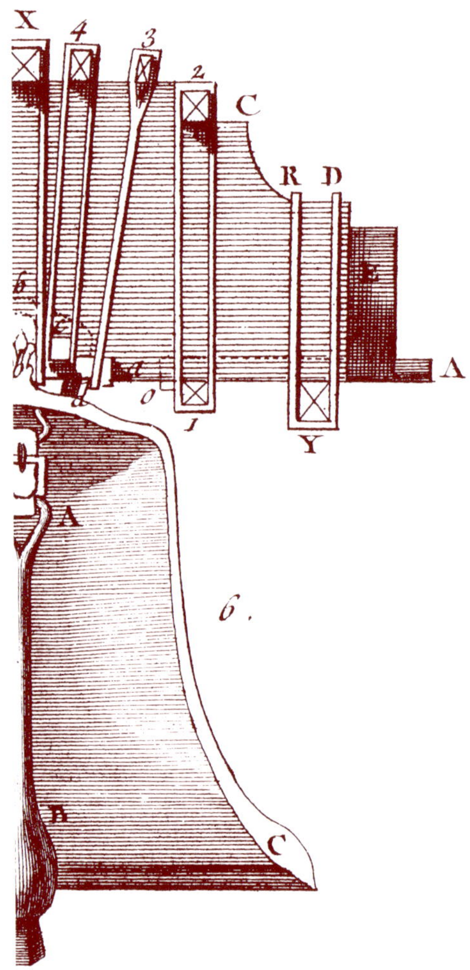

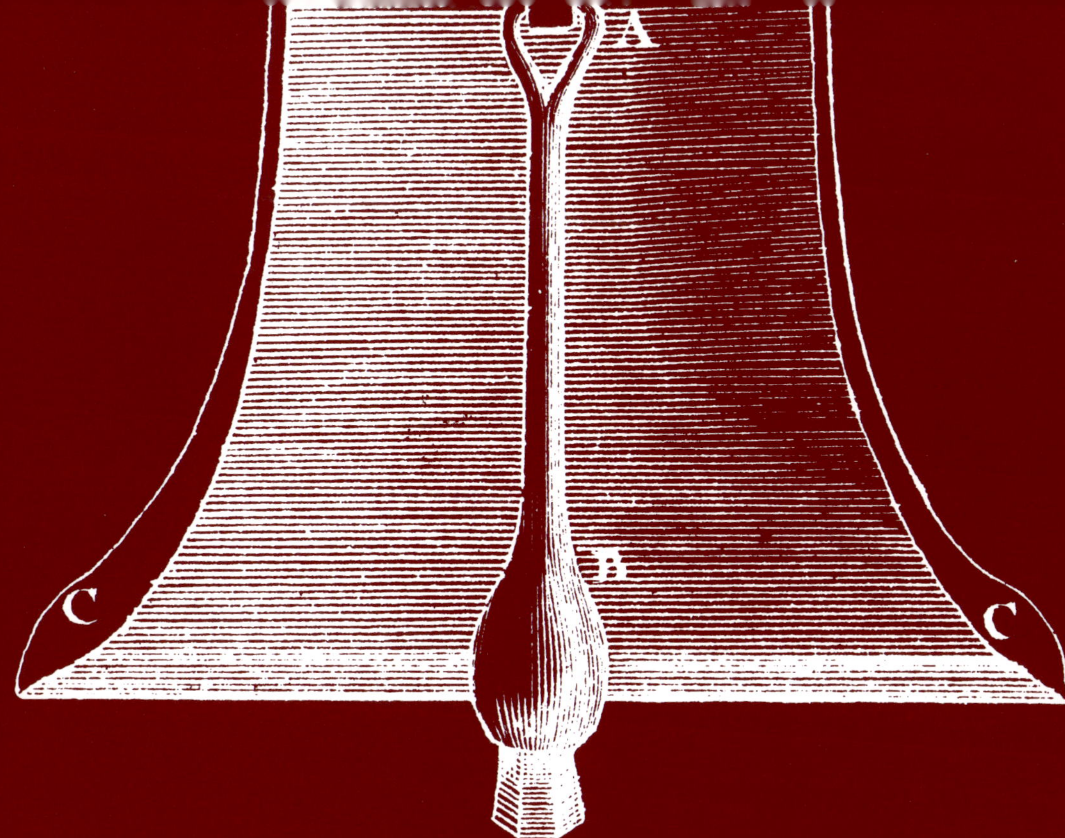
A
B
C
C

X
3
4
4
3
2
2
C
C
D
R
R
D
E
b
c
c
a
a
o
o
d
d
1
1
Y
Y

Wo

rds

Acknowledgements

This book pays tribute to a great building and to the creative efforts invested in it. I would like to thank the National Park Service and the team of architects, planners, city officials, community leaders, and builders who brought us Liberty Bell Center and inspired this book. In particular, my gratitude goes to Bernard Cywinski, whose architectural vision is the main driving force behind the building; Kenneth Mitchell, who was the project manager; and Jeff Lew, project architect for Liberty Bell Center who also played major roles in this book's creation. Thanks are also extended to Michael Conner, Marika Simms, and Sterling Alexander III, of Bohlin Cywinski Jackson; and Karen Stevens, archivist for Independence National Historical Park, for their assistance in assembling the materials for this book. The collaboration with Laurie Olin on the Independence National Historical Park and the master plan set up the most favorable conditions for the development of the center. I am grateful for the insights he generously offered in this book. I also thank Richard Sommer for the historical and critical perspective he brought to the subject. I am indebted to Oscar Riera Ojeda and Gordon Goff at ORO *editions* for supporting this book and wisely guiding its editorial development and production.

—Rodolphe el-Khoury

Foreword

"Yet still while the sweat pours from his brow, that old Bell-keeper hurls the iron tongue, and still–boom–boom–boom–the Bell speaks to the city and to the world."

—From *Legends of the American Revolution*, 1847, by George Lippard

Eloquent in its silence, the Liberty Bell still calls the world to hear its stories. Tales of freedom achieved and liberty denied, of protest and commemoration, of a Bell that stands as symbol of our nation–imperfect but enduring.

Echoing the Founders who forged a new nation, the National Park Service and its partners developed a radical transformation of the Independence Mall–a brilliant plan that included the National Constitution Center, the Independence Visitor Center, and a new home for the Liberty Bell.

The challenge for the Park Service and the design team was to fashion a space appropriate for the icon of freedom, to give millions of visitors the opportunity to learn about the Liberty Bell, and to have that singular life experience as they came face to face with the Bell itself.

While history will always be the final judge, our visitors' feet are their ballots, and the result is a landslide victory for the Liberty Bell Center. For the many dedicated National Park Service employees, partners, and members of the design team, the move of the Liberty Bell in October 2003 was a defining moment in our lives–the Bell continues to speak to the world.

Mary A. Bomar, National Park Service, Northeast Regional Director, former Superintendent of Independence National Historical Park

Introduction

Liberty Bell Center and its Double

Rodolphe el-Khoury

On October 3, 2003, the Liberty Bell Center, the new home of the Liberty Bell, was opened to the public. The building, designed by Bohlin Cywinski Jackson, is one of the highlights of Philadelphia's reconfigured Independence Mall and the latest achievement in a long planning and building process that continues to unfold with the maturation of Independence National Historical Park.

Laurie Olin, one of the key players on the planning team, gives a detailed account of the process in this book, while Richard Sommer provides an historical perspective on the mall's evolution and the building's present-day context.

As noted by Bernard Cywinski, the architect who led the design team, the building seeks to embody the ideas that drive the master plan as well as the values we associate with the bell. This is a relatively small building, dedicated primarily to the display of a single historical artifact. But given the importance of the Liberty Bell, and its resonance in the international community, such aspirations are not misplaced or unexpected. Cywinski explains how ideas are translated from the ambitious program to every aspect and detail of the building.

Oblique view The architects' intentions are perhaps best evidenced by the way in which visitors encounter the Liberty Bell and Independence Hall. Mitchell/Giurgola's pavilion, the former home of the Liberty Bell, offered a frontal view of the hall as a distant backdrop to the Liberty Bell, displayed on axis in a glazed hall. 1 The Bell Chamber in Bohlin Cywinski Jackson's building is positioned and designed to yield an oblique view of Independence Hall behind the bell. 2

1

Both buildings effectively exploit a familiar rhetorical device by displaying the bell with a direct visual connection to Independence Hall in the background.

2

1 Former Liberty Bell Pavilion 2 View of the new Bell Chamber 3 Serlio drawing 4 Galli-Bibiena drawing

The shift from frontal view to oblique view is a small but critical difference. It is analogous to a much-studied shift in the evolution of scenography, from one-point to two-point perspective. Thanks to ingenious designs by the Galli-Bibienas, the family of scenographers who dominated the European scene for several generations, the taste in stage-set design shifted very rapidly in the early eighteenth century from static frontal views, well illustrated in Serlio's familiar genre studies, to a Baroque model where scenes are set obliquely, in dynamic tension with the proscenium. 3

The Galli-Bibienas' *scena per angolo* was much admired and immediately adopted on the European stage, especially in Italy. In retrospect we attribute its success to a resonance with emerging theatrical practices that reflected fundamental shifts in the Baroque worldview. 4

3

Connected Spectatorship The oblique view extended the space of the stage virtually into the auditorium, bringing the scene closer to the real world. With the Galli-Bibienas, the action that was tightly bound and framed by the proscenium was allowed, at least conceptually, to spill into the world of the spectator.

In Serlio's scenographic model, the implicit assumption is that the viewer is looking through the proscenium at a world that is separate and different. It functions as a window into another fictional realm that is governed by different spatial/temporal laws and representational conventions.

The framed oblique view implies continuity between what is behind and what is in front of the frame. It imitates a visual structure commonly found in cities where public squares, streets, and buildings interlock in mutually framing perspectives.

On the Baroque stage, theatrical representation is highly stylized, but the oblique introduced a touch of naturalism in its imitation of urban experience. The frontal view places the stage and auditorium in polar opposition; the oblique engages them in a visual dynamic that is modeled after chance encounters in the city. The theatrical structure implied by the former is predicated on separation, both physical and conceptual, while the latter strives for connection.

The visual structure of Liberty Bell Center is most literally theatrical in the Bell Chamber. The theatrical model is evident in the anamorphic geometry of the room, which optimizes the staged view by means of a forced perspective. It is designed according to the Galli-Bibiena model: a one-point perspective (proscenium) framing a two-point perspective (scene).

Thanks to the oblique view, Independence Hall is experienced as part of the display in the foreground rather than a detached backdrop. It is dynamically pulled into the space of the exhibit, to directly engage with the bell in one continuous urban scene.

The connectedness is also enhanced by the hall's proximity to the bell. The close-up, exaggerated by the frame's accelerated perspective, restores a monumental quality to Independence Hall that was lost in the over-scaled park.

The connection is sustained throughout the building thanks to the glass curtain wall and the lightness of the support structure. Even in the exhibit space where common wisdom is prejudiced in favor of hermetic environments, the architects opted for transparency. Content, in conventional museological practice, is best delivered without interference. Bohlin Cywinski Jackson and Ueland Junker McCauley Nicholson, the exhibit designers, chose to open the building to the city and welcome interference from everyday life. They take this risk because they are committed to the ideas of openness, accessibility, and connectedness that drive the master plan.

The undulating granite wall strikes a contrasting note in this transparent environment. The design process is telling with regard to its conceptual origins and purpose in the built scheme. One of Cywinski's early sketches shows an excavated space, dipping down into the ground like an archaeological dig, perhaps exposing the foundation of the buildings that previously stood on the site. 5 The sketches place the main exhibit gallery between heavy retaining walls, within a material and spatial density that is entirely at odds with the airy transparency of the built structure. The dense, heavy, and coarsely textured stone wall–as well as a gently sloping paved floor–are vestiges of the excavated chamber. Both communicate a haptic sense of rootedness, a grounding in the particular conditions and archaeology of the site while the transparent curtain wall and the lucid superstructure optically resonate with a universal agenda: they evoke the realm of reason and abstraction. This ambivalence is found elsewhere and in different registers of experience. It is also evident in the ambiguous *parti*, combining the universal order of the grid with the willful demarcation of the linear plan.

Relative views The dynamic tension in the *scena per angolo* was also better suited to evolving literary sensibilities of the Baroque.

5 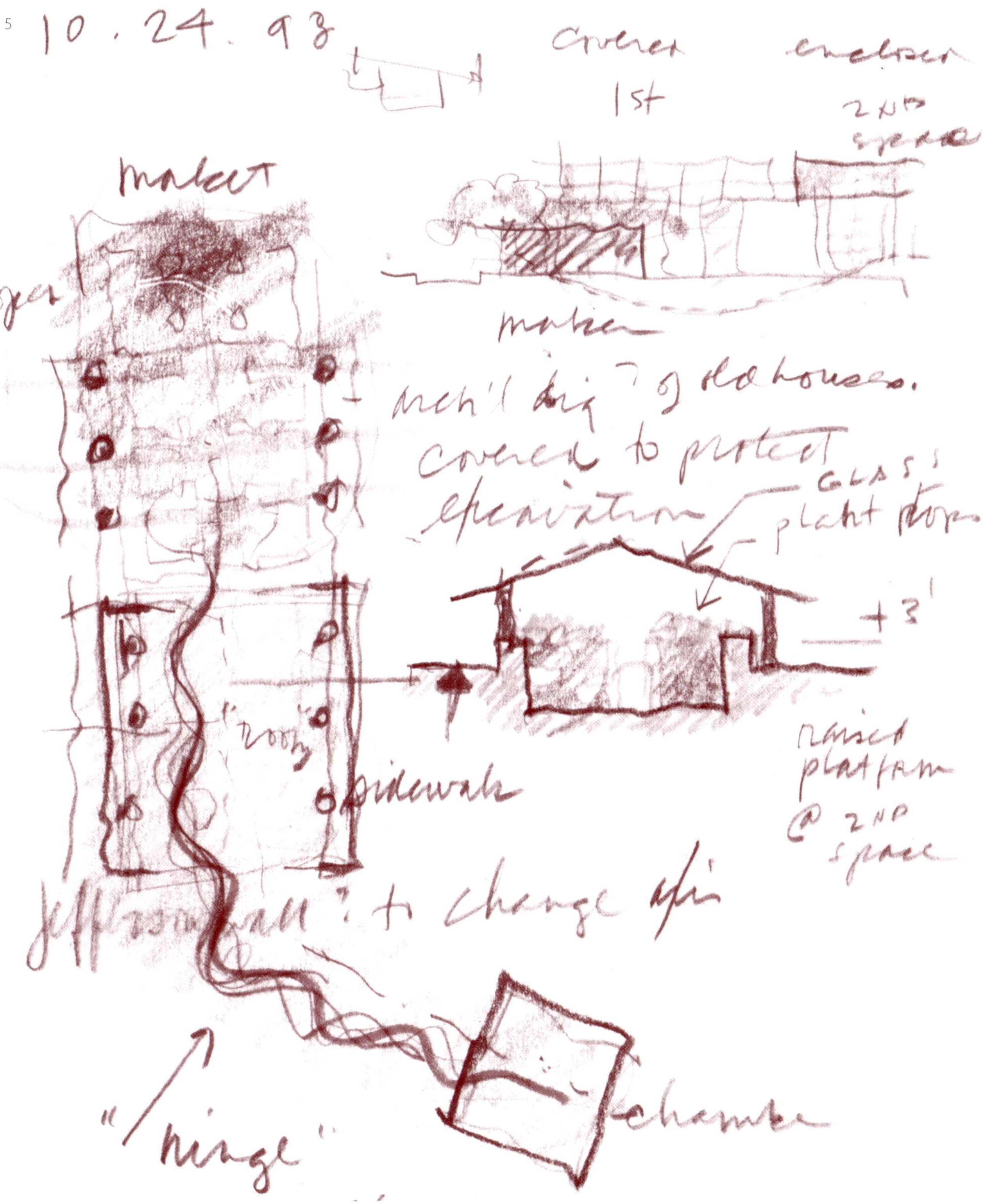

5 Initial sketch for Liberty Bell Center

It coincided with a departure from rigid classical archetypes in favor of more nuanced and conflicted characterizations–a reflection, no doubt, of structural transformations in the social fabric.

This is the time when Europe was still assimilating the material and psychological impact of the New World, as well as notions of an ever-expanding universe. The discovery process paved the way for new hybrid genres and relative frames of reference. There is only one correct frontal view in line with the axis of symmetry; there are an infinite number of oblique views, each with a unique perspective on a given scene. This fact also accounts for the overwhelming success of the *scena per angolo* in the eighteenth-century Italian opera house. In comparison to most European stages that catered principally to the privileged view from the royal box by aligning the vanishing point of the stage design with the position of the sovereign, the Italian scene was less hierarchical, and its audience less rigidly stratified. In Italy's theatres, the oblique view looked right from all angles; it is, in a sense, a democratic view.

In contrast to Serlio's stable and homogenous tableaux, the Galli-Bibienas' angled compositions spoke of complex and varied elements

6

7

dynamically held in a delicate and provisional balance. They also evidenced a shift from the assumed authority of a privileged and fixed view to the multiplicity of partial and relative revelations.

Bohlin Cywinski Jackson's Liberty Bell Center and Galli-Bibienas' stage set designs belong to very different worlds. The cultural and political circumstances behind their inception couldn't be more different. Yet they share a common intuition: the impulse to present the world as a partial, dynamic, and malleable construct.

Instead of the proper axial composition that would automatically telescope and naturalize the historic artifacts in a ready-made and fixed relationship, the Bell Chamber offers an arbitrary–or arbitrated–view, one among many possible others, in which bell and hall are brought into a strategic and provisional alignment.

The deliberate yet fleeting alignment suggests allegorical readings of dynamic and institutional forces at play in a democracy. Also, as stated in Richard Sommer's essay, it "provokes the idea that symbols are malleable and, more important, that history may still be in the making."

6, 7 Street grid with Liberty Bell Center plan overlay   8 Various plan concepts for the Bell Chamber   9 Rodolphe el-Khoury in front of the Liberty Bell

8

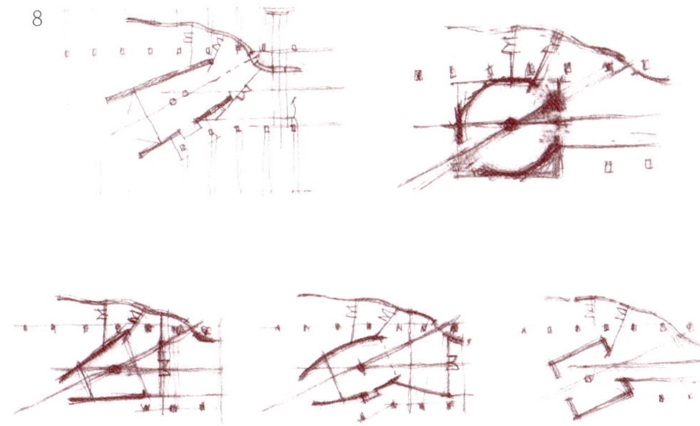

9

Virtual Architecture The highly charged bell/hall scene concluding a carefully designed procession through a chronologically arranged exhibit is the building's–and perhaps the site's–main destination. The procession, which is guided by the stone wall, is occasionally punctuated by perpendicular view corridors aligning with the urban grid. The sporadic intrusion of the cross-axis overlays the open-ended and field-like condition of the city over the directionality and purposefulness of the linear exhibit, rehearsing again the dialectic at play in this building–and, by allegorical extension, in the course and making of history. 6, 7

The lateral counterpoint diverts the visitor's attention sideways, to the urban surrounding, but doesn't distract from the main purpose and destination of the building. It is dramatically unveiled as one leaves the linear path and enters the Bell Chamber. This is a precisely orchestrated transition that the architects calibrated in countless studies. 8

The scene, the *raison d'être* of the building, has an iconic quality that visitors are compelled to record in a photograph, preferably including themselves in the shot–I had this inevitable impulse when I visited the building and, luckily, the architect was there to take the snapshot himself! 9

The composition, which no doubt will be reproduced in millions of photographs taken at the very same spot every year, is striking in its compositional and conceptual clarity. The bell is in the foreground, occupying the lower half of the field, graphically silhouetted against the brighter background. Independence Hall fills the whole frame behind, with the bell tower sitting exactly above the bell in the upper half of the picture.

An office tower with a giant corporate logo looms ominously on the right of the bell tower. In the axial view of Giurgola's pavilion, it stood behind the hall, dwarfing the monument with its overwhelming size. In the oblique close-up it is displaced to the side and reduced in scale. It is a manageable and welcome addition to the symbolic scene, a meaningful glitch that adds yet another shade of complexity to the mythological palette.

The bell, Independence Hall, and, most likely, the visitor, are all framed by the architecture, which here assumes a self-effacing

10

character. Up to this point the architecture is articulate to an extreme, obsessively crafting every connection with exquisite intricacy. In the Bell Chamber, the purpose and destination that it was set up for, it is uncharacteristically mute, a neutral frame that is meant to construct relationships rather than an elaborate architectural setting. Compare this scene to an exterior view of the chamber, and you get a good sense of the restraint and minimalism that were painstakingly invested in its design and construction. The machine-like exterior bristles with structure, layered revetments, and shading devices. It is a complex apparatus that is designed to make the bell/hall/subject scene possible and deceptively effortless while remaining unobtrusive. 10

In comparison, the chamber's interior is an exercise in deferential neutrality where subtle planimetric and sectional inflection are meant to enhance the framing function, rather than add formal intricacy. The Bell Chamber, in effect, is a giant camera that is meant for the production, recording, and dissemination of the bell/hall/subject scene–and the nuanced values that it captures in the angled view.

As an instrument of mass communication, we may think of it as the visual analogue to the Liberty Bell, an instrument that had served the same purpose aurally.

We may also recall that "chamber" and "camera" are, etymologically speaking, the same. The fact points to the *camera obscura* origin of the modern camera but also, obliquely, to the instrumental and cognitive role of architecture in shaping our understanding of the world.

In the Bell Chamber/camera, architecture is distilled to an abstract and quasi-immaterial art, dedicated to constructing intellectual relationships as much as to building material objects. This architecture is perfectly suited for the colonization of virtual space. The architects may indeed be said to have devised a virtual extension to Liberty Bell Center, destined for countless photo albums, books, and magazines. Considering the ubiquity of media representations and their prodigious rate of proliferation, this virtual architecture has arguably a greater presence and impact in the world. The architects of Liberty Bell Center understood and exploited this fact.

10 Bell Chamber, southeast corner 11 Stone wall at interior

Bohlin Cywinski Jackson designed and built two homes for the Liberty Bell. First, the actual building on the mall is a handsome structure that is replete with the fine tactile qualities that have earned the firm's international reputation. This building excels in situating the bell in its particular historical and physical context and is epitomized by the stubborn materiality of the stone wall: a substantial and singular feature in counterpoint to the optical logic of the building, with its impenetrable and tactile presence. 11

There is also another building, a virtual construct that was tailored with no less precision and ingenuity for the universal resonance of the Liberty Bell. It is based on optical effects and is implied in the building's dematerialized features. The virtual building with its characteristic structure, the oblique view, is likely to supplant the first with the dissemination of media representations–to become the Liberty Bell's privileged home in the collective imagination.

We have Bohlin Cywinski Jackson to thank for the complexity and richness that is now built into the iconic representation, home, of a most cherished symbol.

Rodolphe el-Khoury, BFA, BArch, SMArchS, MA, PhD, is involved in design practice as much as in research and writing. He is currently an Associate Professor at the University of Toronto and Canada Research Chair in Architecture and Urban Design. Mr. el-Khoury launched ReK Productions, his independent design practice, in 1997; from 1982 to 1997 he was a partner in Office dA, a Boston-based firm that has received international recognition and awards for architecture and urban design projects in the US and abroad. His publications include a book on eighteenth-century French architecture, *See Through Ledoux: Architecture, Theater and the Pursuit of Transparency*; a critical monograph, *The Work of Office dA*; translations and critical editions of Dominique Laporte's *The History of Shit* and Jean Francois de Bastide's *The Little House: An Architectural Seduction*; an exhibition catalogue, *Monolithic Architecture*; and edited compilation of essays, *Architecture: In Fashion* and *Shaping the City: Studies in History, Theory and Urban Design*.

11

What Becomes a Democracy's Monuments Most?

Richard M. Sommer

Building a better future often requires refiguring the past. This is especially true in the United States, where the still radical promise of democracy puts an onus on each generation to challenge and rewrite the histories it receives. Constructing historical accounts is, of course, not just a matter of writing and reading. History can also be adduced from the spaces we inhabit and the artifacts we apprehend. Given this potential, how do we best attend to the spaces within which important histories have unfolded, and to the artifacts within them that persist as emblems of our most potent historical ideas or events?

A group of concerned citizens thought they had a good answer to this question. During World War II they proposed, and later achieved, a plan to transform a once discreet set of colonial buildings and artifacts, embedded within a dense urban fabric built up over three centuries, into the Independence National Historical Park. The stated purpose of the park was to highlight buildings and sites associated with Philadelphia's role as the "Cradle of Liberty" during the revolutionary period. Three city blocks were razed for the centerpiece of the park: Independence Mall. The project focused on the Pennsylvania State House Complex, known since the early nineteenth century as "Independence Hall." Independence Hall was the site of the first Continental Congress, the signing of the Declaration of Independence, and the framing of the U.S. Constitution.

The importance of the areas encompassed by Independence National Historical Park and the mall is primarily owed to the historic events that took place in and around the Pennsylvania State House, rather than to the unique architecture or inherently monumental character of the buildings and artifacts found there. The creation of the park should also be understood in the context of a symbiotic relationship that has emerged between historic preservation and ever-escalating modernization. The first "heritage" and "historic" preservation movements came in the wake of the convulsive cultural changes brought by modern industrialism in the nineteenth century, primarily in response to the feelings of loss and nostalgia these changes generated. In the United States, public interest in sites related to the history of the American Revolution and our "colonial heritage" have their roots in this period. After the Civil War, attempts were made to find common origins and heritage around which to unify the country in a time of political friction and rapid industrialization. Moreover, the massive waves of immigration that followed sometimes added a xenophobic edge to these attempts at producing an Americanized national culture. The widespread public reverence for the statehouse and its environs is, more specifically, the outgrowth of a colonial revival movement that was at its peak in the 1910s and 1920s. Before these developments, most people in the United States had little time for history, as such–particularly in growing mercantile cities like Philadelphia.

To put the recent renovation of Independence Mall and the rehousing of the Liberty Bell in a proper historical context, one must revisit the larger motivations for the original creation of the Independence National Historical Park and mall. While a colonial revival was among the forces that influenced the creation of Independence Mall, the history of the colonial and revolutionary period is not the only history that is at play here. History–that persistent concatenation of events and phenomena–rarely stays within such tidy brackets. Even in the radically disrupted environs of this National Park, history persists within a built environment that has developed over approximately 350 years. The critical 40 years between 1760 and 1800, when the nation was founded and

12 Plan of Philadelphia, 1683 13 Plan of Philadelphia, 1796

Philadelphia served as its capital, are only a part of this history. The great challenge taken up by the architects and planners who have recently reformed the mall and resituated the bell, was to find ways to represent and give some spatial sense to the diverse and sometimes competing histories that continue to be at play in the site. In what follows I will attempt to sketch out these "histories" and the salient ideas and inspiration that the contemporary designers have drawn from them.

"From Green Country Town" to Metropolis When the Pennsylvania State House was built in the early 1730s, it occupied a very different city than the one envisioned by William Penn just a half century earlier. In Penn's vision Philadelphia was to have been a "wholesome," "green country town"; a "holy experiment" in religious tolerance combining the pastoral order of a seventeenth-century English gentleman's country farm with the market and communal functions of a city. Penn's originating 1683 "checkerboard" plan, spanning between two rivers with an east-west orientation, was consistent with his desire to balance utopian ideals with the exigencies of real estate and land governance.[1] 12 Nevertheless, the statehouse and its yard were built at the western fringe of a typical colonial port town of crowded blocks with stately Georgian faces and haphazard, sometimes treacherous alleys and mews. The practical orientation of the statehouse, with a south-facing yard and north-facing street elevation, stands in contrast to the east-west orientation of Penn's plan and anticipates the city's later massive expansion to the north. 13

Ironically, the nineteenth century brought both the realization and the eclipse of Penn's colonial plan. The preponderance and extension of the grid as a nineteenth-century planning device coincided with the consolidation, in 1854, of the various townships in Philadelphia County under one municipality. By 1900, Philadelphia had radically transformed from a walking city to a sprawling metropolis. The Old City at the eastern edge of Center City, which contained Independence Hall and the Liberty Bell, had become, in the eyes of many, ramshackle. Factories and other imposing structures from the nineteenth century overshadowed the remnants of the colonial period, and commercial and business interests that had once flourished there were moving westward. Like Penn's ideal plan, the Old City and its statehouse appear to have been twice eclipsed:

12

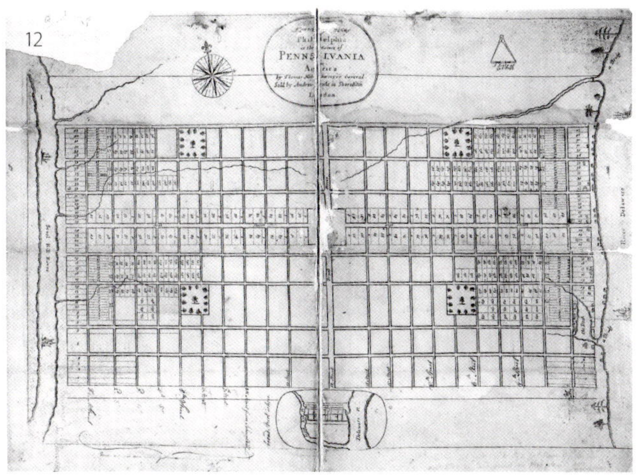

13

first by the completion of the colonial plan and the relocation of City Hall and commercial interests westward to Center (now Penn) Square; and by the recasting of the entire city's geographic limits.

In the early 1900s, anticipating the city's role in the Sesquicentennial of the American Revolution in 1926, Philadelphia undertook a series of ambitious urban planning projects. Two projects, the Fairmont (now Benjamin Franklin) Parkway and the Delaware (now Benjamin Franklin) Bridge drew on the *beaux arts*-derived planning principles of the City Beautiful movement. While essentially transportation-driven, these big projects had the effect of creating two new monumental entries into the city. The new parkway was to function as both a traffic artery from Fairmount Park and the expanding northern and western suburbs into the heart of the city, and a "civic center" of sorts. The parkway slashed diagonally through the city's rectilinear grid, beginning at an elaborate art museum complex atop Fairmount itself, and continuing through to Center Square, where the city had completed a new, gargantuan, Second Empire-style City Hall in 1901. The Fairmount Parkway prefigured Independence Mall by introducing the potential for a progressive, City Beautiful project to renew a "blighted" sector of the city.

14

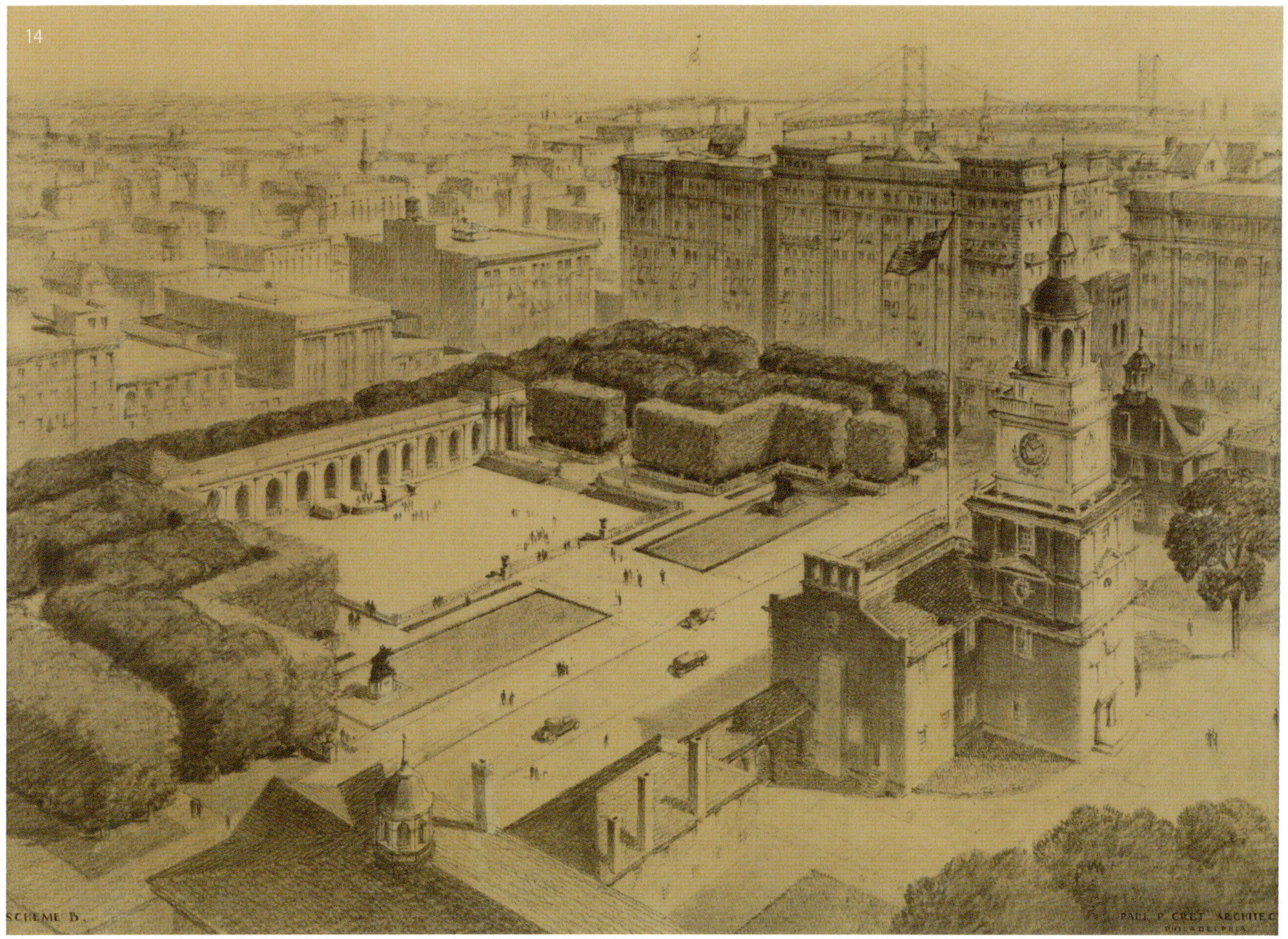

14 Perspective of the block north of Independence Hall by Paul Cret

Precipitated by the growing use of the automobile, the construction of the Delaware Bridge, completed in 1928, followed more than one hundred years of failed attempts to build a bridge that would span the Delaware River from Camden, New Jersey, to the eastern shore of Philadelphia. If the Fairmount Parkway established a planning precedent for the mall, the Delaware Bridge brought direct infrastructural pressures on Old City, especially on the areas around Independence Hall. The massive landing of the bridge fell between Race and Vine Streets, ending in a plaza fronting one of Penn's original squares, now Franklin Square. Drawing twice as much traffic as anticipated, travel on the new bridge allowed for a sweeping panorama of Old City. For the first time the city's citizens could rise up from the labyrinth of the city's oldest precincts and view them, as a whole, from the vantage of their early, maritime formation. The relentless car traffic and the visual scrutiny of the new automobile tourist created pressure to transform the area, particularly the precinct around Independence Hall.

The surge in patriotism after World War I increased the status and veneration of the Independence Hall complex, and the Liberty Bell enshrined therein. Temporary viewing stands were constructed adjacent to Independence Hall on Chestnut Street to serve the frequent patriotic parades, pageants, and rallies held there. Yet, many of the city fathers found the eclectic language, workaday uses, and decaying condition of the older buildings on Chestnut Street facing Independence Hall particularly distasteful and hoped to replace them with a plaza that would more permanently serve patriotic events.[2] Approximately twelve proposals developed between 1915 and the adaptation of the park plan in the mid-1940s, with architect Paul Cret's being perhaps the most sophisticated.[3] 14

A Monument in Search of a Lawn: The Pastoral Machine

The idea to build a vast public green on three blocks facing Independence Hall did not come from planners or architects such as Paul Cret, but grew out of two other, more curious, influences. In 1928 Dr. Seneca Egbert, Professor of Hygiene at the University of Pennsylvania, conceived the scheme that most directly influenced the making of the mall. His proposal was apparently a response to a 1925 Philadelphia City Council proposal to abate traffic congestion at the Benjamin Franklin Bridge Plaza by diverting traffic from the Plaza to Market Street, through the creation of a grand, mid-block boulevard, between Fifth and Sixth Streets. Egbert instead proposed "the development of a Concourse or Esplanade between Independence Hall and the plaza at the west end of the Delaware Bridge that should serve as a permanent and impressive Sesquicentennial memorial of the historic events incident to the founding of the nation."[4]

No drawing is known to exist of this scheme, but Egbert did draft an elaborate report outlining his proposal. Several aspects of the scheme he outlined were present in the plan, which was finally approved in the late 1940s and later implemented. Egbert justified his boldest proposition to demolish three city blocks stretching from Independence Hall on Chestnut Street to the bridge plaza on Race Street–over fifteen acres–by citing a widely held fear that at any time a fire could consume one of the area's abandoned or dilapidated buildings and spread to Independence Hall or another cherished colonial edifice. His other influential proposals included the widening of Fifth and Sixth Streets to accommodate increased traffic from the bridge, the creation of a central pedestrian esplanade "possibly as broad as Broad Street," the creation of a plaza for events fronting Independence Hall, the accommodation of underground parking, and the building of a new subway stop.

Perhaps even more influential than the physical proposals was Egbert's supposition that the new mall would raise tax revenues by increasing the assessed value of the three cleared blocks, resulting in an increase in the perceived value of adjacent properties and the district as a whole. Egbert also implied that the historical value of the Old City could be mined to commercial advantage. To achieve a project of this magnitude, Egbert foresaw the need for a structure through which various federal, city, and state agencies could cooperate.

15

Yet, before Philadelphia even considered building the mall envisioned by Egbert, replicas of Independence Hall had been set on a vast green in other places. In the late 1920s, Henry Ford reproduced Independence Hall as the frontispiece for the Edison (later Ford) Museum he was building at Greenfield Village in Dearborn, Michigan. An exact scale replica of Independence Hall was reproduced for New York City's World's Fair of 1939. 15 At the fair, Independence Hall fronted the end of a grand axis of state buildings along a national mall-like reflecting pool within the "Government Zone." In these and numerous other civic buildings that more or less copy Independence Hall during this period, it is worth noting that the yard, rather than street elevation of the original, is positioned as the symbolic front, an indication that the street elevation that now faces the mall was then deemed by many to be secondary to the building's identity.

16

The bombing of Pearl Harbor and the outbreak of WWII brought a renewed interest in Independence Hall and the Liberty Bell as symbols of patriotism. Starting in 1941, Edwin O. Lewis, a charismatic, highly persuasive, and well-connected judge, and president of the Pennsylvania Society of the Sons of the Revolution, mounted a campaign to build the three-block-long mall envisioned by Egbert. Mindful of the potential for federal support for the construction and management of the mall, the project was conceived as a National Park that would eventually include the entire complex of buildings associated with Independence Hall. 16 Lewis engaged the architect

15 Replica of Independence Hall at 1939 New York World's Fair 16 Judge Edwin O. Lewis, President of Independence Hall Association with Edward M. Biddle, Association Treasurer 17 Plan for the redevelopment of the historic area

Roy Larson, a partner of Paul Cret, to make the new plan. Larson had made a proposal in 1937 that cleared the three blocks north of Independence Hall and drew liberally from Egbert's scheme. Larson later revised his plan to have the park scheme include important historic structures on two partial blocks to the east of Independence Hall. This is the plan that was eventually implemented after the U.S. Congress approved the construction of the National Park in 1949.[5] 17

Leveraging the Old to Augur the New The creation of the mall suggests a now common process by which a city's historical form and stock of historic buildings can be leveraged to stimulate both public and private reinvestment in decaying areas. In hindsight, it appears the mall was a critical element in a Faustian bargain made by Philadelphia's civic leaders to leverage the hallowed Independence Hall and the bell it housed–the shrines most central to the city's legend–to a wholesale reform of Old City. In the process, hundreds of buildings and businesses had to be taken by eminent domain and demolished, including the polychrome Guarantee Trust Company and the Provident Life & Trust Company Bank and Office Building designed by Frank Furness.[6]

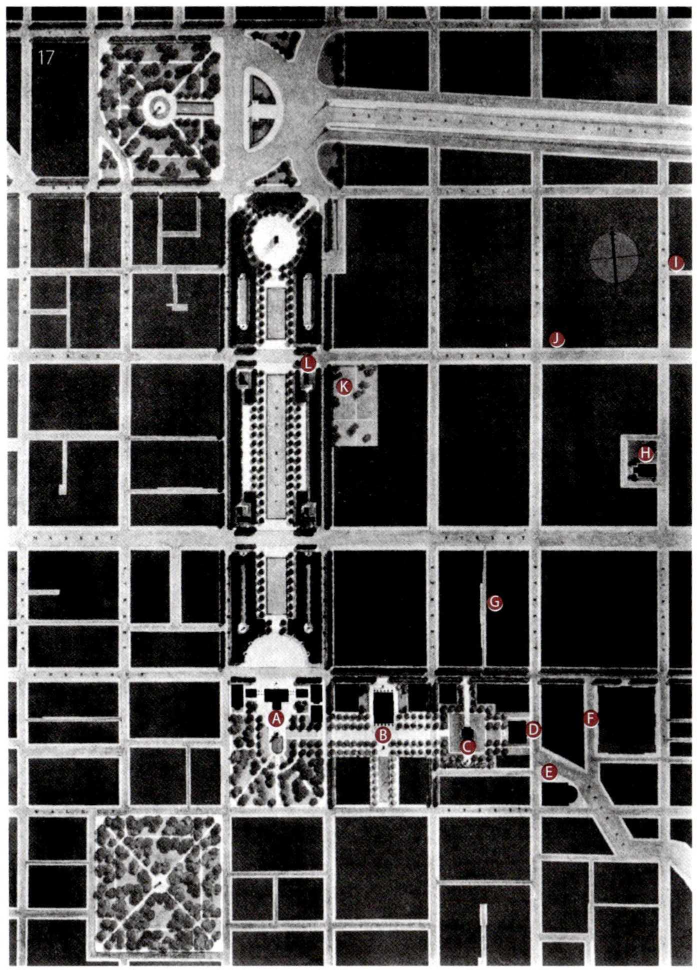

A Independence Hall Group and American Philosophical Society
B Second Bank of the United States (Old Custom House)
C Carpenters' Hall
D First Bank of the United States (Girard National Bank)
E Old Merchant's Exchange
F New Custom House
G Franklin Court
H Christ Church
I Elfreth's Alley
J Betsy Ross House
K Christ Church Grave Yard
L Free Quaker Meeting House

18

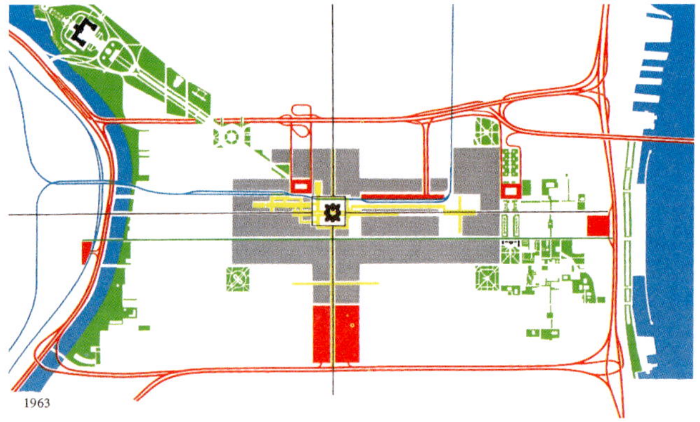

19

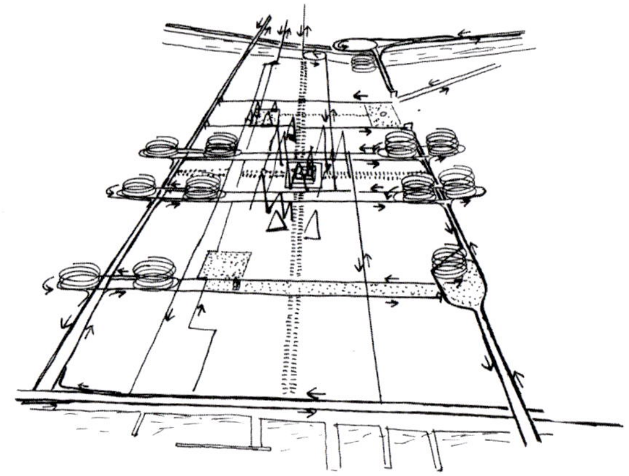

There was an obvious mismatch between the size of the mall and the diminutive scale of Independence Hall–a mismatch that resulted from the divergent planning agendas that coalesced behind the mall scheme. Before the formation of the Independence National Historical Park, Old City's discrete set of colonial buildings and artifacts could be valued for the way their modest form and casual arrangement connoted the humble beginnings of American democracy. Moreover, reverence for Independence Hall received its greatest boost from the colonial revival of the 1920s–a movement that was critical to the creation of a historic preservation consciousness in the United States. Among the many ironies that attend the mall's creation is that by drawing on crudely conceived, eighteenth-century European classicism, the mall erased the monumental commonness that might have been one of the site's greatest assets. The grandiosely scaled mall was mostly intended to do for Independence Hall (the city's old city hall) what the Fairmount Parkway had been seen to do for the new City Hall: create a grand civic corridor to a monumental building, and in the process, manage traffic. The problem is, and was, that Independence Hall is a monument by virtue of its history, not its size.

By relating itself more to a network of national parks and related tourist sites than to the material history of Philadelphia, Independence Mall indicates how, at a time when metropolitan areas like Philadelphia were dissipating into the suburbs, the aesthetic chosen for the symbolic areas at the center was one that put a premium on cleanliness; easy automobile access; and open, verdant vistas. Penn's Greene Country Towne was finally going to be realized in the extreme, but at a scale that could only be appreciated from a moving automobile.

Linking a patriotic-themed memorial to an infrastructure-driven urban redevelopment project was not unique in the early decades of the twentieth century; the roughly concurrent Jefferson National Expansion Memorial in St Louis, which cleared forty-eight blocks of the city's earliest districts, is a prime example of the type. Technically, the Independence National Historical Park was not a "clearance" project. In the areas of the park east of Independence Hall, a strategy was employed of selectively "pruning" those buildings lacking a "history" appropriate to a Revolutionary Era-themed national park. Nevertheless, the park and mall literally cleared the way for a similar regentrification of Old City in general, and nearby Society Hill in particular. In this and other ways, Independence Mall presaged the larger redevelopment of Philadelphia's downtown in the postwar period.[7]

When the city planner Edmund Bacon was appointed the executive director of Philadelphia's Planning Commission in 1949, he assumed the mall project as one of the lynchpins of his renewal schemes. The mall took more than a decade to complete, but was central to Bacon's notion of treating Old City, below Sixth Street, as if it were a colonial Garden City annexed to the mega-projects he was developing for the midtown area. The unprecedented degree of power Bacon assumed during this period allowed him to propose, and partially achieve, a plan that wrapped the original borders of Penn's colonial plan with a ring of expressways. 18 Bacon's scheme, and a similar, more artistically rendered proposal by Louis Kahn, in essence isolated the "original" city from the rest of Philadelphia in a manner similar to the way in which Independence Mall had isolated the hall complex from the city that had grown up around it. This reification of the city to the essence of its old and new formations is captured in a famous sketch by Kahn from 1952, in which Independence Hall appears to be the only building left standing in a city protected at its original borders by citadel-like parking structures. 19

18 Plan of Philadelphia from "Design of Cities" by Edmund Bacon

19 Plan of Philadelphia by Louis I. Kahn

Changing the Subject: Toward a New Mall Half a century after Independence Mall was conceived, a team of architects and planners were faced with the task of remaking the mall and the re-housing of the Liberty Bell. In their studies of how to better utilize the fifteen acres of the mall, several issues came into play. How could the space of the mall be altered to more respectfully frame Independence Hall? How could one program the site anew and somehow better connect the mall to the surrounding context? How, in the age of Disney, could one engage, and manage, a touring public of large numbers in a site of historic importance, while simultaneously maintaining the site's potential to sponsor more spontaneous activities and thereby serve the everyday needs of the city? Questions of architectural character and the application of a historical versus a modern language also had to come into play.

Ultimately, though, the team entrusted with the project had to address the question of what sort of architecture becomes a democracy's monuments most. While a deity, a monarch, or a military triumph is celebrated with classical devices, this team had to summon alternative landscape, planning, and building-based techniques to contend with how one frames, or even defines, a monument in a democratic society. The United States Constitution poses the radical notion that all people, regardless of background, have equal rights and access to opportunity and the pursuit of happiness. What, or who, does a society committed to these principles celebrate in its monuments? In a modern democracy, we do not just celebrate the great men and their buildings. The lives, deeds, and places of the "common man" (and woman), the Unknown Soldier, the slave, the immigrant, and the pacifist Quaker should all be celebrated as well. How, then, do we monumentalize the very site where these romantic ideas of democracy coalesced, where the seeds of American democracy were first planted?

The original scheme for the mall tried to elevate Old City's (and by association, the nation's) colonial heritage above all else by setting Independence Hall on a stage of national proportions. The assumption of a national heritage depends, like an individual's birthright, on the transmission of traditions, unquestioned, from one generation to the next. Yet, the very idea of heritage runs against the grain of American history, where successive waves of immigration and open access to wealth and property have fundamentally challenged the notion that values and culture are inherited, rather than made. Competing accounts of the histories that we share–as opposed to the heritage we inherit–are constantly being amended and are part of the critical process by which the promise of democracy is renewed. For example, in 1838 a group of abolitionists raised funds to build "Pennsylvania Hall," approximately three blocks from Independence Hall along Sixth Street, for facilitating free speech around the issue of slavery. The proximity to Independence Hall was certainly intended to expose the hypocrisy in the state and federal government's refusal to take up the question of slavery. In an expression of the growing hostility toward the activities of these abolitionists, in which both women and African Americans took, for that time, unusually public roles, a mob torched the building three days after it was opened. Although it saved nearby buildings, Philadelphia's fire brigade allowed the hall to burn. Pennsylvania Hall's construction, short life of sponsoring protest, and torching is a part of the history of Independence National Historical Park, alongside the better-known revolutionary events it celebrated there.[8] In the same vein, knowing that George Washington lived, however briefly, and housed slaves on the very parcel on the mall that now enshrines the Liberty Bell does not diminish our first president or sully the bell as a symbol.

20 View of Franklin Court 21 Sketch of Independence Mall locating historic streets and alleys

Quite the opposite, these histories illuminate the nation's unfinished and hard-fought movement toward a more expansive definition of human rights and social emancipation.

From Heritage to Histories, Revised, Recast, and Approximate

The new master plan for the mall developed by the Olin Partnership, Bohlin Cywinski Jackson, and Kise Straw & Kolodner leaves room for the acknowledgement of a more nuanced view of history. The shift in sensibility from the original, heritage movement-induced, Williamsburg-like scheme of the Independence National Historical Park to the sensibility represented in the new plan, can be traced to Venturi, Rauch & Scott Brown's scheme for Franklin Court of 1972. Their approach at Franklin Court, and elsewhere in Old City, promoted the referencing of history over its dogged reproduction. 20 The Franklin Court scheme gives priority to a visitor's subjective capacity to read various built and rebuilt fragments, mappings, and tracery of historical patterns as a two- and three-dimensional tableau in which the "story" of a site unfolds. In the approach that they pioneered, contemporary, everyday qualities of the city are maintained alongside historical references. There is the old, the new, and everything in between.

Venturi, Scott Brown & Associates' preliminary master plan and conceptual design of Independence Mall proposed certain ideas–and outlined certain challenges–that greatly influenced the General Management Plan that was eventually developed. One statement from Venturi, Scott Brown & Associates' planning document sums up the main challenge facing those seeking to reform the mall:

> *There is an intention to salute the world-shaking political steps that were taken in Philadelphia in the 18th Century, but a reluctance to recognize that American Democracy was achieved (and is maintained) through agonized and untidy processes set within an American tradition of realism and pragmatism. Lively clutter and contrast might be a more appropriate physical metaphor for American democracy than peace and serenity.*[9]

Following this ethos, Venturi, Scott Brown & Associates proposed to "emphasize the egalitarian gridiron city over beaux arts formality" and implied that the bilateral symmetry that extended for three blocks in the original design should be broken. Philadelphia's grid was invoked to ensure a sense of free access. While, for example, movement through the institutional venues on the mall might constitute a hierarchical sequence (i.e., arrive at the visitor center, proceed to the bell and then Independence Hall), other less proscribed activities should be sponsored and encouraged on the mall. After all, the mall is large enough to serve many constituencies and uses over time: national tourist shrine; recreational park, and protest and political rally site among others. Breaking the *beaux arts* symmetry would also allow for the two-fold effect of softening the visual relationship between the mall and the hall and at the same time acknowledging the difference in scale between the Benjamin Franklin Bridge off-ramp to the north and Independence Hall to the south. In a radical sketch proposal for a north-south section through the mall titled "Evolution via Section" (and other related sketches included in the study) Venturi, Scott Brown & Associates proposed buildings ascending in scale as they move north from Block One to Three. The scheme reconceived the three blocks as a historical allegory, each assigned a distinct scale, with Block One modeled on the "18th century Towne;" Block Two, the twentieth-century "Big" City, and Block Three, the twenty-first-century "Huge" scale of the "Region" (the nineteenth century appears to be missing).[10]

21

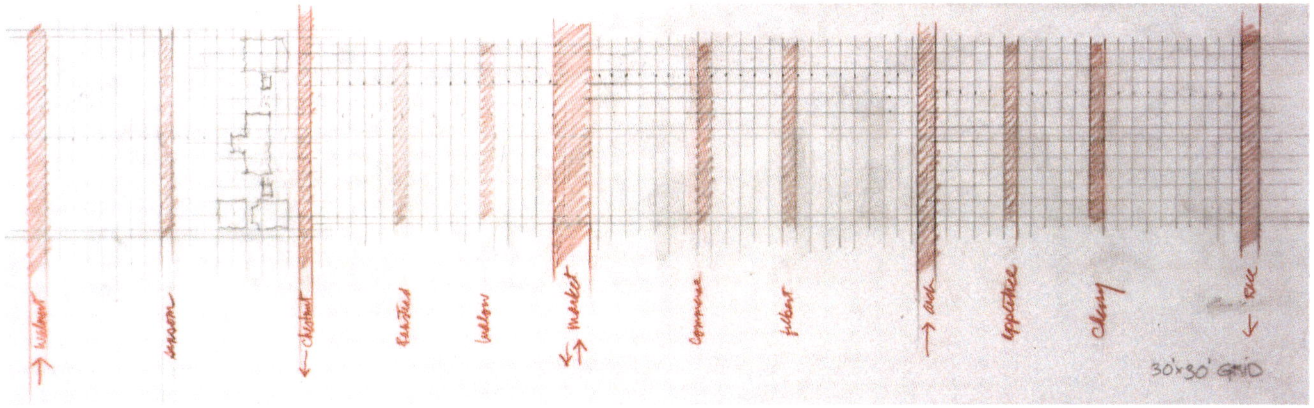

Some of Venturi, Scott Brown & Associates' ideas conflicted with the Park Service and other constituencies vying for the future of Independence Mall. Yet the Olin Partnership team entrusted with developing the master plan respected principles set forth in the General Management Plan, enhancing and even expanding upon them in unexpected ways. The Olin Partnership's plan plays, in particular, on the difference in character between the areas lying to the east and west of the mall. The difference in these areas has become much more pronounced since the mall was first conceived. Redevelopment during the Bacon era generally downsized, greened, and gentrified Society Hill, and Old City to the east, and further promoted metropolitan-scale growth in areas to the west. Thus, the Olin Partnership scheme built up the western edge of the mall with new buildings and defined the eastern edge with landscape and greenery.

Respecting Philadelphia's gridiron plan over *beaux arts* symmetry, the master plan called for the reintroduction of the pattern of smaller alleys and streets that once ran through the large blocks that now constitute the mall. 21 The intention behind reintroducing these patterns was to somehow link to the still existing passages to the east and west, and to recall, as Franklin Court does, the rich "inner life" once contained in these blocks. The reintroduction of the tertiary east-west streets and alleys proved to be challenging. In the early versions of the master plan, the line of buildings bordering Sixth Street was broken into a series of parts that implied public passage through the buildings at mid-block. In practice, as the building programs developed on each respective block and issues of security and crowd management came to the fore, the possibility of literally continuing the streets and alleys through the mall fell away. Nevertheless, the master plan's design guidelines tried to compensate for this lack of literal passage by inscribing the old grid in two related ways. First, there was an attempt to extend the grid of the surrounding city into the mall to establish a shared geometry and planning grid across the extent of the mall. This geometry was proposed as a means to knit together what was intended to be a mix of buildings of somewhat different character. An important expression of this unifying pattern was the provision of an arcade–or, more precisely, a hybrid of a loggia and an arbor–arrayed along the eastern, mall-facing border of each of the buildings. In addition to using the grid as a planning device, the master plan called for the maintenance of view corridors where literal openings were not possible, and for the old patterns to be inscribed as landscape pathways and changes in surface cladding material.

The principle of requiring buildings to defer to Independence Hall and to only increase in scale as they move northward–so boldly rendered by Venturi and Scott Brown–was primarily intended as a control on height. Yet the master plan took this to heart in both the vertical and horizontal dimensions, proposing to step buildings aligned to the western edge out toward the center of the mall, such that their footprints would increase as they moved north, block by block. This stepping effect allowed the creation of a distinct and clear vantage point toward Independence Hall from the principal, mall-facing front of each of the new buildings on each block. These views are now quite palpable from the three main buildings on the mall: National Constitution Center; Independence Visitor Center; and Liberty Bell Center. Yet, owing to the differing function of these three buildings, and the divergent approaches of the architects who designed them, each takes a crucial station point toward Independence Hall as a different opportunity.

23

24

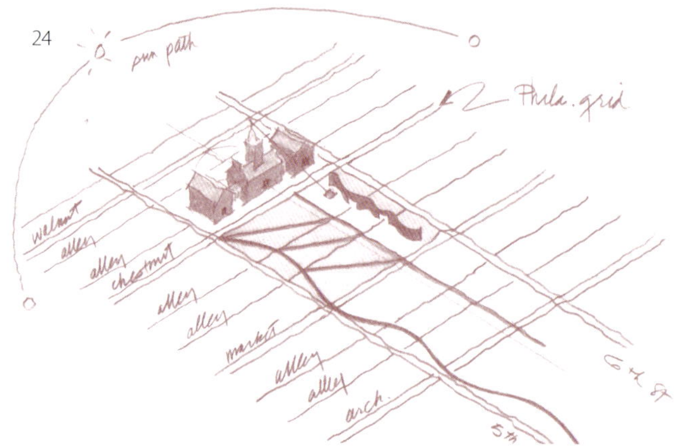

The Bell Comes First Independence National Historical Park encompasses six city blocks and contains numerous historical spaces and building artifacts. Despite this expanse, the Liberty Bell is by far the park's main attraction. As members of the team that developed the master plan, Bohlin Cywinski Jackson was well positioned to design a building to rehouse the Liberty Bell. The firm's design for Liberty Bell Center reveals and exploits a number of interlocking architectural and historical themes embedded in the master plan. The most striking aspect of the new pavilion is the way in which its form responds, albeit in miniature, to almost all of the ambitions that have been brought to bear on remaking the mall as a whole. Among these ambitions is finding a way to accommodate the conflicting need for the mall's spaces to both act and be perceived as an open, accessible public park, and for them to function in a more orchestrated manner, carefully staging a particular sequence of experiences. Both the gridiron plan of Philadelphia and the serpentine paths of the romantic garden are dynamically deployed on the mall as a way of facilitating, and evoking, free movement within a roughly symmetrical plan occupied on one side by buildings, and on the other, by more open, planted areas. Liberty Bell Center achieves the same effect by creating a long, tectonically expressive shed and then orchestrating movement through it–and subdividing its use for exhibits–by configuring an undulating granite wall against the built-up street edge. 22-24

Liberty Bell Center's ultimate goal is to properly frame and contain a revered relic–the Liberty Bell. The center achieves this with two main parts: a filigreed exhibition shed acting as a preamble and staging area for the bell; and an airy chamber housing the bell itself. There are probably people who would argue that the ideal context for the bell would be its "original" home in the statehouse tower. Nevertheless, the Liberty Bell and Independence Mall are not only heritage sites, but are subjects of, and to, history. The "Liberty Bell" did not really exist until the abolitionists coined the phrase and adapted it to the old statehouse bell. Later, from 1885 to 1915, extensive, national railroad tours brought the bell out to the expanding nation and allowed it to be understood separately from its place in Philadelphia. It is suspected that these train tours also caused the bell's fractures to spread, thus highlighting its fragility and status as a relic that needed to be protected and properly enshrined in Philadelphia.

The Liberty Bell was first enshrined within Independence Hall and then on the mall in a beautiful, albeit temporary, crystalline pavilion designed by Mitchell/Giurgola Associates for the 1976 Bicentennial. A new facility was needed that could serve both the pedagogical function of explaining the history and various meanings of the bell and managing the large numbers of people who want to "experience" the bell itself. While it refers in its scale and its infill brick to the colonial architecture of the Revolutionary Era, the highly expressive architecture of Liberty Bell Center's shed more than anything else evokes the kinds of proto-modern, nineteenth-century structures that were once plentiful on and around the historic areas of the city occupied by the mall. The bell has been carefully positioned in the center so that as one enters the Bell Chamber it appears aligned with the tower of Independence Hall.

Yet, the bell appears at the tower's base, rather than the top, roughly where it was displayed in the ground floor of the hall from the late nineteenth century until the Bicentennial.

I do not mean to imply that Liberty Bell Center is a building with a nineteenth-century orientation, but rather that it was the history of the nineteenth century that was most aggressively erased by

22 Alleyway passing through building 23, 24 Early sketch of exhibit hall (left) and influence of street grid on plan of the building (right) 25 View of Bell Chamber

the original mall scheme and that this history should rightfully be recalled in the recomposing of the site. Liberty Bell Center's subtle use of various modes of transparency; its nuanced relationship to Independence Hall; and its layering of materials from a visually porous exterior to the sensuous yet mute walls encasing the bell, make it an entirely contemporary building. While respectful, it presents the bell within a visual tableau that through its composite image may just give Independence Hall's street façade the monumentality it appeared to lack once it was exposed to the mall. Before the construction of the mall, most popular postcard representations of Independence Hall and almost all of the built reproductions (i.e., the New York World's Fair) had taken the hall's bolder, more picturesque, south-facing yard elevation as their front. Collapsed together, the increase in the Liberty Bell's status, by virtue of perceived scale, is brought to bear on Independence Hall. Now, in just a few moments in Liberty Bell Center, the bell-tower montage provokes the idea that symbols are malleable and, more important, that history may still be in the making.

1 For an account of the first plans for Philadelphia, see John W. Reps, *The Making of Urban America: A History of City Planning in the United States* (Princeton, NJ: Princeton University Press, 1965), pp. 152-53. **2** *Cultural Landscape Report: Independence Mall, Independence National Historic Park* (Denver, CO: United States Department of the Interior, 1994), pp. 27-28. **3** Among the approximately twelve proposals made between 1915 and the adaptation of a plan in the mid-1940s, Paul Cret's was perhaps the most sophisticated. Clearing a half-block of buildings north of Chestnut Street to Ludlow Street (one of the built-up secondary alleys), Cret proposed two similar schemes, the first with a semicircular plaza and the second with a square plaza. Cret's schemes kept the plaza small and located a flight of steps below grade, a gesture that would have limited long views of the diminutive colonial statehouse, thereby increasing the perception of its scale. **4** For a full account of Egbert's proposal, see *Cultural Landscape Report: Independence Mall, Independence National Historical Park*, pp. 29-32. **5** Ibid., p. 63. **6** For an account of opposition to the wholesale clearance of the mall site mounted by the Park Service's architect, Charles E. Peterson, see Constance M. Greiff, *Independence: The Creation of a National Park* (Philadelphia, PA: University of Pennsylvania Press, 1987) pp. 49-58. See also Lewis Mumford's later criticism in "The Skyline: Philadelphia-II," *New Yorker* (February 9, 1957). **7** For a further account of Independence Mall in the context of Edmund Bacon's planning, see Richard M. Sommer, "The Urban Design of Philadelphia: Taking the Towne for the City" in E. Robbins, R. El-Khoury, eds. *Shaping The City* (London, UK: Routledge 2004). **8** See Pennsylvania Hall Association, *History of Pennsylvania Hall which was Destroyed by a Mob on the 17th of May*, 1838 (Philadelphia, PA: Merrihew and Gunn). **9** See Venturi, Scott Brown & Associates, Inc. "Gateway Visitor Center and Independence Mall, Master Planning Programming and Conceptual Design, Phase I" 1996, p. 5. **10** Ibid., p. 21.

25

Richard Sommer is a partner in the design firm borfax/B.L.U and Associate Professor of Architecture and Urban Design at Harvard's Graduate School of Design, where he is also the Director of the Urban Design Program. Mr. Sommer's design work, writing, and exhibitions explore new roles for architecture within the complex political geography, culture, and history of the contemporary city. His recent research has focused on how the changing aspirations of American democracy have challenged–and radically transformed–traditional modes of monument making.

Giving Form to a Creation Story — The Remaking of Independence Mall

Laurie Olin

The urban scene embracing Independence Hall in Philadelphia has been an almost continuously evolving situation since construction of the hall was completed in 1753. Built on what was then the western edge of the city, subsequent urban infill and density were anticipated by its authors. Accordingly, it was set back from the street and normal building line to form a small but noticeable public space–less than a square and more than a walkway–along Chestnut Street. This small piazza was to become the site for numerous gatherings, demonstrations, and protests as citizens gathered in attempts to influence and argue with the provincial and local authorities that met within. 26 Behind the State House, as it was then known, on the sunny south side, the remainder of this city block was developed as a public garden. It is from this garden where the *campanile*, or bell tower, comes to the ground that the familiar iconic images of Independence Hall framed by stately elms, oaks, and sycamores have been made. By the end of the nineteenth century, the surrounding community had become a somewhat worn district of fading shops, small industries, and crowded deteriorating housing. 27 Commerce and respectable living had moved away to other quarters of the city and enticing new suburbs. Between 1915 and 1930 several plans for renewal were made in the form of plazas, malls, and parks. In 1954 a scheme championed by Edmund Bacon was adopted, and several distinguished architects and landscape architects were employed to develop the design of this new park. This plan grew to include the creation of a park extending eastward from Independence Hall for three blocks. Hundreds of buildings, many superb products of America's finest nineteenth-century architects, were demolished to create a "historical" park devoted to the eighteenth century, the period of the Revolution and the early Federal years when Philadelphia was the nation's capital. What began as an urban renewal venture for the City of Philadelphia and the State of Pennsylvania eventually was translated into one of the nation's first truly urban national parks, albeit an oddly non-urban one, which radically disrupted the built fabric of the city. Not only were buildings and streets eradicated, but alongside the three blocks north of Independence Hall, which came to be called "Independence Mall," a series of nondescript federal facilities was built–a Federal Courthouse, a regional headquarters and office for the Federal Reserve Bank with a parking garage, and a U.S. Mint. Other nearby blocks ended up with corporate headquarters and back offices for banks, while some stood empty for a decade. It would be hard to imagine a less friendly and less active set of neighbors for a public park. 28-30

26

27

26 John Lewis Krimmel, "Election scene, State House in Philadelphia" (1815)

27–29 Aerial views of Independence Hall facing north in the 1950s, 1970s, and in 1997

30 Independence National Historical Park in the context of the City of Philadelphia

28

The mall, as designed, also proved to be problematic. Block One, the first block north of Independence Hall, was popular with local office workers, largely because it had two intimate and heavily planted terraces raised slightly so as to overlook a simple grass panel in the center, which afforded views to Independence Hall from the park, and Chestnut and Market Streets. The next block to the north, referred to as Block Two, contained a below-grade parking garage and two brick, arcaded, stoa-like structures and a series of elevated terraces; walls; steps; planters; and a large fountain. The garage fell into disrepair, and the fountain stopped working in the late 1970s. The terraces became overgrown and shelters for the homeless.

29

Block Three, designed by one of America's most distinguished landscape architects, Daniel Urban Kiley, was an exercise in geometry and historic recall. Kiley was inspired by particular Moorish urban landscape designs for fountains and watercourses such as those at the Alhambra in Granada and in the bosques of orange trees at mosques in Seville and Cordoba. It was beset by problems from a lack of use and maintenance. By 1998 its historic merit and integrity were called into question, despite Kiley's authorship and reputation. The National Park Service (NPS) decided that Block Three could be demolished and redesigned for an appropriate new use.

30

At the northern end of Block One near Market Street, a small, handsome, modernist pavilion had been designed by the highly regarded firm Mitchell/Giurgola Associates for the Bicentennial of 1976 to display the Liberty Bell. In subsequent years, as the number of visitors and crowds increased, the National Park Service concluded that it was too small and inadequate to handle the volume of visitors and their needs. Also, there was a sentiment that it was not possible to properly interpret this icon, to tell the stories about it and its changing meaning through time in this constrained structure. It needed to be replaced, but how?

By the late 1980s it was clear that these three entire blocks of the park needed to be redesigned. The National Park Service initiated a public process that was a precursor to developing a new General Management Plan, which could be used to re-imagine and direct the redesign and improvement of this park. While there were problems with some aspects of the park to the east of Independence Hall as well, the main emphasis of the Management Plan would be upon the northern blocks. The principal elements of the plan included a new enlarged bell pavilion that would offer a significant amount of interpretive material regarding the bell and its evolution into a symbol of national and individual liberty, including its use by the antislavery movement of the nineteenth century. A second element was to be a major visitor center. Not only was it to assist visitors to Independence National Historical Park with their questions and needs (such as bathrooms, maps, schedules, and timed tickets for the hall, which was experiencing long lines and waiting times) but also to help with tourism for the City of Philadelphia and the region, especially pertaining to the many historic sites, entertainment, and lodging.

As Blocks Two and Three had become largely unused and presented barriers of walls and ramps to the street and the adjacent city, the reworked park was to be more open and possess lawn or other open spaces suitable for large gatherings for annual and special events. An area suitable to accommodate 250 people demonstrating or exercising their First Amendment right to protest was to be incorporated and designated as such on Block One within view of the hall. Additionally, the General Management Plan called for facilities for the many charter buses and various tourist vehicles, which had proliferated, crowding the streets and blocking movement and views in several directions.

While this plan was being developed in the early and mid-90s, an independent group of citizens had formed that was interested in creating a new facility devoted to honoring, explaining, and interpreting the United States Constitution. While it is generally known by most Americans that the Declaration of Independence was written in 1776 by delegates to the Continental Congress (Jefferson, Adams, Madison, Hamilton, and others) in Independence Hall, many forget that the U.S. Constitution was also conceived there ten years later. It is the oldest written constitution for governance of a democracy. We still live by its propositions, use it, and argue about it every day. It is a living and evolving document. Therefore, this new organization argued that it was in some ways more important than the Declaration, and needed a facility of some sort to present and interpret its history, contents, and workings. Forming a non-profit organization, the National Constitution Center (NCC), they began to lobby the city, state, and federal government for space and assistance in creating such a facility north of Independence Hall in the park, commissioning studies and proposed concept plans from various designers.

With all of this activity surrounding the re-conception and desire to rebuild and transform the three blocks of the mall, the National

Park Service conducted several small exercises with local designers to see what a new park might look like, and to test the program that was emerging from the development of the General Management Plan. Encouraged by this progress, The Pew Charitable Trusts funded a feasibility study for new visitor and bell facilities. Venturi, Scott Brown & Associates was commissioned to prepare a concept design plan. At the urging of the NPS they engaged Hanna/Olin (now the Olin Partnership) as landscape architectural consultant, as well as several engineers and a cost estimator. The Venturi, Scott Brown & Associates team chose to combine the new home for the Liberty Bell and visitor center into one building. Following the lead of Cret and Grebier, architects of earlier master plan concepts, they proposed to place it on the north end of Block One, extending the width of the block from Fifth to Sixth Streets. The two blocks to the north, they argued, could be parkland and could contain facilities for the buses, access to the garage, and a new maintenance, storage, and equipment facility desired by the NPS and mentioned in the draft General Management Plan. The NPS balked at this proposal, feeling that the proposed two-story building would wall off the two blocks north of Market Street, continuing to render them dead and useless, a vacuum in the urban scene. Robert Venturi and Denise Scott Brown argued that the park was too big; that it should never have been created as a giant axis; that Independence Hall was too small a building to successfully terminate such a gesture and view; and that Cret and others were correct–the two northern blocks should contain buildings rather than open space.

The NPS requested that they develop an alternative with facilities on the first and second blocks. Venturi, Scott Brown & Associates split the program, with the bell pavilion on the south side of Market Street and a parallel building on the north side for the visitor center that was also to include the park maintenance facilities. Behind this second building, further to the north, the Olin group attempted to devise an outdoor bus terminal of quality, with trees and canopies that would work with the local streets and this visitor center. Studies utilizing either Block Two or Block Three were made. The architects also proposed covered walkways, arcades of a sort extending along both Fifth and Sixth Streets south from the bell pavilion to protect and lead visitors to Chestnut Street and crossings to Independence Hall. While Venturi, Scott Brown & Associates's plan might have functioned perfectly well, the NPS was dissatisfied with the buildings blocking views from the streets to the north, and the leftover quality of the two northern blocks.

At the same time the National Constitution Center saw an opportunity presented by this scheme. They came forward asking to locate their proposed center on the second block, which in the Venturi, Scott Brown & Associates scheme was largely empty. The City and The Pew Charitable Trusts saw the advantage of having this additional attraction and encouraged the NPS to include them. Plans began to develop for a multiple partnership between the National Park Service, the City of Philadelphia, the State of Pennsylvania, The Pew Charitable Trusts, and the National Constitution Center to implement a master plan for the park and buildings.

The Master Plan Design Team Early in 1997 the General Management Plan was published and a Request for Proposal was issued by the National Park Service for design professionals to prepare a new master plan for the three blocks north of Independence Hall. This plan was to accommodate the program as suggested in the General Management Plan. Numerous teams with nationally prominent design and planning firms responded. We began to consider the nature of the project, the client, and what sort of team might be best to tackle such a project. At the same moment James Kise of Kise Straw & Kolodner, a firm of planners, architects, archaeologists, restoration, and conservation specialists with offices on Broad Street in Philadelphia, was having the same thoughts with his partners, and called me to solicit my interest. When Dennis McGlade, one of my partners, and I met with Kise, the probable need for adding others to the team came up. Kise proposed securing a nationally prominent architect, an exhibition/historian consultant, transportation and other engineering specialists, as well as a cost estimator. After discussion I suggested the architecture firm of Bohlin Cywinski Jackson which had an established national reputation and had offices in three different cities in Pennsylvania–Philadelphia, Pittsburgh, and Wilkes-Barre–and had won the American Institute of Architect's 1994 Architecture Firm Award and many significant design awards. Kise recommended Avi Dector of History Now as a person who could be very helpful regarding historic interpretation. Dector had played such a role in the development of the design and program for the enormously successful United States Holocaust Memorial in Washington, D.C., designed by James Ingo Freed. Our team was completed with Urban Engineers and International Consultants Incorporated cost consultants, also of Philadelphia, making it a local team entirely composed of firms within walking distance of the site.

When the team assembled to plan an approach to the project and the interview tasks were developed and assigned, it was decided that the Olin Partnership would take the lead as prime professional, as the project was to prepare a master plan for a park. All the others were to be consultants for contractual reasons. I made a strong commitment to working collaboratively with the others on the project, regardless of contractual arrangements, should we land the job. Bernard Cywinski, a principal in the Philadelphia office of Bohlin Cywinski Jackson, was to play a major role as the program for the three major facilities was analyzed. Filled with enthusiasm, the group prepared carefully for the interview, studying the many groups and constituencies that we would need to work with for a successful plan to emerge. Regarding the plan itself, the team was well informed from the earlier involvement of the Olin Partnership in the Venturi, Scott Brown & Associates exercise, about some of the pitfalls and issues of concern to the National Park Service and the city. The interview committee, consisting of representatives from the National Park Service, The Pew Charitable Trusts, and the City of Philadelphia, awarded the contract to our team in late spring of 1997 and by mid-summer work commenced on the plan.

The Plan Several fundamental problems raised by earlier studies, but still unresolved, needed to be addressed. Where should one locate and arrange the principal structures on the three blocks so that each could have a view to Independence Hall without blocking that of the others? Where should the bell go? What should be done with the large number of tour buses that were paralyzing and blighting the local streets? How should the awkward and intrusive garage on the second block be dealt with? How could the park be reconceived so as to help put the city back together, to reconnect the areas on each side to the east and west between which the park acted as a barrier? Finally, how, if at all, in the forms and elements of a plan was one to respond to the early history of the area, and specifically to the events being honored by the park and its buildings, without falling into the traps of ersatz historical styling?

As the summer progressed each of the team members delved into analysis of a gamut of particular technical, functional, and programmatic issues. These included: pedestrian circulation; parking for buses, automobiles, trolley tour vehicles, and horse-drawn carriages; public transportation via bus and subway, which had a station at Market and Fifth Streets; utilities; adjacent

31 Edward Hicks, "Peaceable Kingdom"

properties–their current use and future plans; lighting; security; and what was known about visitors to the park–their habits, problems, needs, and patterns of attendance and behavior. Cywinski, Kise, and I met frequently to ponder the ideological and formal/physical issues regarding the bell and the parts as we were beginning to understand them. I delved into the history of events between 1760 and 1800–the period of the Declaration of Independence, the Revolutionary War, the Continental Congress and the drafting of the Constitution, and the decade when Philadelphia was the new nation's capital. I became convinced that the task was not only to arrange some buildings and design an attractive park, but more importantly, the challenge was to give physical form to a creation story–the settlement of the city and the founding of a nation. I was particularly interested in the evolution of Philadelphia's urban structure and fabric, especially its condition of *Rus in Urbs*, or of the country in the city. Although Philadelphia may have been the world's second largest English-speaking city at the time (after London) and a powerhouse of economic importance, scientific thought, learning, and ambition, there were numerous gardens and farms within the city. Transportation at the time was still largely on foot, two- and four-legged, and there were numerous barns, pastures, and livestock ponds about, as can be readily seen on early maps and plans of the city. As described in letters written by visitors of the time, the city was full of orchards, gardens, and trees along the streets. On its edges, the western one of which was east of Broad Street, were scraps of forest and pasture, and fields with crops. Horses, cows, and Georgian and Palladian architecture were thoroughly mixed together. While urbane and cosmopolitan, an open city of commerce and mixed races, ethnicity and religions, Philadelphia was perched on the edge of a continent and wilderness.

During this period the seeds of our contemporary suburban devotion to trees and lawn, as well as our habits of loose-fit urbanity, were planted in colonial settlements from Maine to the Carolinas. The near-pastoral setting that surrounded Pennsylvania's statehouse existed for only a brief moment in time, but it was re-created repeatedly as this and other state capitols decamped to rural settings away from the dense centers of commerce. Accordingly, some sort of reciprocity between buildings and greenery, ideas of representation between town and country, culture and nature seemed in order for the new plan for the mall.

In a way this was the landscape and urban design equivalent to the allegorical paintings of Edward Hicks, an eccentric, early nineteenth-century Quaker preacher who painted numerous renditions of a Peaceable Kingdom, wherein he brought together disparate strands of thought, tradition, and events, conflating them into one coherent yet multifaceted image. 31 In many of these, Hicks depicted William Penn meeting with Sachems of the Lenne Lenape (the local constituents of the native American Delaware people) under the "Treaty Oak" at Shakamaxon on the bank of the Delaware River just north of the future city of Philadelphia. The river as he represents it bears a remarkable resemblance to the Tiber as painted by Claude Lorrain in a series of highly influential paintings that helped launch landscape painting as an important branch of art in the seventeenth century. The Tiber, of course, was the river where Aeneas ceased his wandering after the fall of Troy to establish a new home, thereby founding Rome. Thus we see Penn founding a new community, and by implication, a new civilization, based upon the principles of freedom of religion and respect for the individual. Themes of tolerance and peaceful coexistence, central tenets of Quakerism, are underscored by a group of animals derived from remarks of Isaiah in the Old Testament, depicting a "peaceable kingdom" in which the lion shall lie down with the lamb, the ox with the wolf, goats with bears, and so on. In several of these, a small pie-faced Quaker child appears with garlands and wearing a Phrygian or liberty cap symbolic of both the American and French Revolutions. These are remarkable paintings, complex and simple at the same time, that are laden with meaning for Hicks' contemporaries and still accessible to us today while remaining delightful unto themselves. It seemed that our task was also to create such a unity from an equally disparate set of materials, namely the various elements of the NPS's program.

32

First we tackled the problem that has bedeviled architects and planners for the past century. How should visitors view Independence Hall? How could the new design offer views of the building that respect its dignity and significance considering that the sponsors of all three proposed buildings wanted Independence Hall to be visible from their buildings.

When Independence Hall was built, it was one of the largest and most impressive structures on the continent. While the clearing of the mall created unprecedented views along the multi-block axis,

32 Axial view of Independence Hall 33 Nolli plan of former park 34 Oblique view of Independence Hall tower

a pair of large insurance company buildings had been built on the block immediately south of Independence Hall; consequently, in Ed Bacon's straight-on view, the hall appears as a diminutive old building collaged against nondescript, backlit monoliths. 32, 33 Moreover, numerous critics and historians have objected to the axial plan based upon the fact that in colonial and early Federal times there were buildings immediately across the street.

We found a way to see Independence Hall once more as a large building with only trees, smaller structures, and the sky behind it. Early views of the hall were all from diagonal perspectives, from the intersections of Chestnut and Fifth or Sixth Streets. This was because the block across the street was occupied with buildings and this was the furthest distance one could be away from it and take in the whole of the front façade. Standing on the southwest corner of Block One and looking up through the leaves, one could see the tower tall against the sky and hardly noticed the taller twentieth-century structures to the right. 34

That was the answer: the new bell pavilion should be positioned in the southwest portion of Block One to make the strongest

33

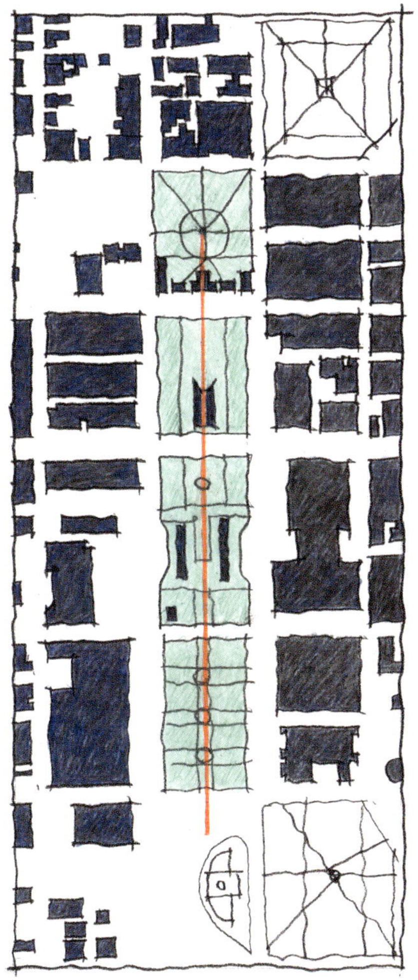

34

connection to the hall and clear the way for longer views from the other blocks to the north.

After an analysis of the relative size of each of the desired facilities and their probable visitation and service needs, the design team concluded that the National Constitution Center and the NPS maintenance facilities could not be squeezed onto the second block along with the new visitor center. These buildings had to be located on the third block. The National Constitution Center leaders and the mayor's office argued that this was too far from the hall,

35

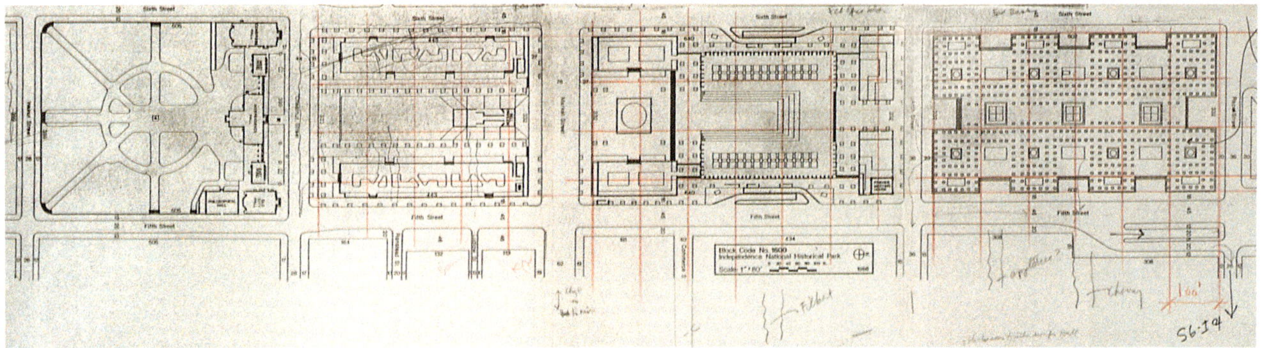

36

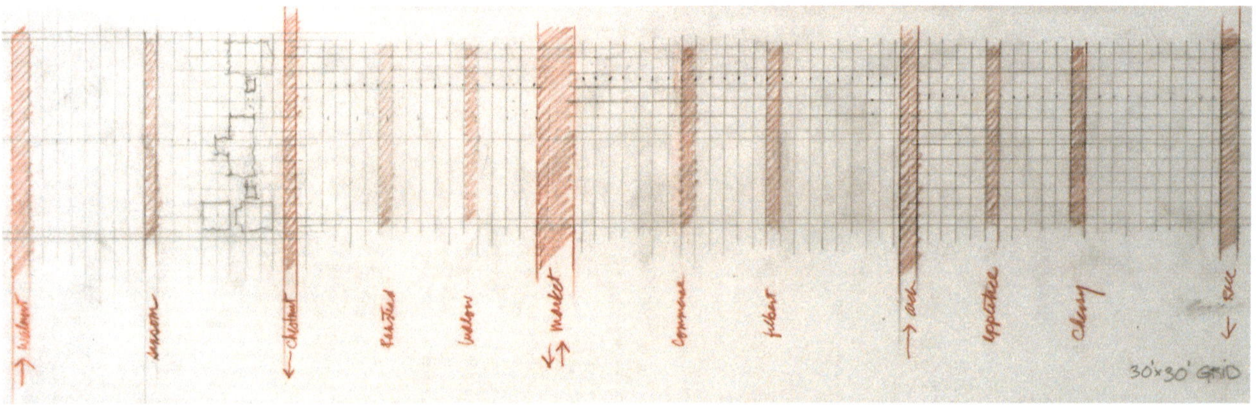

37

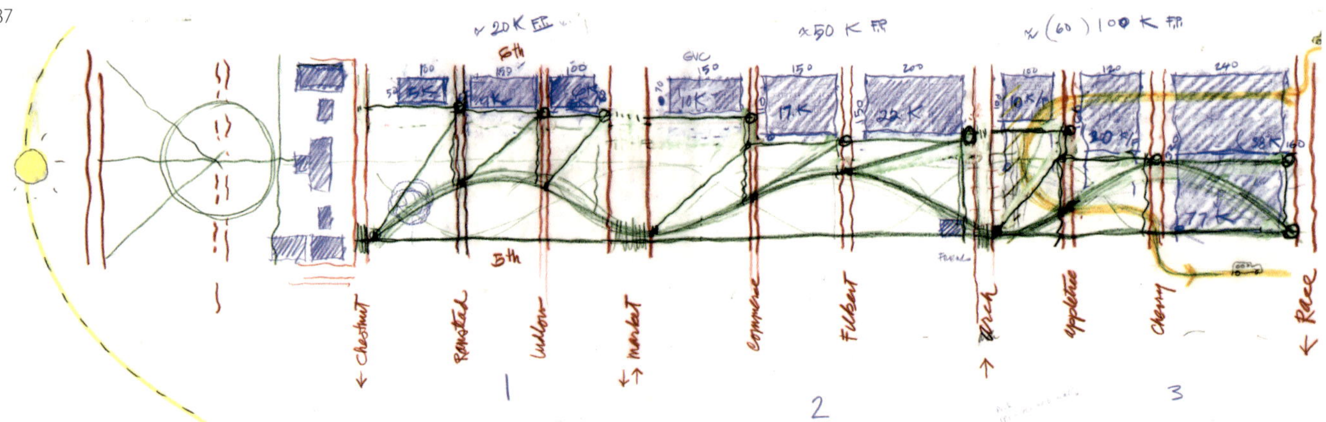

that it would hurt their visitation and economics. Conversely, the design team explained that having a major facility on the third block would enhance the dynamics of the park, and that what had been perceived as a problem of distance in previous experience was actually a problem of the earlier design. A destination such as the National Constitution Center would completely change things. At the same time the Olin Partnership began exploring the possibility of placing a bus drop-off facility on the third block as well. It appeared that this block could not support parking for all the buses, the automobile garage for the National Constitution Center, and the National Park Service's maintenance facility. As a result, the city and NPS found a remote parking facility for the buses to get them off the mall, with only drop-off and pick-up at the center.

With numerous functional elements becoming more and more clear, the central issue of the overall arrangement of parts became more pressing. Finally, in late summer, Cywinski and I met on a weekend to sit down and solve it. In preparation of this meeting, Cywinski made several studies, which proved to be pivotal. 35-37 Laying a grid across the entire site from south to north, he filled in squares on each block approximating the program square footage

35 Former park plan with 100' grid 36 Positions of streets and alleys in 30' grid 37 Circulation and building placement diagram 38 Restored historic Philadelphia alley

38

for each of the facilities where the team had concluded they must be located. He'd also marked off the cross alleys and small streets that I had fixed upon from studying the historic maps of the area. Together the two of us sat and methodically laid out the program, first symmetrically, as per the earlier Bacon plan, if only to prove to ourselves that it really was unworkable. That plan would require breaking the facilities apart into pieces that would be dysfunctional and too expensive to operate. It was also clear to us that the new facilities couldn't extend across the blocks east to west (from Fifth to Sixth Streets) as those on each block to the north would not be able to see past to Independence Hall. Cywinski said that they'd have to go on one side or the other. The programs for these facilities, each one larger than their southern neighbor, suggested that they be arranged in plan to resemble a progressive shallow curve on the park-side flank, analogous to the rake of seats in a theater. This would provide dedicated sight lines and a sequence of views from each building and every portion of the remainder of the site toward the hall. Together we realized that this must be on the western side along Sixth Street, given the earlier conclusion about the need to place the bell on the southwest corner of Block One. This could, in effect, continuously frame Sixth Street from north to south with buildings, with doors, and windows facing the government and corporate facilities opposite, making it a normative urban street once again. Also, if the new structures were placed along Sixth Street, they would help to visually screen the large and rather banal twentieth-century buildings from the park. Requirements for large open areas for crowds of 5,000 or more necessitated generous amounts of open space. It can be very hot and humid in the summer at times when visitation is the heaviest and shade is most desirable, suggesting the need for trees, canopies, porches, or arbors extending the length of the mall. Without preconceptions of how to arrange them, Cywinski and I had assumed since the beginning of the project that there should be canopy trees throughout the mall. Now it became clear that they had to occur continuously along Fifth Street if the center was to remain open to allow a view to the hall from Block Three. Cywinski drew a series of curves on each block leading in and out to the corners where people would be crossing and entering from Old City. I filled in the shapes with trees. It seemed a bit too pat, but it solved many of the functional problems.

With the buildings roughly drawn in on the west, groves of trees and garden spaces on the east, and greensward in the middle, we then carefully put in the former east-west alleys. We provided two alleys per block, to serve as pedestrian paths and service lanes, as well as markers, scaling devices, resting places and traces of the former colonial urbanity. With their evocative names–Ranstead, Ludlow, Commerce, Filbert, Apple Tree Alley, Cherry–they also made literal, visual, and physical connections to the neighborhoods beyond, on both sides of the park; and despite jaywalking between major intersections, they could allow people to enter and leave the park from a large number of locations. 38 Some still existed in the adjoining blocks, as well as providing views such as the one to Christ Church steeple on Second Street and physical access to other important attractions such as the Atwater Kent Museum to the west on Seventh Street, and the Jewish Museum and Synagogue and the Christ Church Cemetery east of Block Two.

To strengthen the urban quality and further frame the city streets, small pavilions were suggested to be built on most of the park corners to serve a variety of needs: bus shelters; entries to the Market Street subway; public restrooms; and interpretive events. To further facilitate movement and openness, diagonal paths were introduced across the central lawns leading from corners and park

39

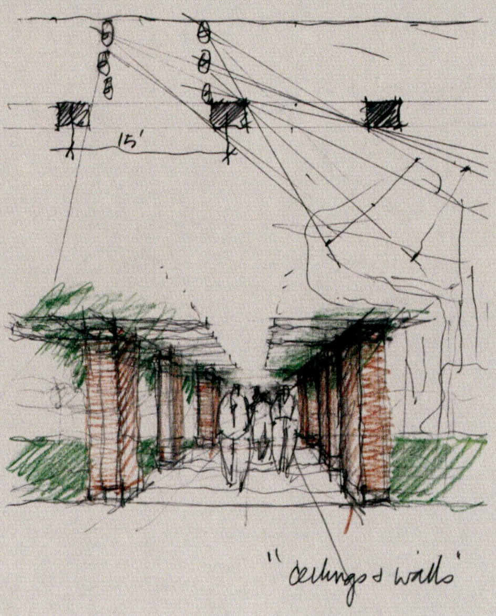

40

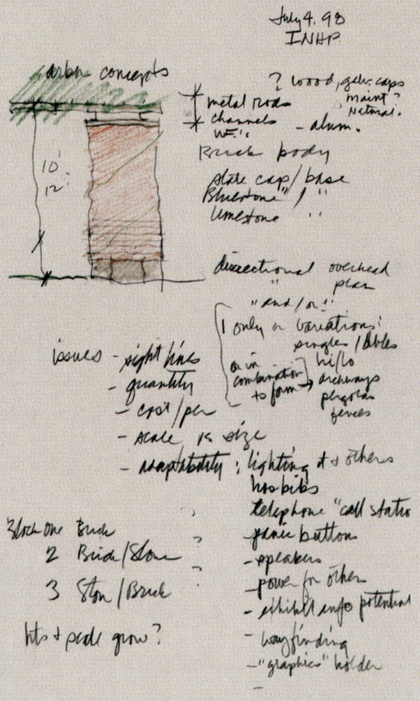

41

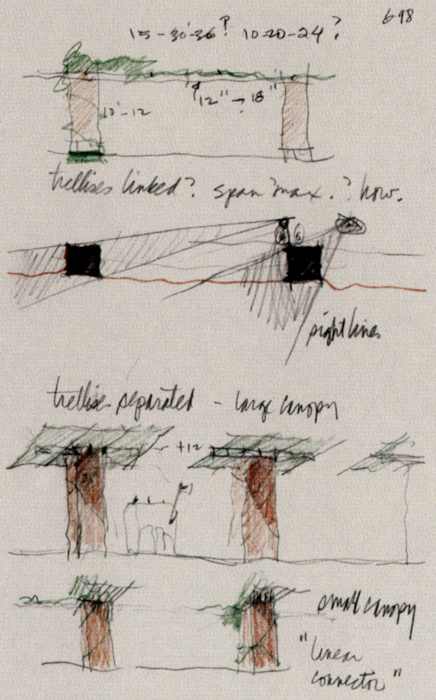

42

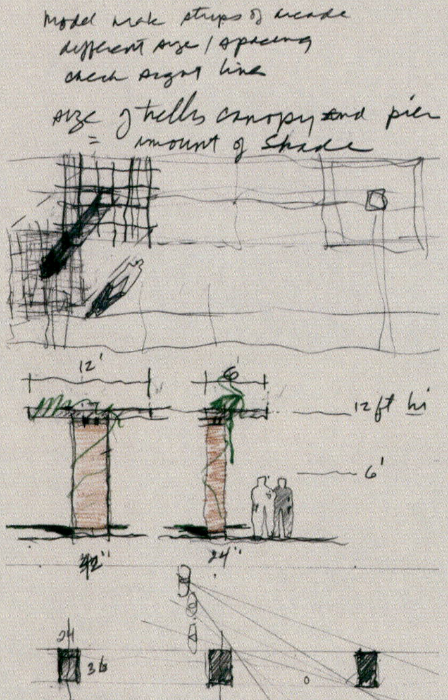

43

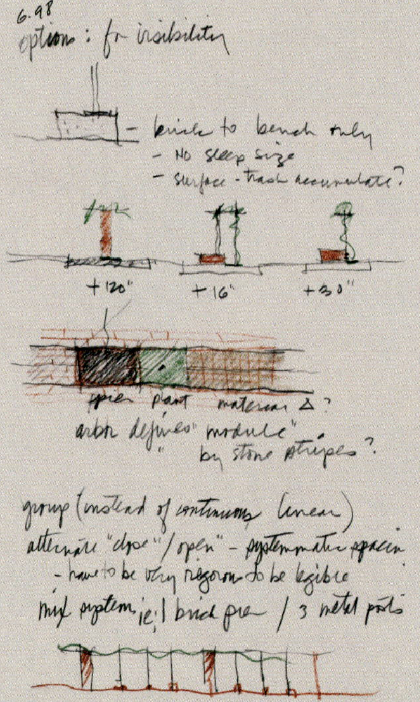

44

39-44 Sketches of the brick pier arborway   45 Sketch of Independence Mall concept plan

45

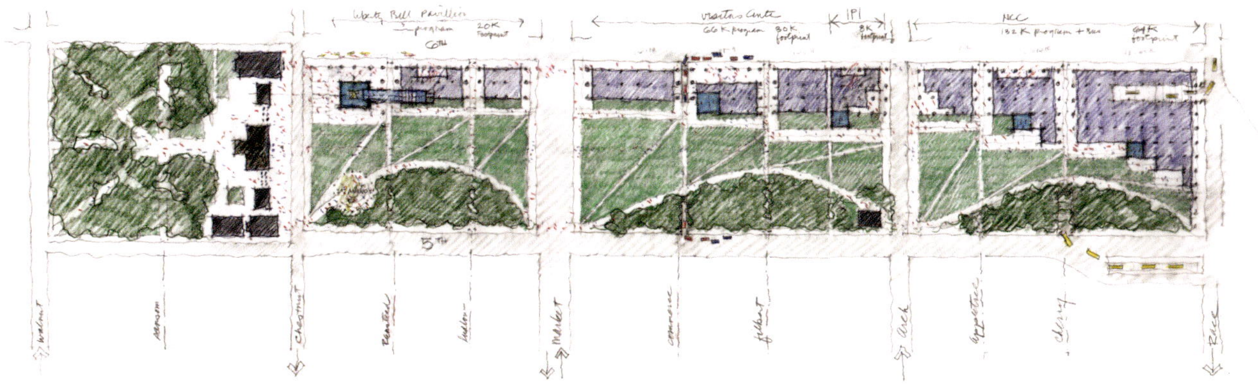

entries on the mid-block alleys to building doors and entries. A major north/south walkway was also located in the park along the east side of the buildings on the first and second blocks. This promenade created an architectural transition between building and landscape and provided for service vehicle access throughout the park. Concerned about shade for this walkway but not wishing to add more trees here, Cywinski suggested that a two-block-long arbor might solve the problem. Further, it would help unify the project while tempering the scale of the facilities, helping to insure that they felt more like park pavilions and less like large institutional structures, emphasizing the prominence of Independence Hall. 39-44

The plan that emerged by the end of that work session, while not symmetrical in the conventional sense, was balanced. 45 Groves of trees and gardens were to stand opposite the buildings with lawn in between, opening views from each part to the other. The plan reconnected the park to the city. It rebuilt the urban fabric along Sixth Street and provided a continuous, permeable greensward along Fifth Street. Here trees, after several years of growth, would also help to mask the large twentieth-century buildings, such as the United States Mint, for visitors on the paths and lawn of the park. The city was to be put back together physically while an armature for interpretation, performance, and memorials was created.

Independence Hall is given back its prominence, though not in a manner that makes it look weak like a diminutive or foolish dictator. The view from Liberty Bell Center would reinforce the memory of its former situation atop the old statehouse. It is basically the same view that people had in the eighteenth century when buildings across Chestnut Street forced views to be oblique, and from a near distance, bringing emphasis to what was an imposing civic building.

After this session with Cywinski, further meetings developed the ideas inherent in the *parti*. The arbor was to be planted with grape vines to remind us of the early hopes for vineyards and wine (not so workable at the time, as it turned out); roses brought from England; wisteria from China (named for the early, scientifically inclined Wister family of Philadelphia); and native plants such as clematis, Virginia creeper, trumpet vine, and Dutchman's pipe. On the second block, an outdoor café and small kiosk are to sit on an elevated terrace, sheltered and surrounded by plants of the sort that can be found throughout the ecologically rich valleys around Philadelphia–trees (tulip poplar, hickory, oak, chestnut, and white pine, to name a few); under-story trees (dogwood, redbud, sassafras); shrubs such as native azaleas and mountain laurel; and ferns, herbs and wildflowers. As with other elements of the park, there is no attempt to reproduce an early scene or particular place. Instead, plants were selected for their contemporary needs and their ability to provide interpretation of the society; individuals; place; and events that formed the setting for the Independence Movement, Revolution, Constitutional Convention, and the initial Capitol of the United States. As direct products of the Enlightenment, Philadelphia and its early inhabitants participated in developments in science, especially in the collection, identification, propagation, and exportation of American plants. It seemed natural that a park charged with interpreting the setting for the Revolution should employ plantings that contribute to the many narratives to be presented there.

A final aspect of this memory of *Rus in Urbs* lies in the fact that each of the new buildings was proposed to survey an expanse of lawn, as British and American country houses of that period did, and as so many of our homes and institutions do today. The situation of modernity and sophisticated up-to-date urban life is meant to rub up against native plants, gardens, and open vistas that echo those with which Philadelphia began–albeit serving a new situation: namely, that of a secular pilgrimage shrine, an urban oasis, and an education and entertainment venue for visitors and tourists.

Work continued through the autumn and into the winter as we fleshed out the plan in detail and worked with the NPS and city to resolve a series of issues. One issue concerned the size and architectural character of the proposed buildings, another was the development and layout of Block Three, and yet another concerned the traffic plan and what to do with the buses. It was unknown, at that time, who the architects for the buildings would be, or how they would be funded. The Park Service, therefore, asked us to prepare architectural guidelines for the bulk, mass, height, location, and materials of the new buildings.

The team had been concerned for some time about the underground parking garage on Block Two and its interface with the streets, park, and visitor center. We identified a number of liabilities with the garage: the long vehicular access ramps on Fifth and Sixth Streets forced pedestrians to walk in a narrow path between street and ramps and limited entry to the park and the visitor center; the absence of public space, light, and orientation devices to welcome visitors to the park above; the state of general disrepair; the structural inability to accept additional load; and finally, the potential cost of corrective work that would be required. We solved the vehicular ramp/pedestrian access issue by replacing the long, straight ramps with compact spiral ramps. Cywinski, in sectional studies, located a five-story-high atrium entrance for the public along the street edge that welcomed visitors from the street and from the three levels of parking below in a spacious hall filled with natural light and vegetation. 46 This grand arrival space to the visitor center and park became a major feature of the master plan. Working with Cywinski, conceptual plans were developed, integrating street, garage, visitor center, and park circulation–generating Block Two's role as the principal gateway to all destinations.

46

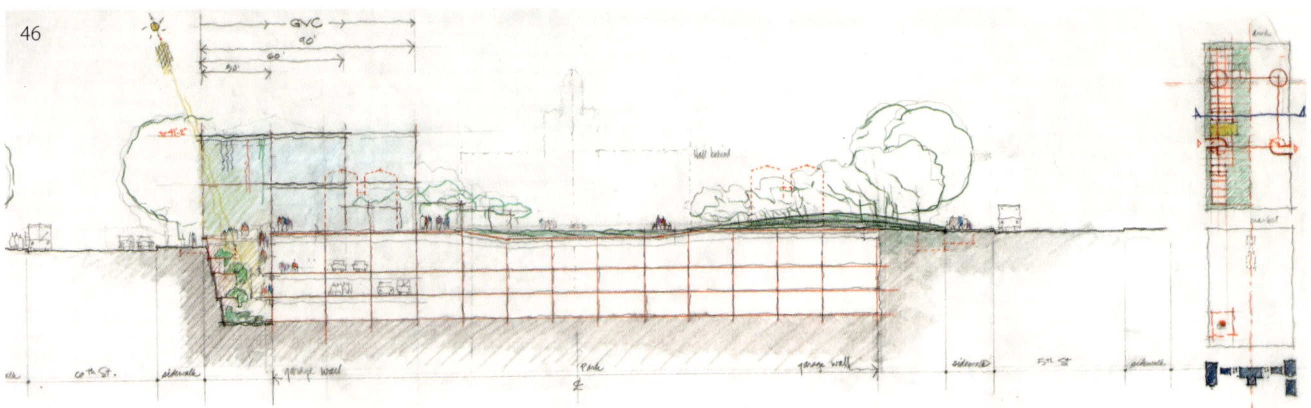

As the design guidelines were being developed, the team unanimously agreed that the new buildings were not to be neo-colonial. Copying Georgian detailing was forbidden, as were

46 Section through Block Two parking garage and future visitor center 47 Block One building placement diagram 48 Block Two building placement diagram 49 Block Three building placement diagram

semicircular masonry arches and coated or reflective glass. The range of excellent institutional, commercial, and domestic buildings nearby led us to suggest a transition in scale from one end of the park to the other, beginning by using brick and a little bit of metal and stone for the bell center; brick and a more liberal use of stone and metal on the visitor center; and the possible use of stone and glass exclusively on the constitution center. The guidelines required these buildings maintain a street wall along Sixth Street, with a greater portion of solid wall than openings, while providing a large amount of transparency on the side facing the park to animate it and to help light it at night. 47-49 These structures were also expected to acknowledge the reinstated alleys through the liberal use of entries and openings, further helping to break down their scale and animate Sixth Street.

The cornice of Independence Hall, about forty feet above the pavement, was set as a height limit for the structures in the first two blocks. For these two relatively narrow buildings (by contemporary institutional standards) a gable roof was mandated. The building in the third block, which had turned out to be much larger as the constitution center board and staff developed their program, was allowed to be taller on the back (northern) portion of the site, and a flat roof was permitted.

Plans and perspective sketches of the scheme were developed; the guidelines were finalized; and meetings were scheduled with officials from the city, state, and federal government. When officials from the

47

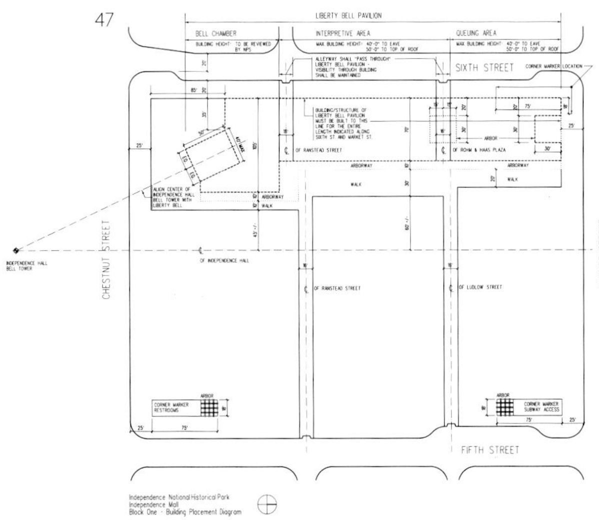

48

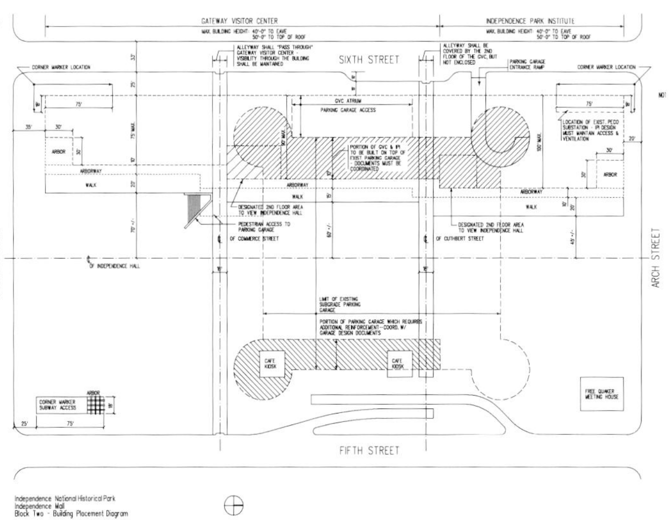

49

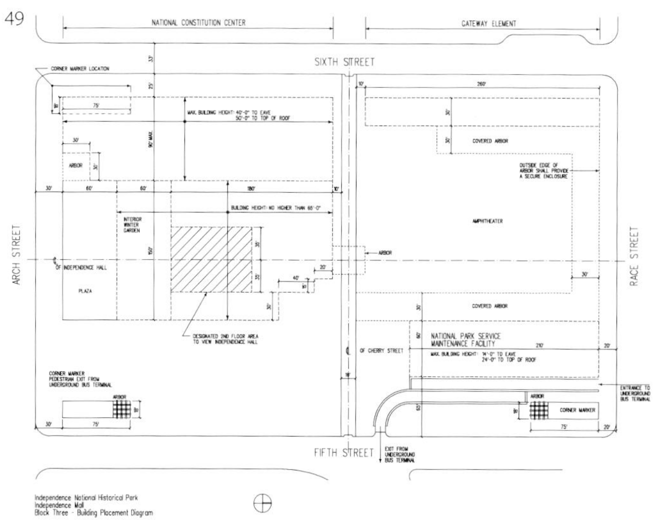

50 Independence Mall master plan

51 View from the National Constitution Center toward Independence Hall

52 Wireframe drawing

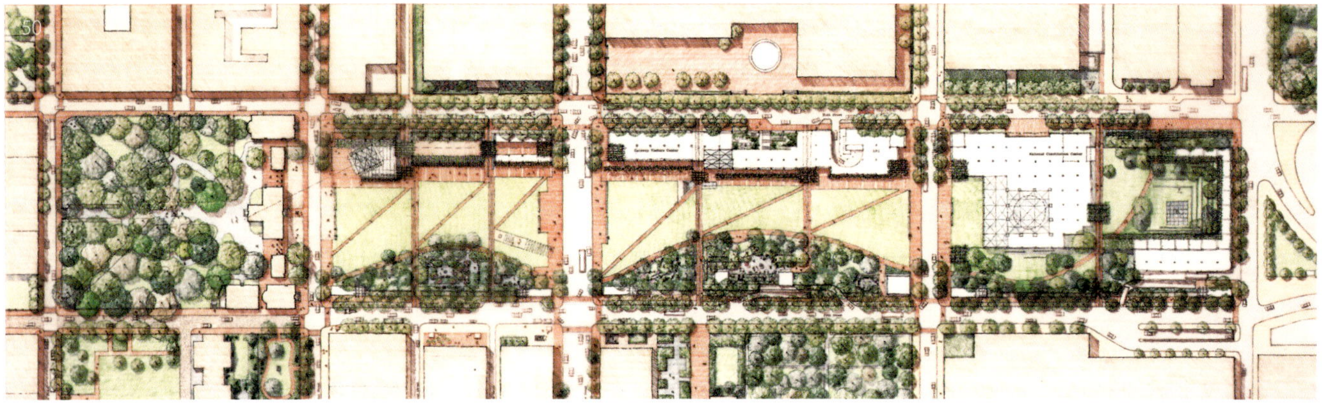

51

City of Philadelphia and the National Constitution Center first saw the plan, both objected to the position of the proposed facility on the northern end of Block Three. The team had unanimously agreed from the earliest days that the building needed to be placed across the entire block from Fifth to Sixth Streets, with a major room of some sort on the central axis facing south, terminating the view and ending what I frequently referred to as a scene that wandered off "as though in North Dakota." If the space was too long for Paul Cret and Robert Venturi at one block in length, letting it extend to the plaza at the end of the Benjamin Franklin Bridge and the Callowhill district of North Philadelphia, as it currently did, was absolutely unacceptable. Thus, the placement of the largest building on the third block was seen as desirable and necessary. The design team raised it slightly so it could see nicely over its front lawn and down the extent of the other two blocks. We also proposed placing a parking garage and bus facility beneath it along with the NPS maintenance works. Mayor Rendell and the National Constitution Center leaders stated that it was unacceptably distant from the hall, and after serious debate, insisted that it be moved south to the building line on the sidewalk of Arch Street. I argued, along with others on the design team, that this would produce a thrown-away half block of park behind the building that would be unusable and a social problem. Sensing a potential deal-breaking crisis, the NPS directed the designers to move the building and reconfigure the space behind so as to alleviate the problems they feared. So, with much more at stake, the plan was adjusted, and the final plan showed the National Constitution Center in this southern location. 50 - 56

A public presentation took place in October 1997 in the auditorium of the existing visitor center at Third and Chestnut. A large crowd attended along with local television and journalists. Despite an impassioned protest from Edmond Bacon, who opposed the project, the plan moved forward. Budgets were developed, funds allocated, and client committees and project managers selected. The NPS proceeded, working closely with The Pew Charitable Trusts and the city on the master plan and visitor center. The National Constitution Center prepared to manage the programming, design, and construction of their major new institution, working with the University of Pennsylvania and other local and national institutions. The NPS, working without a complete budget for the mall or the bell center, approached the private sector for financial assistance so that they too could begin implementation.

Design, Architecture, Politics Just weeks after the plan was approved, requests for qualifications were solicited nationally from architectural firms to be considered for the design of the three major facilities and the park: Liberty Bell Center; Independence Visitor Center; National Constitution Center; and the three-block park with its additional features—café, restrooms, pavilions, First Amendment Plaza, alleys, walls, etc. The familiar process of developing short lists and conducting interviews led to the selection of Michael

52

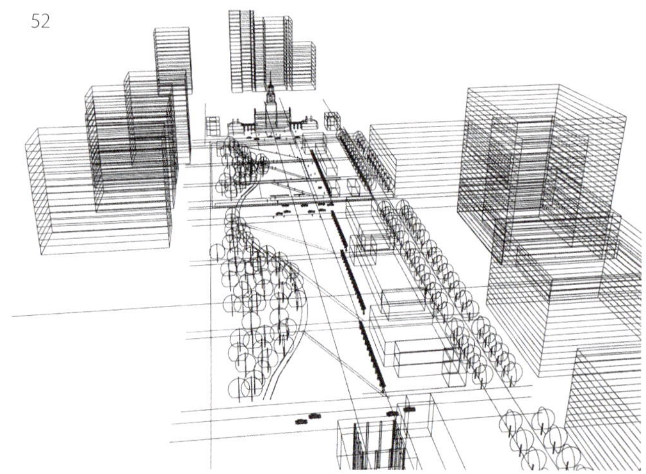

53 View of café on Block Two of Independence Mall 54 View of Independence Hall from the new visitor center 55 View from inside Liberty Bell Center 56 View of Independence Mall from Independence Hall

53

54

55

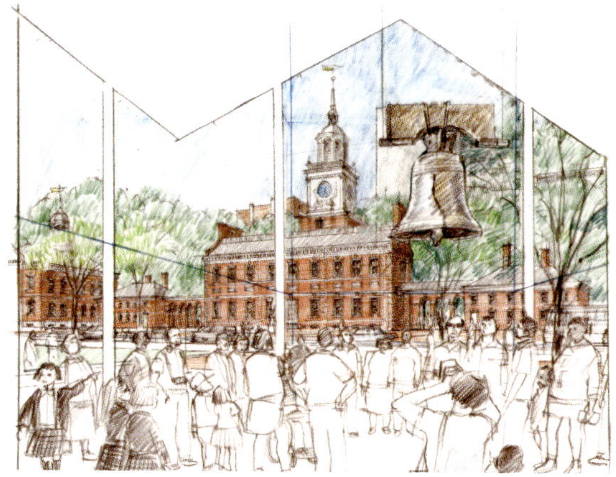

McKinnell of Kallmann, McKinnell & Wood Architects from Boston as the design architect for the visitor center; Henry N. Cobb of Pei Cobb Freed & Partners from New York as the design architect for the National Constitution Center; and Bernard Cywinski of Bohlin Cywinski Jackson of Philadelphia as the architect for Liberty Bell Center. The Olin Partnership was retained to design the first two blocks of the park by the National Park Service, and was also chosen as landscape architects for the National Constitution Center and Liberty Bell Center by their architects and clients. The hope of the NPS was that the landscape architect would help to keep the vision of the master plan, coordinate the efforts of the three distinguished architects, and help them to work together.

As Cobb and I had worked together for years; Cobb, McKinnell and I had been colleagues on the faculty at the Graduate School of Design at Harvard; and Cywinski and I had just collaborated on the master plan, we all were optimistic about working together. Shortly after Cobb began work, he independently concluded that the bulk of the constitution center should be at the north end of the site, with a portion extending south along Sixth Street. He also concluded that there should be an open area of lawn between Arch Street, and a great room in the middle of the facility and site. Ironically, this was almost identical to the *parti* of the earlier suppressed scheme presented by the master plan team, who now embraced it heartily on its return. Upon further review, the National Constitution Center client also accepted Cobb's suggested design. Additionally, the combined bus/parking/maintenance facility that was proposed to go beneath it was deemed too costly. An automobile garage and the NPS maintenance facility were developed below grade, but the buses ended up on grade along Fifth Street, where we had shown them in one of the earliest studies. Here and on the opposite (western) side of the building, Cobb showed the ingenious use of geometry for which his firm is noted. Screening the bus parking, he created a proscenium while leading the passengers out to a "front porch" view to the hall as their introduction to the park and the National Constitution Center.

56

On the western side he created a view between the south wing and the main building, that opens diagonally through the building toward Franklin Square. It was remarkable to find a way to situate the National Constitution Center to welcome motorists to the park and city, and to facilitate physical and psychological connections between the park and the square, while working within the original footprint of the master plan.

However, both Cobb and McKinnell, at one time or another, challenged three of the key master plan elements–namely, footprint, arbor, and alleyway–citing difficulty or conflict with their programs or design goals. Cywinski and I, with NPS support, made the case for adherence to the principles behind these elements for the sake of cohesion and coherency among the multiple agendas and diverse personal approaches in play. While debate was intense at times (one of the NPS participants humorously referred to our discussions as the "Clashes of the Titans"), we found common ground after a number of work sessions spanning the winter and spring of 1999. 57-61 During that time, schemes for real buildings evolved. The group of architects, the Olin Partnership, and the NPS visited the site on numerous occasions to talk over issues and material choices; test the master plan and its guidelines; and collaboratively make the decisions on matters of common concern. 62

By the summer of 1999, work had been underway on the parking garage on Block Two; and each of the buildings and park designs had progressed to the point that detailed cost estimates could finally be produced. The result was sobering. Each and every piece was discovered to now cost far more than originally envisioned

57

58

59

57 Bernard Cywinski, Laurie Olin, Henry Cobb, and Michael McKinnell   58-61 Master plan team meetings to review designs of all new buildings in the mall

when the overall plan was completed a year and a half earlier. The reasons were many, but the two most fundamental were: 1) the construction situation in Philadelphia and the region had changed, with prices increasing dramatically; and 2) the condition of the parking garage structure was worse than anyone had expected, drawing more money into its reconstruction and the requirements for placing the new park and visitor center above it. Some radical changes took place to reduce the amount of building while staying true to the master plan design principles. An educational facility, the Independence Park Institute, was postponed; the extent of arborways reduced; and all the corner pavilions along Fifth Street eliminated except for the public restrooms. The visitor center suffered the most, cutting back on architectural detail and substantially reducing the scope of the atrium/entrance connecting street, building, and park. Building finishes, park furnishings, interpretive and art works were also simplified, reduced, or eliminated.

60

Compounded with the challenges of the overall cost of the project were archaeological artifacts that were unearthed once construction began on this historic site. Excavations for the new buildings unearthed unexpected and provocative discoveries. Block Three proved to be rich in archaeological findings, ranging from the remains of a Native American settlement with fire pits, artifacts, and early trading goods to the bits and pieces of daily life in the Revolutionary Era. Next, it unfolded that important figures in the development of African American self realization had lived and met on a portion of the National Constitution Center site along Fifth Street. Excavations on Block Three also exposed a pre-colonial street and a portion of a graveyard in which many skeletons were found. Block One was equally fertile ground, yielding artifacts that reinvigorated the interest of local historians and the African American community. Remains of the Robert Morris mansion at Sixth and Market were recovered. The house is significant because it served as the executive mansion for George Washington and John Adams during their presidencies and was the forerunner of the White House. Around that time, it was publicized that Washington brought and kept a number of slaves during the years he lived in Philadelphia on the very site that the Liberty Bell was being honored. This publicity led to demands that the NPS create a memorial to the enslaved Africans who lived there.

61

Independence National Historical Park after 9/11 The terrorist attacks of September 11, 2001 dealt another blow to the realization of the master plan and the park. Everyone in the United States has been affected by the events of that tragic day and no one factor in our lives has changed more than our sense of safety. In the name of providing security, we now go to great lengths to protect our citizens and the icons of our culture, often in ways challenging our cherished beliefs in democratic freedoms.

The impact on the Independence National Historical Park was among the worst in the country. Within hours of the attacks, Independence Hall was cordoned off and Chestnut Street closed. Suddenly, foot and vehicular traffic between Old City and Society Hill were cut off from the rest of the downtown to the west. Within days, physical barriers and armed patrols appeared; and, ironically, after the Liberty Bell was moved into its new home, a temporary security screening facility was set up in the vacated 1976 Liberty Bell Pavilion. After impassioned pleas, Chestnut Street was eventually reopened to traffic; but the fences, barriers, and guards remained to guide the visitors along very defined routes between Liberty Bell Center and Independence Hall.

The Park and its Future By the end of 2003, all three major buildings were opened and serving a visitorship that quadrupled in the first two years of operation. By mid-2006 the park, whose rebirth is the *raison d'être* for the new quarters constructed for such high purposes, was nearly finished. Only a small portion of the master plan remained to be constructed on Block One. Most of Block Two was completed or under construction; and Block Three landscape was realized, albeit possessing a somewhat adolescent quality to the planting, which should only improve with age. The barricades might yet come down as they should, and the park will, in time, be fully realized. When that happens, all the effort of so many people will be justified. Visitors and residents alike will be able to walk freely through this most American city and visit the single most important structure in our land, Independence Hall. They will be able to see the Liberty Bell and understand why it has become such a symbol to all those who have, and are still struggling for, freedom and self-realization. They will learn about the system of laws and rules crafted by a group of unusually prescient men that still guide us through our difficulties and differences, while taking pleasure in the seasons and each other out of doors in the heart of the metropolis. It is not too much to hope for in William Penn's *Greene Country Towne*, the host to a series of the most amazing events in Western history. The vicissitudes of the early years of the twenty-first century will be weathered; and the Independence National Historical Park will be completed to celebrate our history, reaffirm our beliefs as a society, and stand as an extraordinary American place for all to enjoy.

Laurie Olin is a distinguished teacher, author, and principal of the landscape architecture firm, Olin Partnership, in Philadelphia. He is currently Practice Professor of Landscape Architecture in the School of Design at the University of Pennsylvania. Mr. Olin's numerous award-winning design projects include campuses, urban design, and parks. His work extends to Bryant Park and Battery Park City in New York; the Getty Center in Los Angeles; and social housing in Frankfurt, Germany. Mr. Olin's major planning and design projects at academic institutions include the University of Pennsylvania, Yale University, Stanford University, MIT, and a new campus for Harvard University in Allston, MA. Mr. Olin is a John Simon Guggenheim Fellow, an American Academy of Rome Fellow, an honorary member of the American Institute of Architects, a Fellow of the American Academy of Arts and Sciences, the 1999 Wyck-Strickland Award recipient, a member of the American Academy of Arts and Letters, and a Fellow of the American Society of Landscape Architects.

62 Revised master plan drawing based on actual designs for new buildings

Liberty Bell Center: Architecture and Symbol

Bernard Cywinski

The design of Liberty Bell Center began unofficially while we were deeply involved in the creation of the master plan for Independence National Historical Park with Laurie Olin, Jim Kise, and their respective firms. In thinking about the future home for the Liberty Bell, we knew we had established a clear direction for the development of its new site. By imagining how a design could evolve in its historic context and by adopting the master plan's intellectual goals, we believed the master plan created a very favorable environment for the new home of the Liberty Bell.

We were delighted to continue working with Laurie Olin as our consulting landscape architect for the roughly one-acre site that would accommodate the building and its special gardens, arborways, and walkways. With Laurie, we knew we could explore the relationship between landscape design and building design in a profound way, find ways to make seamless the solutions concerning the land and the building, and also raise the awareness of those who would experience this place. One of the great pleasures of our collaboration was our pencil-in-hand conversations over drawings that were shaped with enthusiasm for mutually conceived ideas. 63 We asked Joe Nicholson of Ueland Junker McCauley Nicholson, another Philadelphia firm, to join us as exhibit designer, with the intention that together we would truly integrate exhibit design and architecture into an interdependent, singular experience. Joe, being an architect and exhibit designer, saw the potential of this idea and proved to be a great collaborator as the design progressed, finding ways to dissolve the boundaries between building and artifact. 64

Any discussion of Liberty Bell Center must begin with an understanding of the center's role relative to Independence National Historical Park's mission and the realization that the center shares the same set of goals and principles that guided the rebirth of the park. Before the Liberty Bell Center project became reality, the National Park Service's broad goals were firmly

63

64

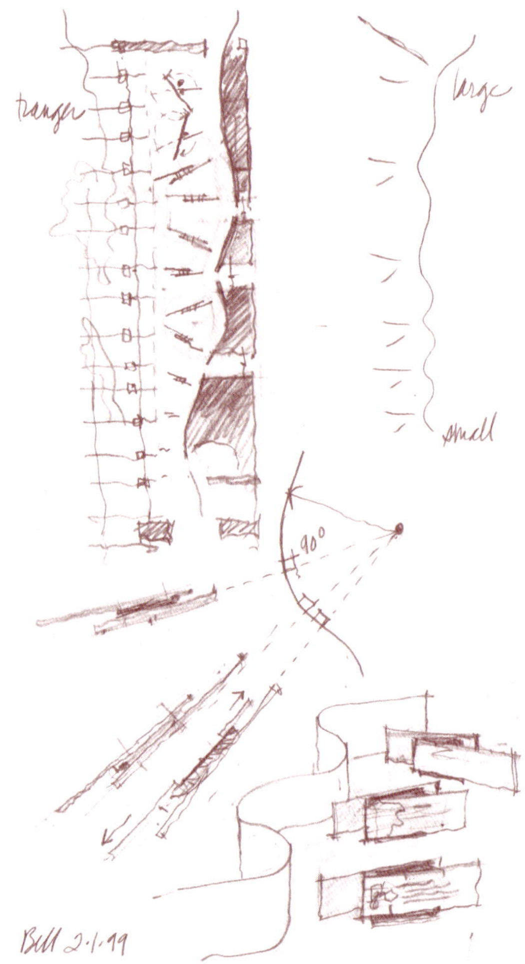

established in the General Management Plan for Independence National Historical Park. This document laid out the Park Service's philosophical position and stated the underlying urban design principles for the large-scale reconsideration of the park's constituent built and open spaces. 65 The Park Service's intentions were to reestablish a park as a setting appropriate in size and use for Independence Hall, enhance the visitor experience, and strengthen physical and symbolic connections between the park and its urban surroundings. 66

Great attention was to be given to the scale of Liberty Bell Center and the other new buildings, as well as outdoor spaces, with the intent to favor Independence Hall's "visual and intellectual power, which is derived from its relative smallness and the enormous impact of the ideas formed in and symbolized by it." The General Management Plan recognized the importance of taking advantage of how design can enhance experience in sensory ways: views and vistas to appreciate Independence Hall and its surroundings; axes, asymmetry, and sequence to locate key indoor and outdoor spaces; and circulation and hierarchy to enhance accessibility and order.

65

66

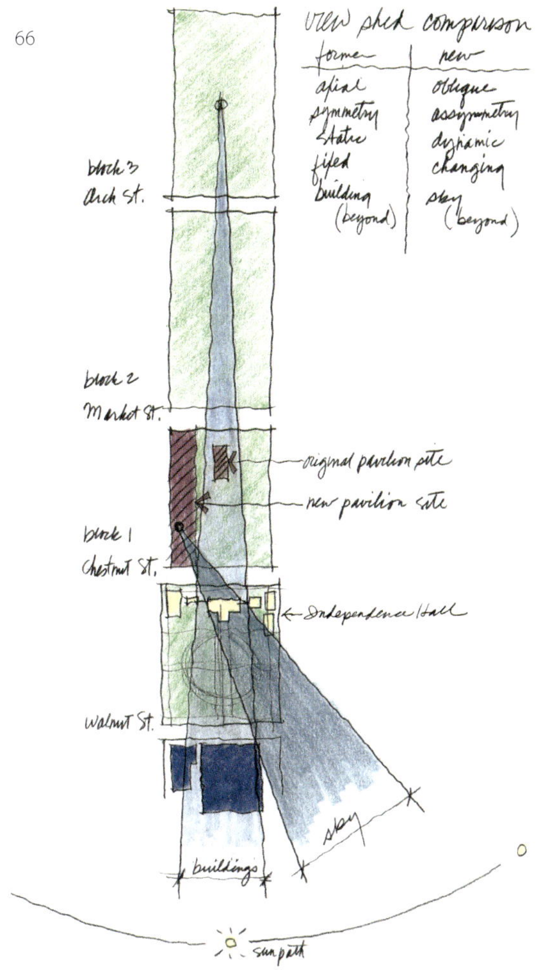

Looking beyond the confines of the park, the General Management Plan noted the value of arranging buildings in keeping with "William Penn's grid plan, in which buildings and spaces derive their importance from factors other than physical position, is inherently communal and egalitarian, very much in the spirit of the park." The General Management Plan goes on to stress the Park Service's desire for reintegration with the city around it through provision for a pedestrian environment that encourages free movement diagonally across the mall and supports "interconnection between the mall, its buildings and the city fabric and its civic life." [67]

The National Park Service believed that a reconstructed park would better celebrate American history, ideals, and purpose–and would reaffirm Independence Hall's primacy as the centerpiece of the park. The Liberty Bell was to be the keystone in the arch of important artifacts, which represent the democratic principles and ideas that define our nation. The Liberty Bell and the United States Constitution were to be housed and displayed, their stories told in individual buildings that would complement the richness of those stories. The stories would be supported by a presentation of artifacts and documents and provide the visitor the opportunity to interact with history in ways that were previously unavailable. Added to this agenda was a third building, the new Independence Visitor Center, which was designed to welcome, inform, and arrange journeys for visitors to Independence National Historical Park, as well as to the many historic points of interest in and around Philadelphia and in the eastern Pennsylvania region.

With the background of this well-articulated plan, the Park Service gave reasons for replacing Aldo Giurgola's 1976 Bicentennial Liberty Bell Pavilion. Held in praise by many and disdain by others, the Park Service realized that while it responded well to its original program, changes in the numbers and composition of visitors demanded new modes of interpretation and greater response to a wider range of interests. [68] At a pragmatic level, a more sophisticated environment was needed in terms of air quality, humidity and temperature control, lighting, security, and like preservation matters. Most importantly, a larger space was required to tell an expanded story to larger and more diverse audiences.

Moreover, many of their key desires were socially oriented and qualitative: the desire to offer a variety of learning experiences responsive

67

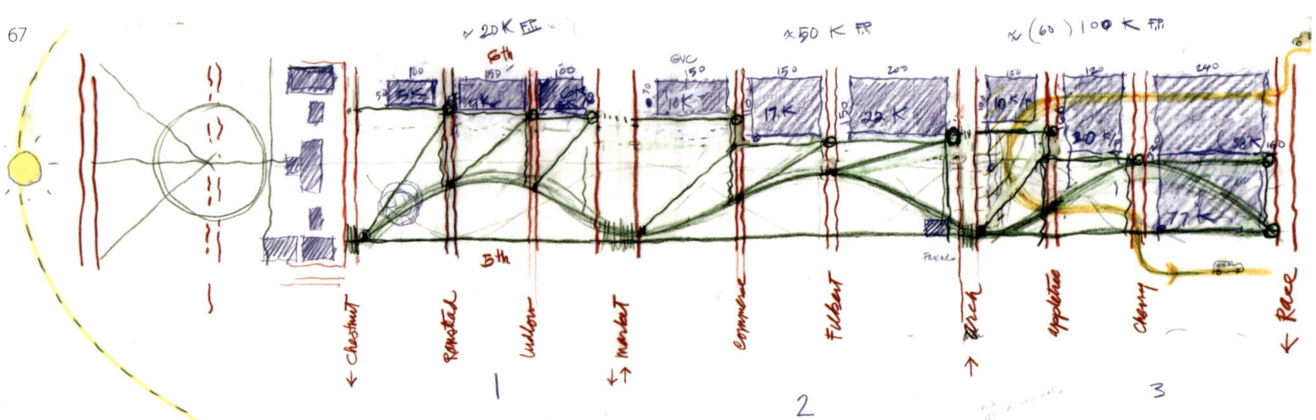

67 Circulation and building placement diagram 68 Mitchell/Guirgola's 1976 Liberty Bell Pavilion 69 Liberty Bell detail

to different learning styles; the ability to address the needs of the increasing numbers of foreign visitors; the means to communicate the history and significance of the Liberty Bell in ways that are intellectually sound and enjoyable to experience; and, most importantly, to enable the visitor to encounter the bell intimately and in silence. Bohlin Cywinski Jackson clearly saw the Liberty Bell Center design goal to be one of providing an authentic, moving, and memorable encounter with this icon of American and world history in an architecture that resonated with the profound events that took place in Philadelphia.

68

We were enthusiastic about the rich set of circumstances, expectations, and mystery that this project held. Our practice, from its beginning, has been dedicated to design principles that celebrate the spirit of place, the craft of building, and the making of architecture that is responsive to context, technology, and human nature. The design of Liberty Bell Center would provide an extraordinary challenge, especially due to its atypical nature: a structure to house a single object venerated by our society and recognized by the world as a symbol of freedom and the human spirit. 69 We were moving forward on unknown and difficult terrain and had to negotiate a balanced path between information and entertainment, monumentality and accessibility, solemnity and conviviality.

The task of designing a new home for the Liberty Bell and all of what that means philosophically, historically, and contextually had very few, if any, precedents. What other iconic object in American history has been so celebrated? What emotions should the encounter touch to impart a sense of awe, joy, and pride and make the personal experience a memorable event? Capturing the spirit of this place and celebrating the union of bell and hall while deferring to the importance of Independence Hall and its place of primacy on the mall were our

69

70 Master plan detail of Block One 71 Oblique view of Independence Hall 72 Oblique view studies

72

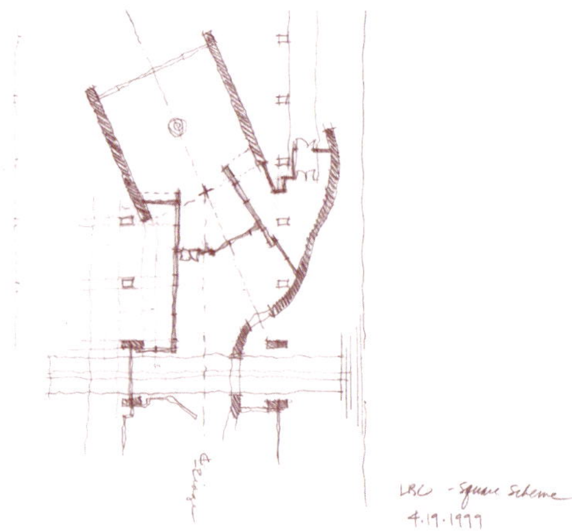

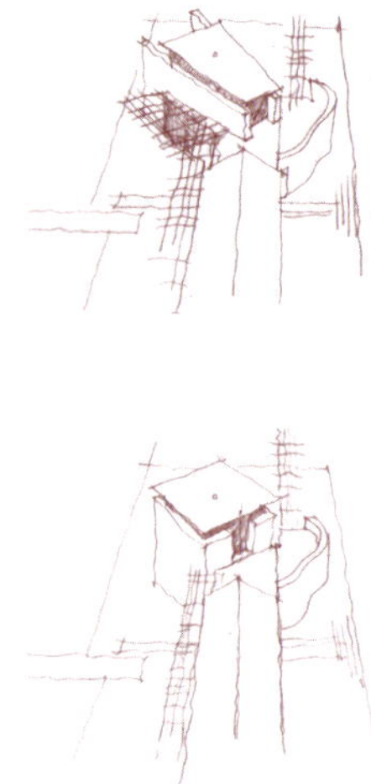

first concerns. We also wanted the center's place to be "of the park landscape" while asserting its presence as structured space situated on historic ground, clearly marking where the Liberty Bell resides.

Our involvement in the master planning for the park allowed us two distinct advantages: the time to fully understand the cultural legacy of the site; and an opportunity to contemplate the melding of meaning, place, site, building, and program in a comprehensive presentation of the Liberty Bell.

While we worked on the master plan, we did not know the ultimate size of the building or its detailed program. However, we did know that the bell would be located in a position of deference to Independence Hall. 70 The physical location of the bell was to move from the existing Liberty Bell Pavilion that was centered on axis with Independence Hall on the north side of Block One. The new new location for the bell would be much closer to Independence Hall and on the southwest corner of Block One. Where formerly the view of bell and hall was overwhelmed by a twenty-story office building directly behind the hall, now both would be clearly seen with the hall's spire silhouetted against an open sky. 71

Locating Liberty Bell Center's structure off the mall centerline and closer to Independence Hall required an "axial shift" between the center's exhibit space and the Bell Chamber to present the desired alignment of bell and hall. 72 The requirement for a direct oblique view from bell to spire of Independence Hall was perhaps the most telling design requirement derived from the master plan. The subtlety of how one turns direction, shifts people's movements, and reveals the bell in a powerful and authoritative setting would be a major focus of our design energy. There were two other components that gave the master plan special meaning: the alleyways and the arborway. We would find that

70

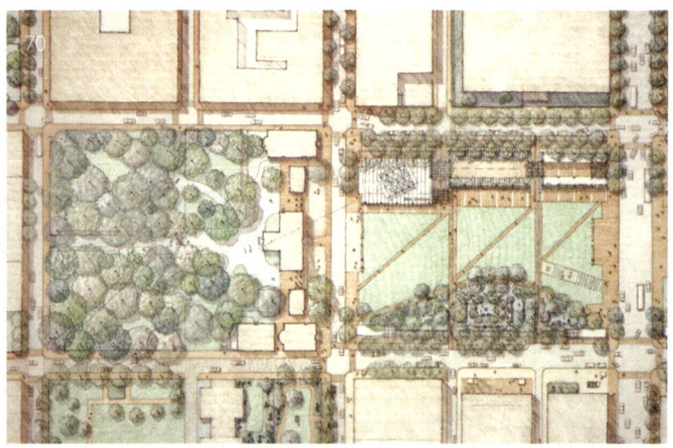

71

73 System of alleys and streets knitting site to urban context 74 Restored historic Philadelphia alley 75 Alleys define exhibit space

these same features would serve to define the essence of the architectural plan and section of Liberty Bell Center.

In an effort to give scale, and in particular a Philadelphia scale, to the park, we reintroduced to the master plan the alleyways on Blocks One and Two of Independence Mall. The alleyways connect the landscaped east side to the west side of the mall where contemporary buildings form an urban edge sheltering the landscape from the heavily built-up twentieth-century Philadelphia. They also allow us to contrast the urban western perimeter strategy with a natural landscape of indigenous plantings along the eastern edge that, during the eighteenth century, marked the city's limits. The park's former symmetry about the axis of Independence Hall was replaced by a balance of equal masses: buildings on the west and arboreal landscape on the east. Together these elements flank a great lawn, an idealized American space of openness and grand vista. 73, 74

The intersection of alleyway and structure served to lock in the positions of arrival and entry, exhibit and queuing, and the Bell Chamber encounter. The two alleyways divide the plan segments, yielding a northern zone for outdoor gathering; a central zone with storytelling exhibits occupying the 150-foot by 50-foot space between alleyways; and, finally, the chamber zone in its prominent southerly position, presenting the bell in a grand space. The alleyways were scribed into the floor plane as a reminder of the past. The materials that formed the exterior alleyway slip under the exterior glass wall and become the floor of the interior, creating a seamless connection between inside and out expressed in brick, bluestone, and granite. 75

74

73

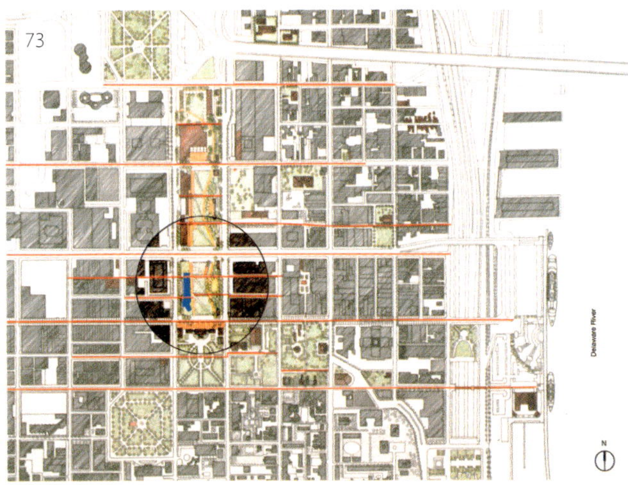

75

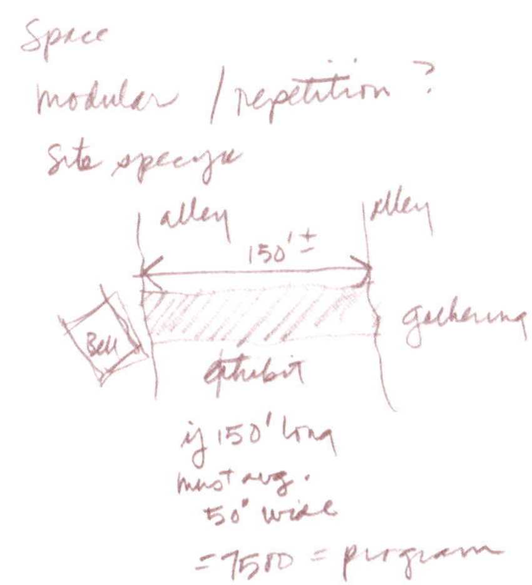

76

In the master plan the arborway, composed of brick and stone piers supporting metal trellises, provides an architectural transition element between landscape and buildings. 76-79

The arborway unifies the three blocks and provides a human-scaled element at the park's western edge. The arborway would be both landscape and architecture, with flowering vines entwining the trellises above, filling the walkway below with dappled sunlight.

77

We were asked at the architect selection interview, "What do you think the building will look like?" We said that we viewed the arborway piers as "beginnings of buildings" and that one could

78

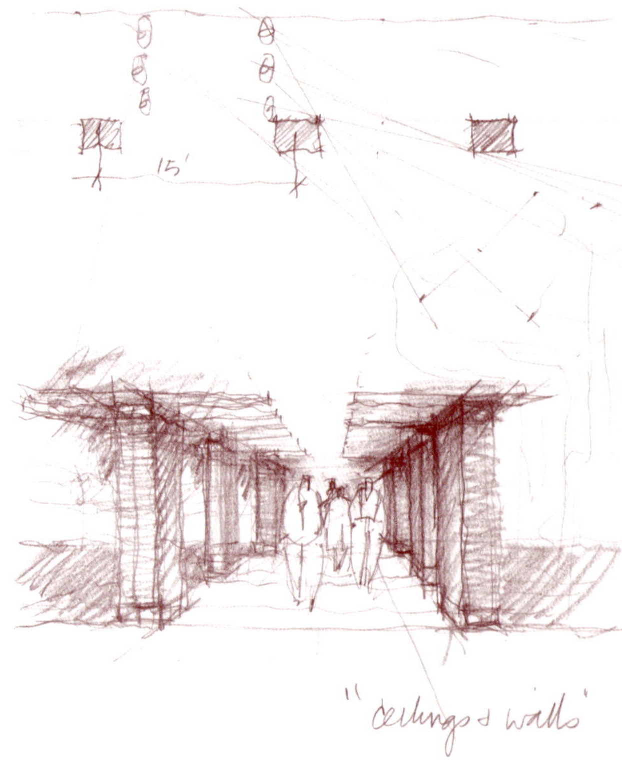

imagine the arborway morphing into a building. The piers would become columns of support; glass walls would span between piers to enclose the interior; and the arborway would have a roof like those of the train and market sheds of historic Philadelphia. 80, 81

We also believed from the beginning that the new home of the Liberty Bell should be a pavilion in the park, highly transparent so one would never really leave the park to enjoy the experience of encountering the bell and its history. 82 This desire for transparency, which is traditionally avoided in an immersive gallery environment, became a guiding principle for the building and the exhibit. We could tell the bell's story with a constant awareness of surrounding historic circumstances embodied in the site, with Independence Hall to the south and the National Constitution Center to the north. Finally, our design should resonate with the history, site, and landscape of the park to create a lasting architecture.

The National Park Service had very explicit goals for the visitor experience and firm beliefs regarding exhibits. The bell receives a diverse and ever-growing visitation; and as technology, media, and industry have increasingly raised our expectations about experiential environments, the need to present a more comprehensive, engaging, and informative visit was key. Beyond a higher level of intellectual understanding of the bell's history and meaning, the Park Service hoped for an architecture and interpretive exhibit that engendered

80

81

82

80, 81 Historic Philadelphia headhouses 82 Study of transparency and exhibit 83 Mediums for exhibit storytelling 84 Circulation diagrams 85 Plan sketches

83

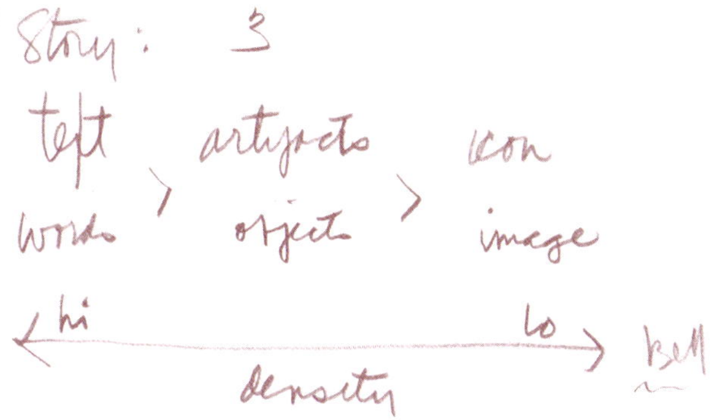

84

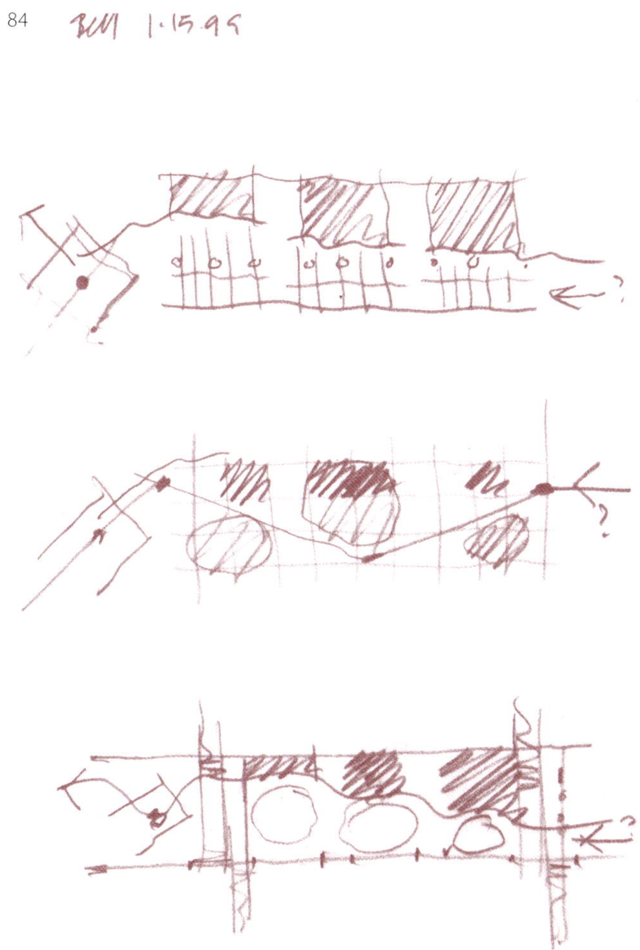

85

respect and appreciation for the bell, but also for an experience that was moving, powerful, and memorable. The exhibit program clearly outlined the content goals for the project: "The exhibit will focus on telling the story of how the Liberty Bell was transformed from a utilitarian object to a relic of the Revolution, to a symbol of America's persistent investment in liberty, to an international icon recognized worldwide for its association with the rights of humankind. 83 Exhibit content will move from the concrete facts of the bell's creation and use to the abstract ideas it has come to symbolize, not only for Americans, but also to people around the world."

This storyline gave rise to the notion that this is a "one-way building." The visitor enters at the beginning of the story, walks through its chapters, and exits after encountering the bell itself. Typically, exhibit visitation consists of entry, circulation in a loop pattern returning to the point of origin, the requisite visit to the gift shop, and then exit. In Liberty Bell Center, the experience is processional and destination-oriented. 84 It culminates with the most dramatic and memorable display, which is a much more powerful sequence. The story unfolds chronologically, and the space is experienced linearly so that the story and building are revealed as visitors advance toward the moment of encounter with the Liberty Bell.

As the design progressed, we continued our discovery of poignant ways to connect architecture, site, and the story. The arborway physically tied architecture and landscape together. The transparency we sought in the building would orient visitors and allow long views connecting building, park, and streetscape. A more subtle connection to the landscape is in the slope of the floor in the exhibit space. It parallels the exterior grades up to a "plateau" three feet above the sidewalk where the bell resides in its chamber. Although the slope is only two percent, you sense your ascendancy through the exhibits and your arrival at the level floor of the Bell Chamber, as well as your descent to the street upon exiting.

We used another landscape device, a garden wall, to continue our dialogue with the land and connect with the exhibit story. 85 Guiding one through the total experience is an undulating wall of Chelmsford granite that originates in the landscape to the north and continues under porch and roof through the building and out into the landscape to mark the end of the visitor's journey at

86

its southern end. The granite wall carries many messages. It is a prominent material shared by Independence Hall and Liberty Bell Center. The stones are guillotine-cut, resulting in a rough, uneven surface that makes the walls appear more handcrafted than machine-made. Additionally, Chelmsford granite has mica content that sparkles when sunlight strikes the surface. 86 The stone wall undulates in plan, diagonally bisecting the rectangular space east to west, forming a tall, narrow opening at the entrance and a wide low space at the exit. The third characteristic of the wall is that its top elevation is consistent, defining a horizontal datum line. Due to the floor's "rising," the wall changes its nature, an imposing thirteen-foot height at entry and a quiet ten-foot height at the plateau of the Bell Chamber. The resulting spatial perception changes softly along its length, from grand to intimate. As the wall never touches the ceiling/roof, it takes on other meanings. Which came first, building or wall? Was this a nod to Jefferson's undulating brick garden walls at the University of Virginia? We did, for a time, consider brick for the wall. However, as brick (a modest, uniformly scaled building unit) was prominently used on the floor and piers, the change to stone gave the wall a stronger presence due not only to the stone's color, shape, and texture, but also because of the change in scale resulting from using large blocks. We also valued its message of importance, permanence, and durability. The wall guides the visitor through the exhibit story, announcing each chapter in incised stone: "Pennsylvania's State House Bell, America's Liberty Bell, The World's Symbol for Liberty." 87

Knowing that people who visit the bell will absorb the experience at differing levels subject to personal time and curiosity, we wanted to offer alternative circulation paths to respond to this inevitability. So that the story could be told quickly in headlines and in-depth exposition, we developed what we referred to as the "fast lane" and the "slow lane." 88 The abbreviated walk through the exhibit takes

87

86 Detail–stone wall 87 Detail–stone signage 88 Flow diagram - fast lane, slow lane 89 Independence Hall brick and stone detail 90 Exhibit hall under construction 91 Exhibit hall section

88

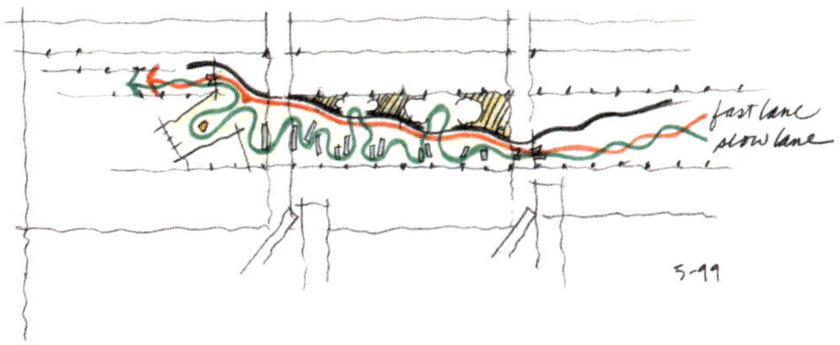

91

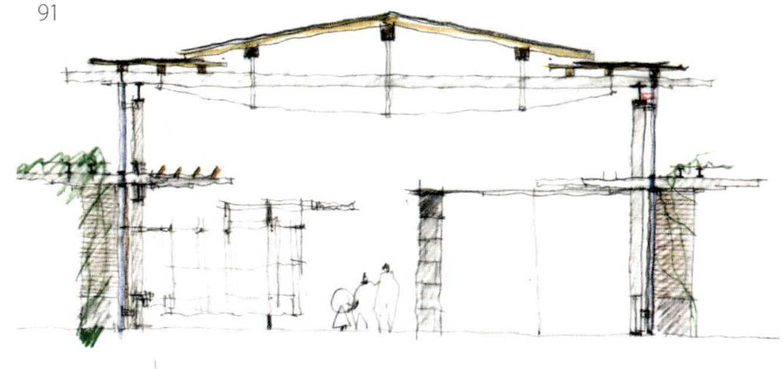

place along the undulating wall, giving people a synopsis of the story with the opportunity to select individual chapters to investigate. The more leisurely walk takes the visitor in and out of the several alcoves where the story is told in more detail. As the visitor progresses through the exhibit, the undulating granite wall veers westward, allowing the exhibit area to expand spatially until one reaches the threshold of the Bell Chamber. The exhibit medium changes from printed word to image and artifact to electronic communication in step with the technology available at the time the events took place in history.

We looked to the external surroundings to inform the palette of materials and details for the building. Independence Hall, the Liberty Bell Center program, and exhibit story suggested using hand-molded brick, a Flemish bonding pattern, and the grapevine mortar joint to mirror that of the hall. 89 Subsequently, the site walls, piers, and building surfaces all use this common language to achieve a greater harmony with their surroundings. The decision to use the arborway pier as the primary structural progenitor of the building gives the building and the exhibit within a great sense of order and scale. The closely spaced piers in the arborway, less than twenty feet center to center and ten to fourteen feet high, support vine-covered trellises outside and light-shielding canopies inside. The interior volume of the exhibit space needed to be higher than the trellises and canopies and above the undulating stone wall. We drew a number of structural options: paired piers; staggered piers of differing heights; and piers combined with taller steel columns in order to increase the building height to something over twenty feet in the exhibit space. Most combinations proved to be overly bulky or out of scale. Jon Morrison, our structural engineer, informed us that by interlocking the brick pier with paired steel columns at mid-height, we could get the lateral stability and stiffness the building needed and the slenderness that we desired for the interior supporting members. 90, 91

89

90

Additionally, the structural bay width of fifty feet could be achieved with economical steel trusses because the tight column spacing along the building's length effectively reduced the load on each span. This solution also gave us the freedom of having no interior columns to constrain the shape of the exhibit area. We continued this approach in the chamber envelope, increasing the scale of the piers and columns and compressing their spacing even more to suit the chamber's higher ceiling and grander scale.

We studied how glass walls and an opaque roof would engage the structure and complete the enclosure. We wanted to express the openness and connection to the landscape but also impart a strong physical presence to the new structure. At the ground plane we minimized the separation of inside and out by having the glass curtain wall meet the sloping floor, relegating ductwork and piping to concealed or screened areas away from the visitor's view. We tested sub-floor, overhead-exposed, and above-ceiling distribution systems. We found that the sub-floor system required a costly structured crawl space and the exposed system to be visually inappropriate. The above-ceiling solution proved to be most suitable in economic and design terms. The final scheme provides

conditioned air from above the ceiling augmented by radiant heat along the walls just above the trellises/light-shielding canopies. The mullion pattern of the glass curtain wall changes based on its location within the building. At the exhibit alcoves the mullions are closely spaced. At selected positions, they have a wider spacing to enhance the park view, and they are broadly spaced at the chamber window behind the bell. We used an ultra-clear low iron glass for the south window wall of the Bell Chamber so the view of the Liberty Bell and Independence Hall appears as if there is almost no glass at all between them. 92

After considering slate shingles, terne-coated metal, and painted metal options, we settled on a roof surface of standing seam copper. From the exterior the visitor sees a simple gable roof: copper cladding on wood decking supported by steel trusses. The master plan design guidelines mandated that there be no exposed rooftop equipment to interfere with views down onto the Liberty Bell Center from the surrounding taller buildings. To keep the roof clean we located mechanical and electrical equipment and ductwork in a basement and above a wood ceiling that rests on the bottom chord of the roof trusses. To provide the proper level of acoustic performance, we integrated sound-absorbing strips above the slotted openings in the wood ceiling. This ceiling design enhances directionality, gives scale, and adds richness of surface.

Lighting throughout the exhibit area is provided by small, cable-supported, low-voltage fixtures. The light cables are strung along the south side of the exposed bottom chords of the roof trusses. The visitor can see only ambient light, as the light sources are shielded from view in the direction of circulation. At the Bell Chamber, with its much higher ceiling, narrow beam spotlights are focused on the bell to enhance the form, surface, and color of this extraordinary object.

Our discussions with Joe Nicholson regarding the exhibit continued throughout the design process as building, storyline, and exhibit simultaneously evolved. As the exhibit program dictated three main chapters to the story, we introduced the idea of physical pauses between them by creating viewways: places to rest momentarily and enjoy views of the park to the east and the city to the west as one walked through the exhibit. People on the city sidewalk would equally enjoy seeing the activity within the building and the greenery of the park beyond. The width of the exhibit area was determined by our desire to stay within the predetermined length of space between the two alleyways. The rather tight spacing of piers, important to give human scale to

92 Liberty Bell Chamber   93 Sketch of architecture/exhibit interface and transparency   94 Early sketch of view to Independence Hall tower from Bell Chamber

the arborway and the building, also preordained the module for exhibits. 93 Most importantly, we believed that Liberty Bell Center should be as open as possible, day-lit, and visually connected to the park. We agreed at the onset that the exhibit would not be a "black box." The language of the exhibit system was to be the language of the architecture, adapting to the grid, using structural metal shapes, layering glass panels of different degrees of transparency. The shade-giving metal trellises on the exterior would extend into the body of the building to protect the interior from glare and to concentrate exhibit lighting in a series of wood baffles attached to the metal armature topping the piers. The architecture quickly became the exhibit medium, offering smaller subdivisions of space within a larger airy volume in which the individual chapters of the story could be nested. We worked together to design the exhibit assemblies, select graphic panel surfaces, and develop connection details using the building's architectural vocabulary. The result of our collaboration was an exhibit armature of aluminum structural shapes bolted together to support graphic panels of various sizes. Spanning between piers or projected from them at ninety degrees, the panels, cases, and imprinted translucent glass screens combine with the exhibit armature to create changing visual compositions of line and surface. The Bell Chamber was, without question, the greatest challenge–and demanded a compelling, authentic, and memorable solution. 94 This four-foot-tall icon would need to be placed in a structure that was properly scaled to the urban park environment, more than 15 acres in size, and compatible with the Georgian architecture of the neighboring Independence Hall. The bell also demanded a home that was both grand and intimate, and that communicated the power of the ideals it symbolizes. The General Management Plan called for a place that is open, democratic–an American place. Our way of giving form to these ideas came through a long process of discussion, drawing, modeling, and testing reactions until we arrived at the solution that needed no verbal assistance in its understanding.

93

While engaged in the project's overall approach of layering landscape, structure, exterior envelope, systems, and interior surfaces, we studied an array of geometries and materials for the Bell Chamber. The Bell Chamber's principal orientation is almost due south. Therefore, the sun's azimuth and altitude throughout the year would influence the geometry and mix of techniques we were to use to prevent any direct sun rays from striking the

94

bell while affording people the prescribed view of bell and hall. We considered predominantly solid brick-walled enclosures, but they felt bunker-like and undemocratic. We looked at totally transparent glass solutions; they felt too vulnerable and exposed to surrounding urban distractions. What resulted was a hybrid solution for the exterior envelope that layered glass walls, metal sun-shielding louvers, brick piers, and paired steel columns. 95 To arrive at a final geometry for the plan and enclosed volume, we first studied the platonic geometries and rectangles. While these shapes allowed centering of the bell, they did not speak to the background of Independence Hall and sky. We then looked at non-parallel walls that either opened or narrowed toward the hall beyond. We chose a narrowing volume that gave the chamber the centered bell location, a directional focus toward bell and hall, and a grand scale resulting from the forced perspective generated by the converging wall planes.

The determination of the height of the Bell Chamber began with our desire to allow a person viewing the bell to see the aligned spire of Independence Hall and the sky beyond. Our sectional studies of the chamber always diagrammed this sightline–visitor's eye to chamber roof edge to spire tip. 96 The resultant height also yielded the appropriate volume for the chamber. The innermost layer of containment is formed by lower flanking cupped walls, like two hands protecting a flame. The multiple layers of glass, brick, metal, and stone brought the scale down from urban at the outermost layer to intimate at the innermost surface closest to the bell.

95

The gently curving walls shape the interior volume of the chamber and frame the view of the Liberty Bell. We considered a variety of materials for these walls–Venetian plaster, domestic marbles, granite, metals, and various coatings–before selecting Carrera marble. The Carrera gave us the soft veining, luster, and uniformity of color that allowed us to lay up the walls in a very delicate ashlar pattern, which gave them both substance and weightlessness and an aura of dignity and repose that make the encounter with the bell all the more compelling. In considering the hard materials and their acoustic implications, we knew by splaying the exterior walls and tilting the vertical angle of the cupped marble walls as little as three degrees, we could soften the ambient sound in the chamber. Beside the acoustical virtues, the converging planes and this ever-so-slight tilting of the cupped marble walls enhance the visual experience by guiding the gaze upward from the bell to the tower. Upon entering the chamber, one's eye is drawn upward to see bell, hall, spire, and sky in one motion. That will become the memory of the experience, one of sudden encounter with the Liberty Bell in its historic surroundings, of exhilaration, of calm reflection, of respect and a sense of connection to this icon at a personal level. 97, 98

95 Exploded axonometric of Bell Chamber 96 Diagram of all-important visitor's sightline to bell and spire 97 Visitors in the Bell Chamber

We aspired to make a building that generated human response: anticipation, discovery, pleasure, and pride. We believe architecture can resonate with its surroundings. Our obligation was to marry an emotionally charged place with this emotionally charged object. By orchestrating a procession from city to park to exhibit to Bell Chamber, we set out to reveal the story of the Liberty Bell and celebrate the visitors' arrival, approach, and encounter with this most cherished icon.

Liberty Bell Center takes its place in Independence National Historical Park to honor the extraordinary events in the eighteenth century. It participates in the contemporary urban setting of Philadelphia, in an ensemble of spaces that defines the essence of the park as civic monument, urban oasis, and personal garden. But most importantly, it uniquely celebrates the Liberty Bell and what it represents to all of us, young and old, man and woman, citizen or guest, as members of a global community for whom freedom is as essential to life as the air we breathe.

97

96

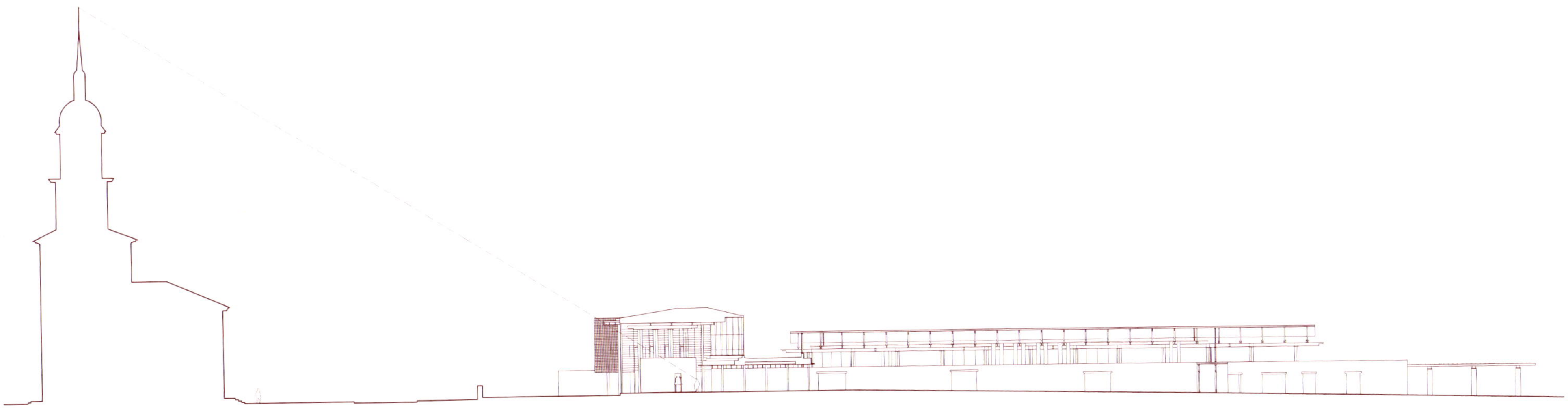

Endnote Liberty Bell Center is the result of many dedicated and hard-working people bringing diverse talents to the task and working together to make a wonderful building. On behalf of Bohlin Cywinski Jackson, I take this opportunity to gratefully acknowledge them for their contributions.

As Bohlin Cywinski Jackson was involved in developing the Independence National Historical Park (INHP) master plan, we were fortunate to work continuously with the National Park Service for seven years. During that time we worked with a number of outstanding individuals The project started when Martha Aikens was the superintendent of INHP. We owe a lot to Martha's clear guidance and leadership, from the development of the General Management Plan, through the master plan, to the design of Liberty Bell Center. Mary Bomar succeeded Martha as superintendent of the park as the construction of Liberty Bell Center was nearing completion. She has become one of the building's strongest supporters and we thank her for all her efforts in making Liberty Bell Center a focus within the City of Philadephia. Current INHP superintendent, Dennis Reidenbach, formerly assistant superintendent to Martha and Mary, provided steadfast continuity on the entire design and construction process. David Hollenberg, the Associate Northeast Regional Director, is an architect we were very fortunate to work with. The design of the building owes a lot to David's aesthetic judgment and perseverance in acquiring the necessary funding to support such a project. In addition to these individuals we also recognize the other members of the INHP building committee: Chris Schillizzi, who gave valuable direction on the content and design of the exhibits; Deirdre Gibson, for her insight on the integration of the building into the landscape; Jack Dunleavy, who provided assistance on the design and construction of the building systems; and all the department heads, who provided feedback at each stage of the design.

The National Park Service's project contract administration was performed through the Denver Service Center. Bob Lopenske and Joe Crystal, both from that office, were key to moving the project forward through the design phase. We would also like to extend our thanks to the National Park Service for graciously allowing Bohlin Cywinski Jackson to reproduce in this book the graphic materials that were generated during the design of this project.

We extend our gratitude to the following organizations for their very generous support for the design and construction of Liberty Bell Center: The Annenberg Foundation; William Penn Foundation; The Pew Charitable Trusts; and the City of Philadelphia.

The building's success resulted from the dedication of many individuals in our office, in particular Peter Bohlin for his sage and incisive design input; Kenneth Mitchell for his leadership of the master plan and the building teams; and Wolfram Arendt, Monica Barton, Joseph Bridy, Jeff Lew, Anthony Pregiato, and Erin Roark for their selfless devotion to every detail in the building.

We could not have designed this building without the many creative and dedicated consultants on our team. Special thanks go to CVM Engineers led by Jon Morrison; Joe Nicholson of Ueland Junker McCauley Nicholson; Mark Giovagnoli from BR+A Engineers; and, of course, Laurie Olin from the Olin Partnership.

Liberty Bell Center was constructed by the Daniel J. Keating Company, the exhibits were fabricated and installed by Maltbie Incorporated, and the construction project manager was Hill International Incorporated. We thank all these organizations for the care and diligence with which they delivered this project.

Bernard J. Cywinski, a principal of Bohlin Cywinski Jackson, holds Bachelor of Arts and Master of Architecture degrees from Columbia University and is a William Kinne Fellow. He is a fellow of the American Institute of Architects. Mr. Cywinski is a long-standing member of the AIA's national Committee on Design and a sought-after lecturer, critic, and awards juror. A monograph on the firm, *The Architecture of Bohlin Cywinski Jackson*, was published in 1994. Two additional books on the firm's work have also been published; *Ledge House*, was released in 1999, and *Arcadian Architecture – Bohlin Cywinski Jackson 12 Houses*, was released in 2005. He has served as design principal for many of the firm's award-winning commissions including the Wallace Social Sciences Building at Princeton University; the New Dental School at the University of Maryland in Baltimore; the Sellinger School of Business at Loyola College in Maryland; the Pennsylvania Higher Education Assistance Agency headquarters; the Keystone Office Building in Harrisburg, Pennsylvania; and the Liberty Bell Center for the National Park Service in Philadelphia.

98 Visitors in the Bell Chamber

Lin

Sketches
Diagrams
Presentation Drawings
Construction Documents

es

Sketches

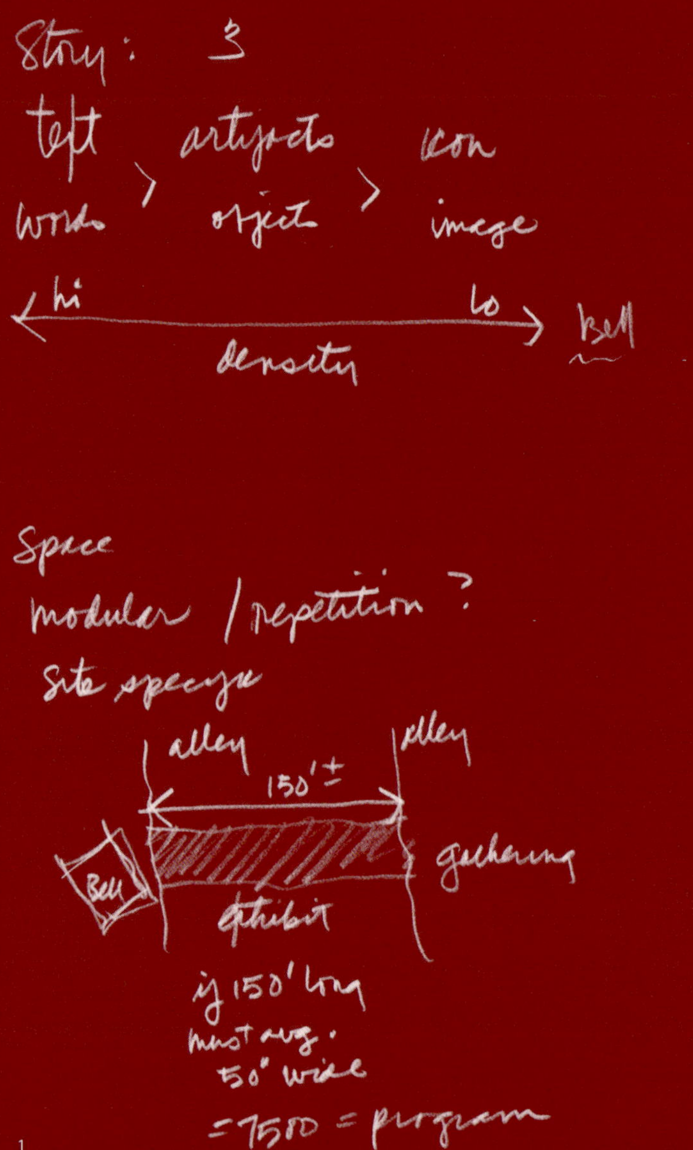
Story: 3
text
artifacts
icon
words
objects
image
hi
lo
density
Bell
Space
modular / repetition?
site specific
alley
alley
150'±
Bell
gathering
exhibit
if 150' long
must avg.
50' wide
= 7500 = program

1 Notes regarding exhibit hall 2 Early sketch of exhibit hall 3 Initial sketch of Liberty Bell Center

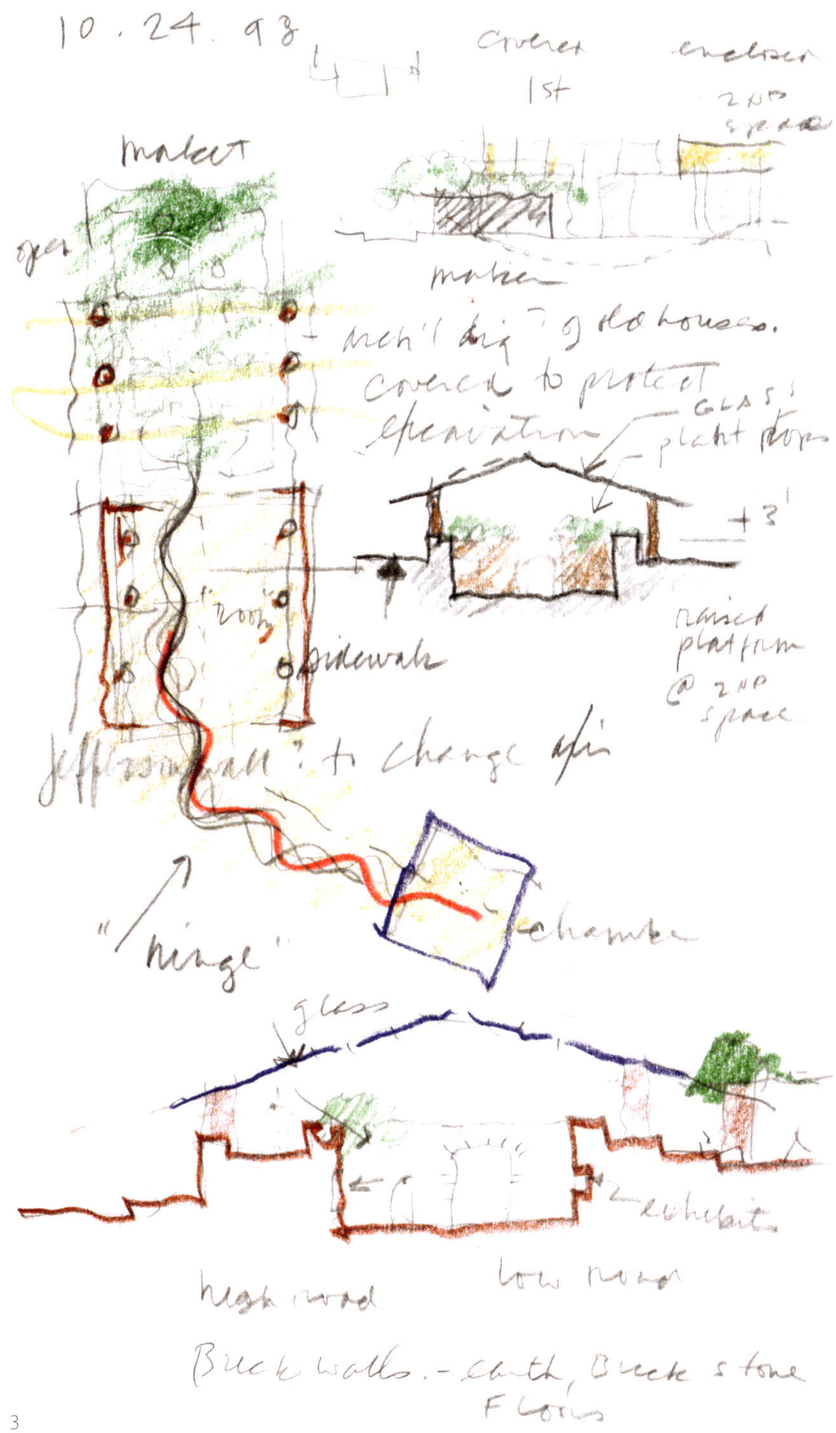

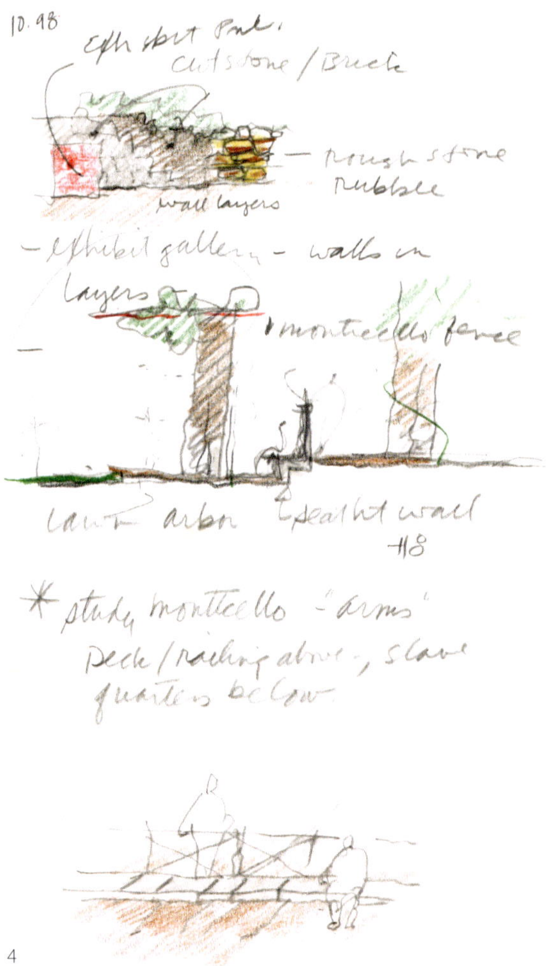
10.98
wall layers
monticello fence
lawn
arbor
* study monticello 'arms'

4

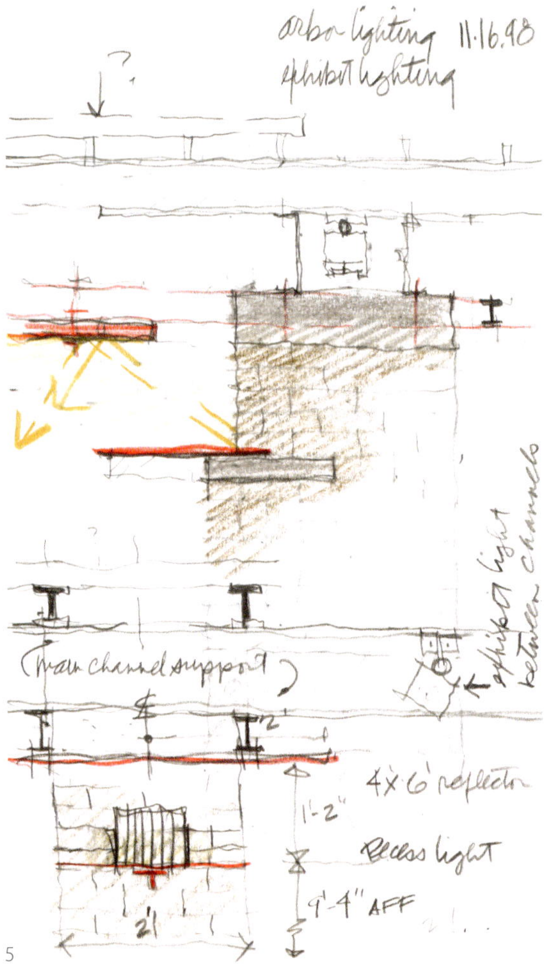
arbor lighting 11.16.98
exhibit lighting
4x6' reflector
1'-2"
recess light
9'-4" AFF
2'

5

N
E
W
S

6

4 Sketch of brick piers and low walls 5-8 Trellis and brick pier studies

7

8

Bell processional
Dark to light
Bell
foreign 600
children 30
landscape
diagonally
* density of info/exhibit
more info - less space
to
more space - less info
or
plan & section

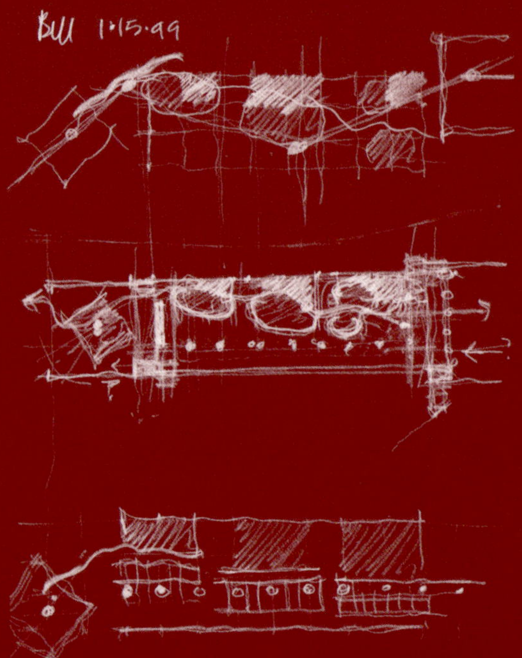
Bell 1·15·99

9

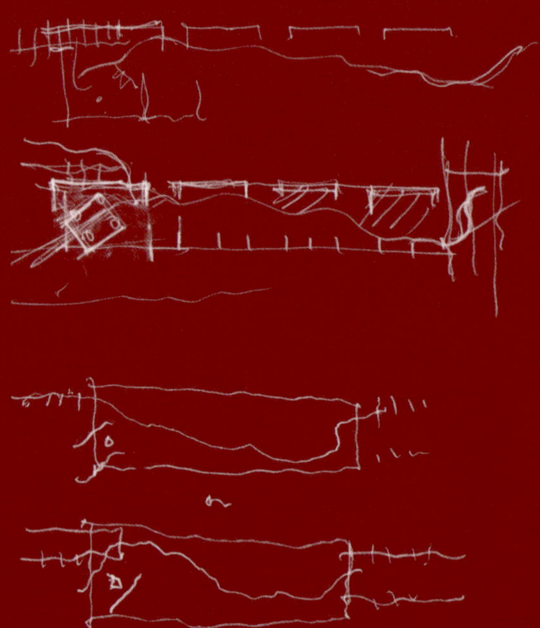
or

10

11

9, 10 Various plan diagrams of building 11 Study of possible ways to progress through building 12 Influence of street grid on plan of the building 13 Fast lane and slow lane for progressing through the exhibit

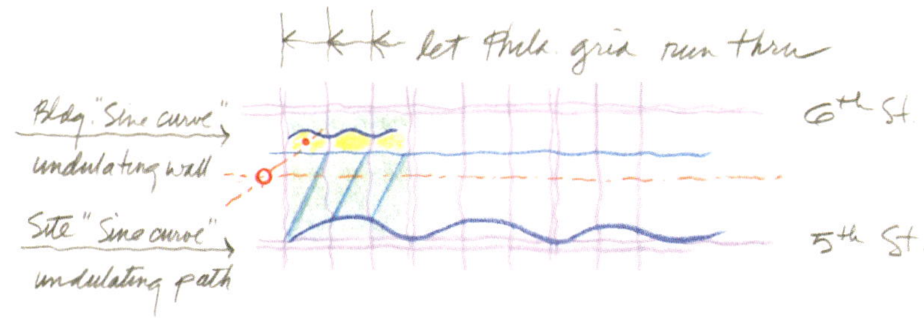

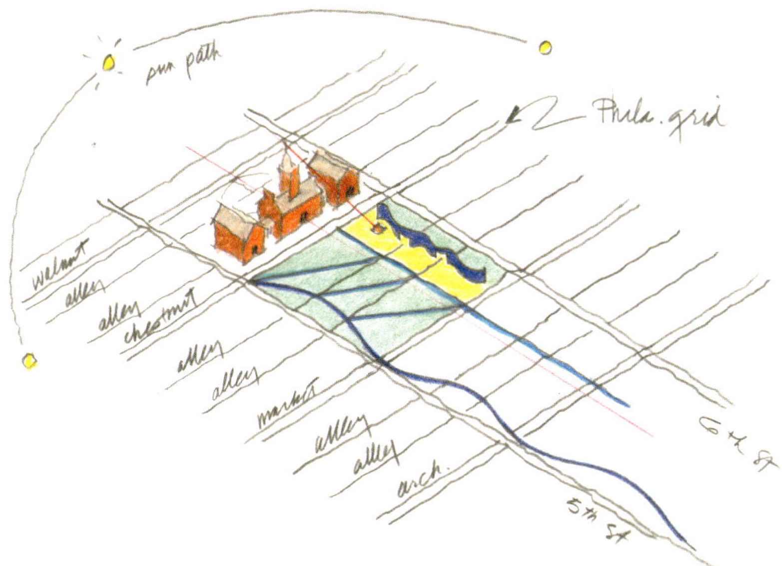

12

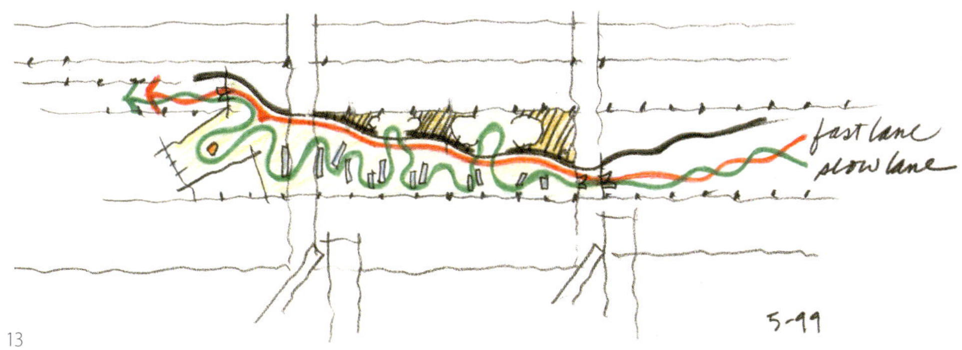

13

82
1.28.99

14 Floor plan/site plan drawing by B. Cywinski and L. Olin   15, 16 Floor plan sketches

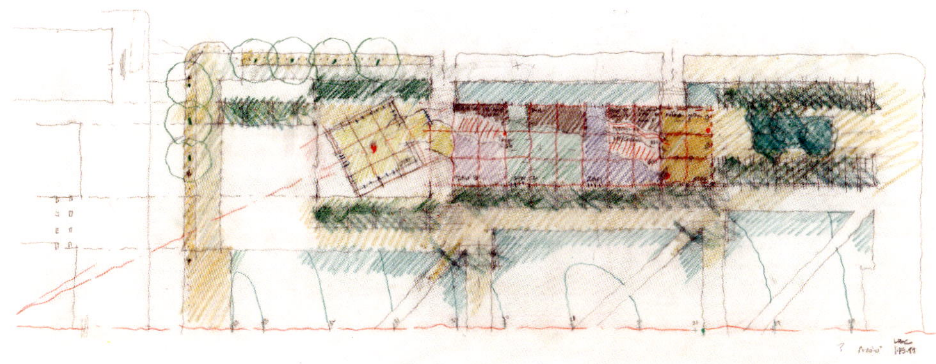

15

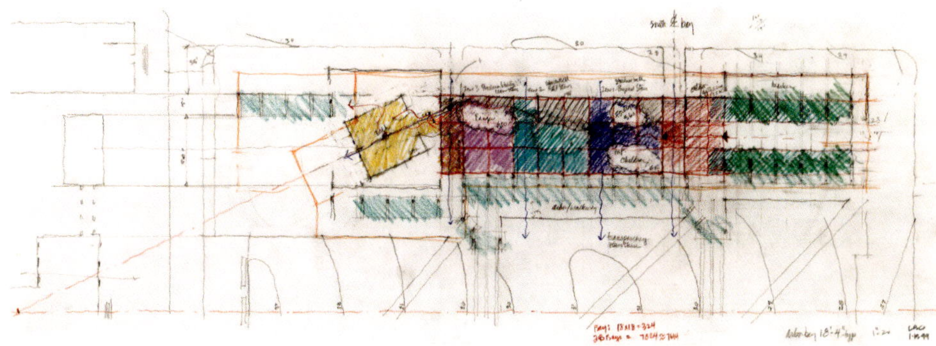

16

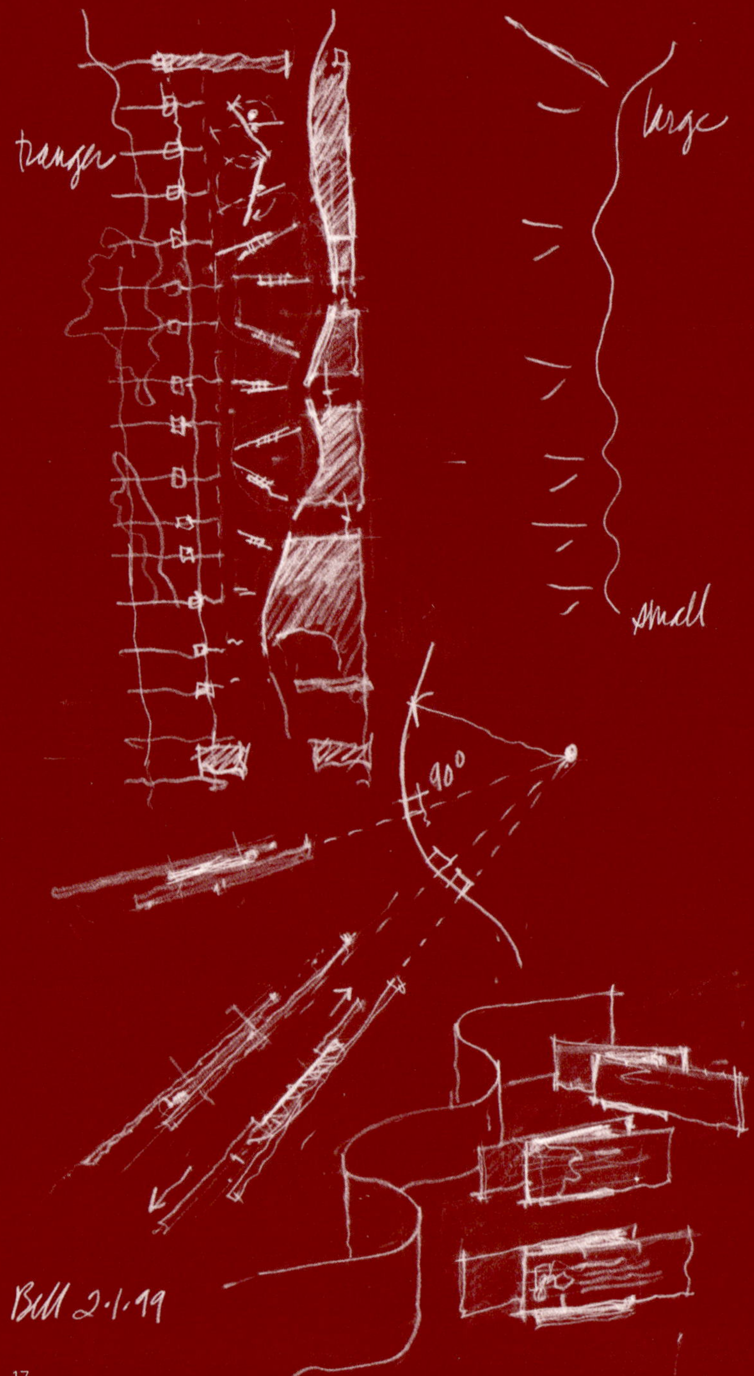

large
small
90°
Bell 2.1.99

17 Study of exhibit panel layout 18–20 Study of possible roof structures and ceilings 21 Study of exhibit panel arrangement and interior trellis 22 Study of interior trellis structure and ceiling in exhibit hall

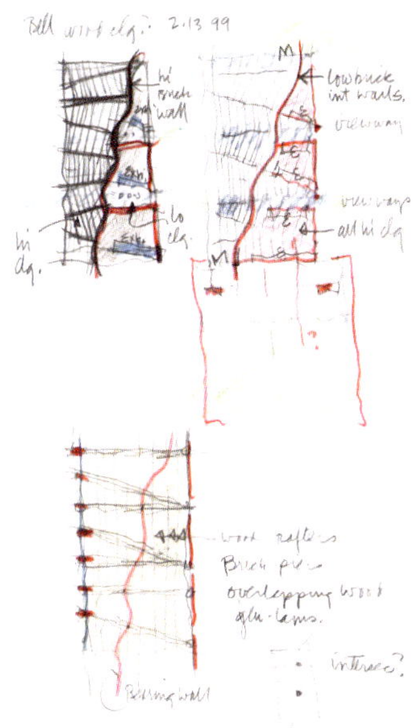

18

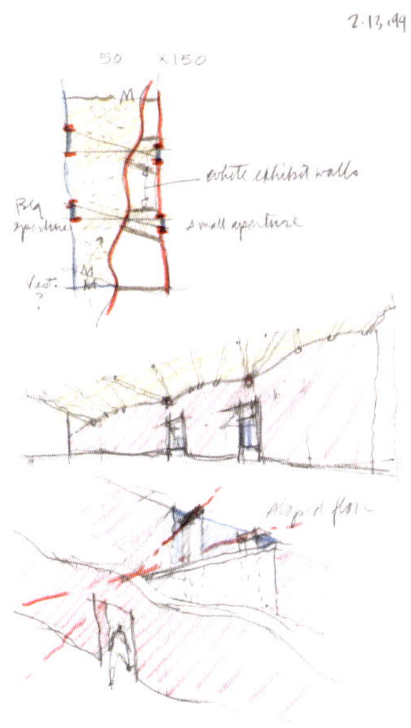

19

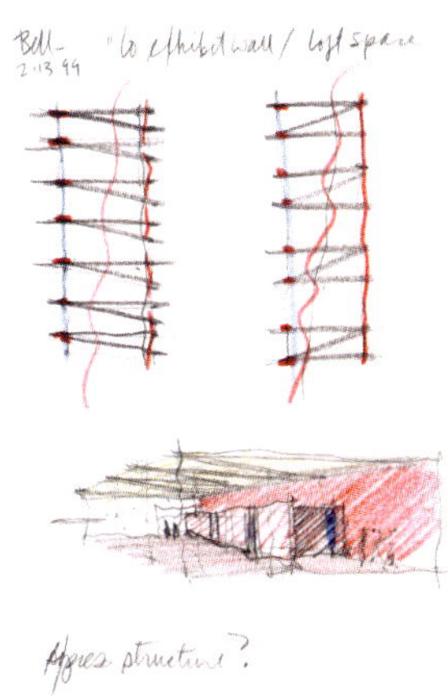

20

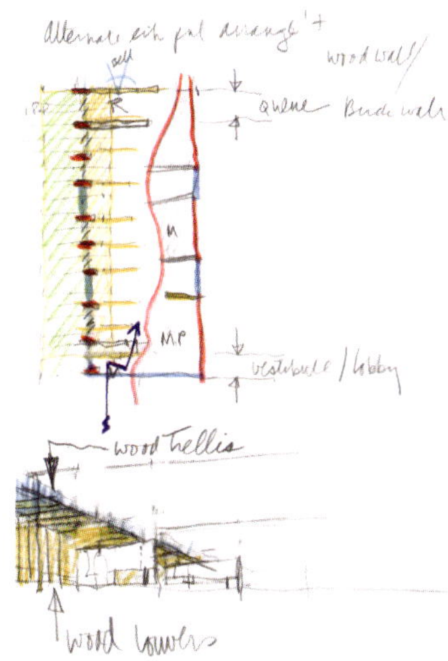

21

22

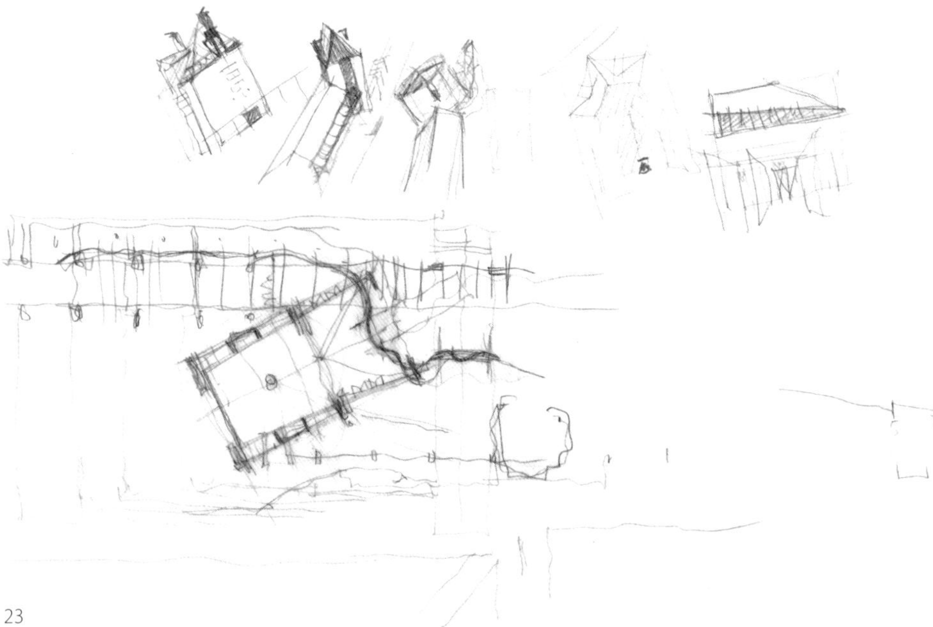

23

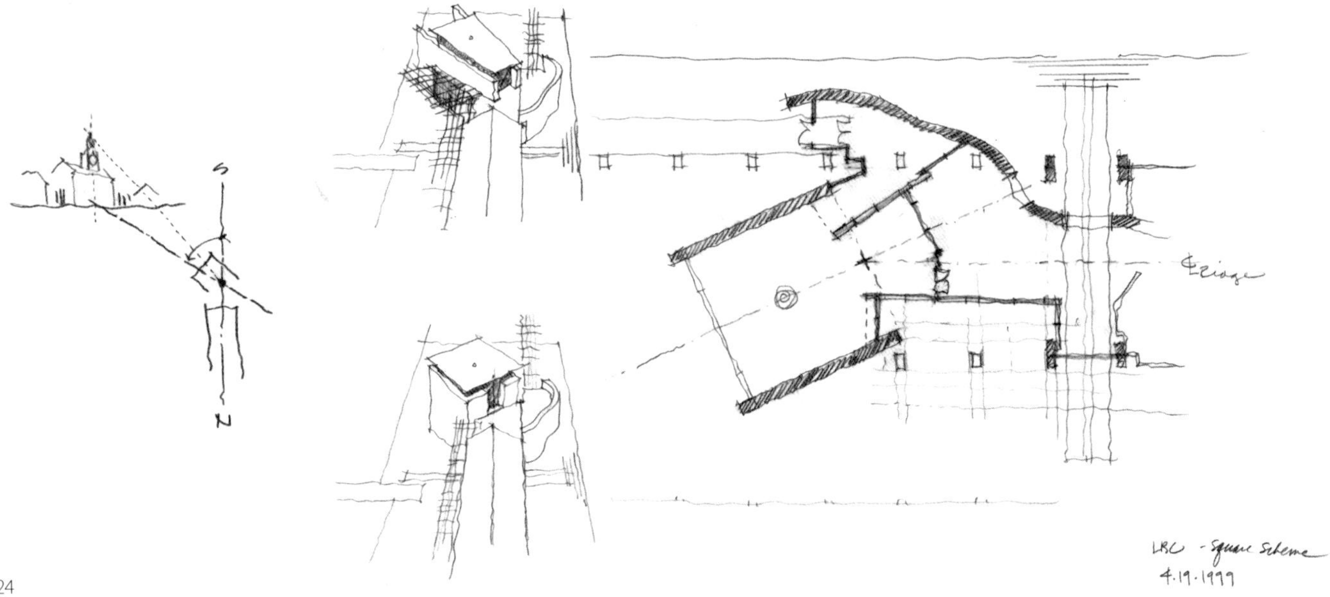

24

23, 24 Plans and perspective sketches of Bell Chamber 25, 26 Various Bell Chamber plans

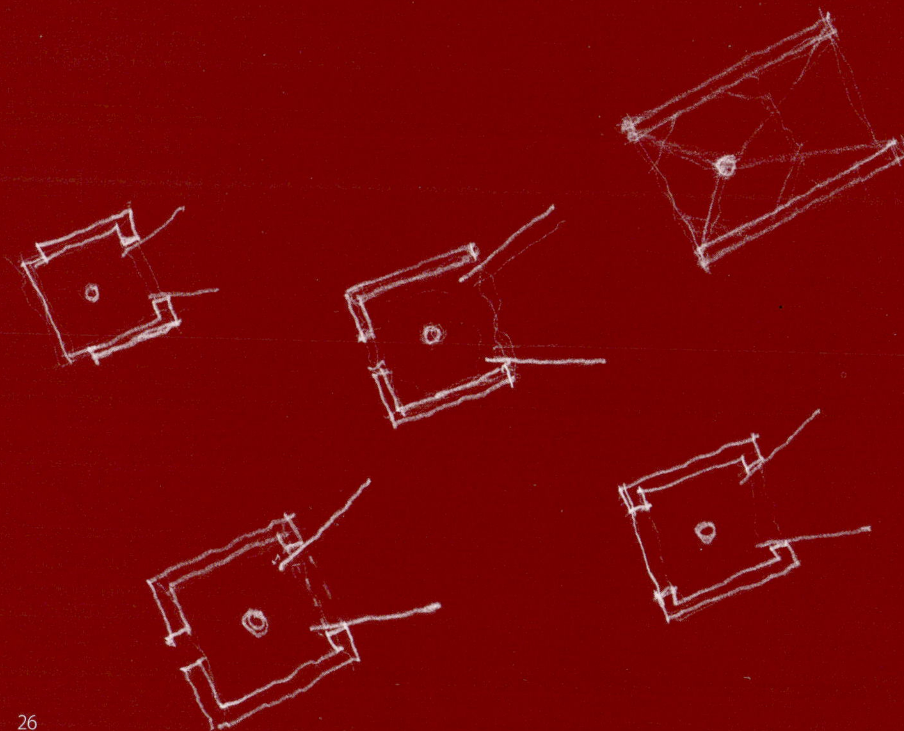

26

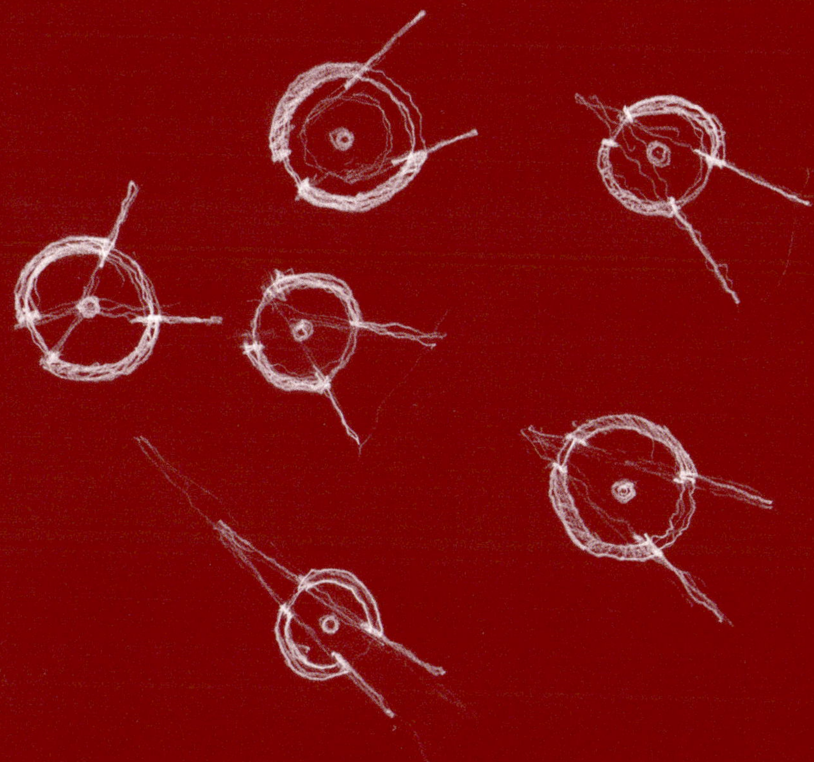

25

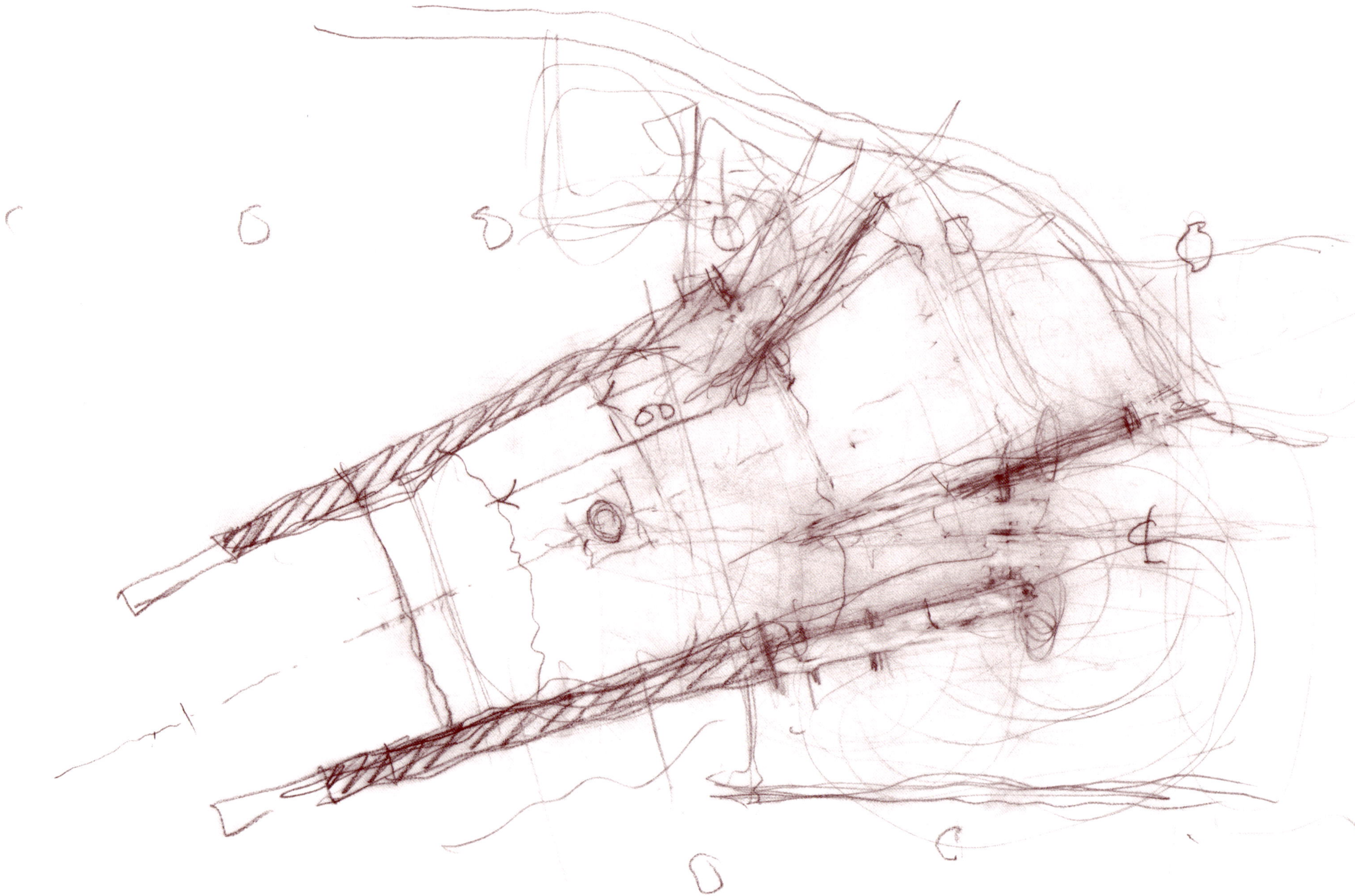

27 Bell Chamber sketch

28 Composite of various Bell Chamber plan studies

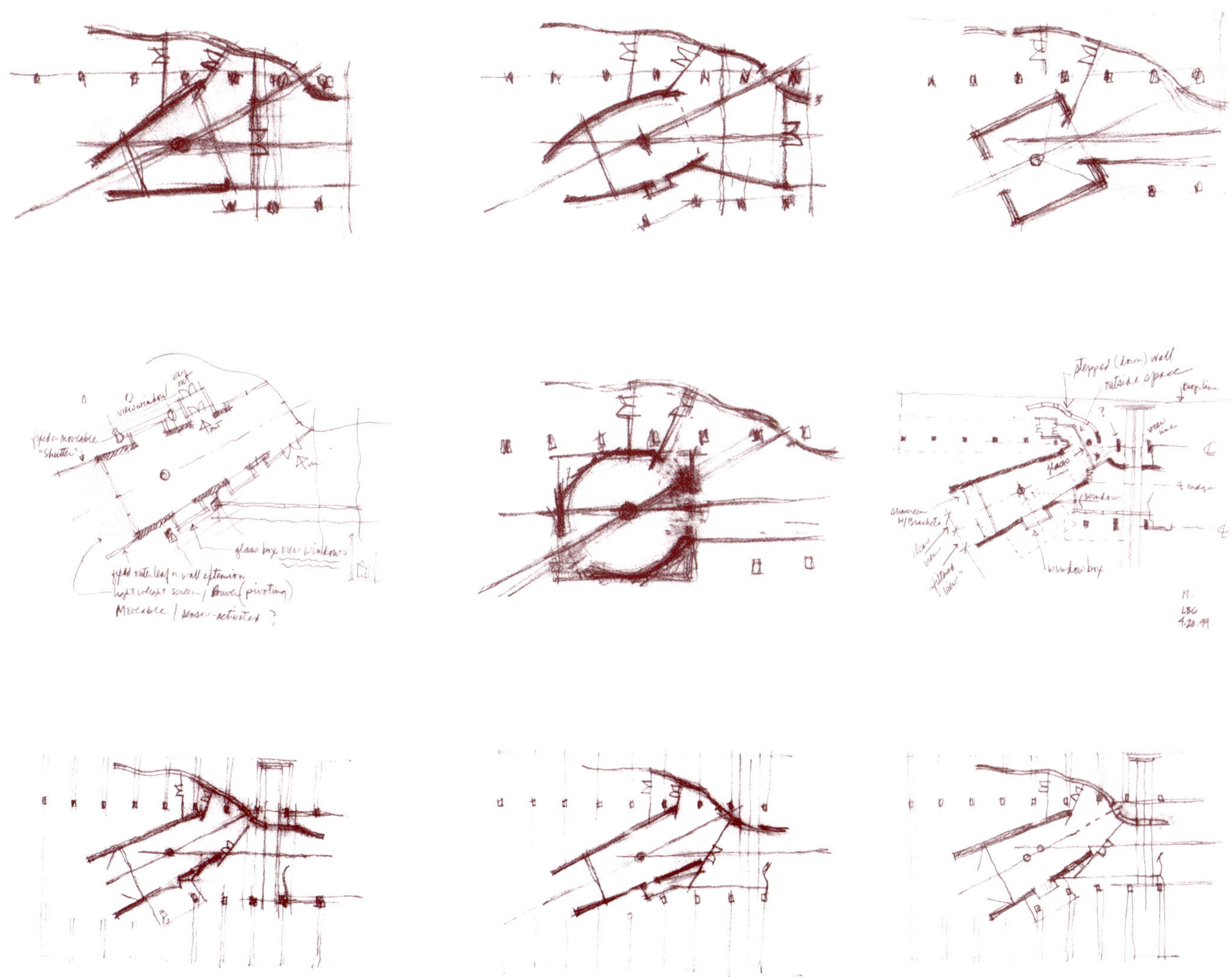

offset (equal spaced) cross beams
"longitudinal" beam
double columns
brick pier (buttress) beyond
column line
199

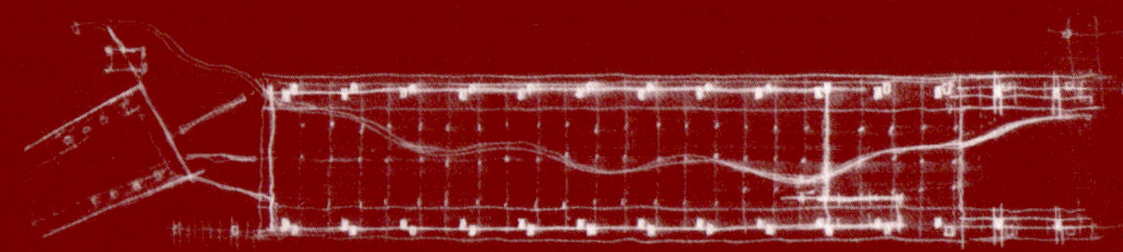

30

12.4.99
LBC
straight @ lintels?
express jointing
smooth stone
surround
rough beyond
smooth
rough
express quoins @ ends of walls
rough
smooth

29

31

32

29 Roof structure sketch 30 Reflected ceiling plan study 31, 32 Stone wall sketches 33 Building section with brick piers and steel columns to support roof 34 Bell Chamber studies

33

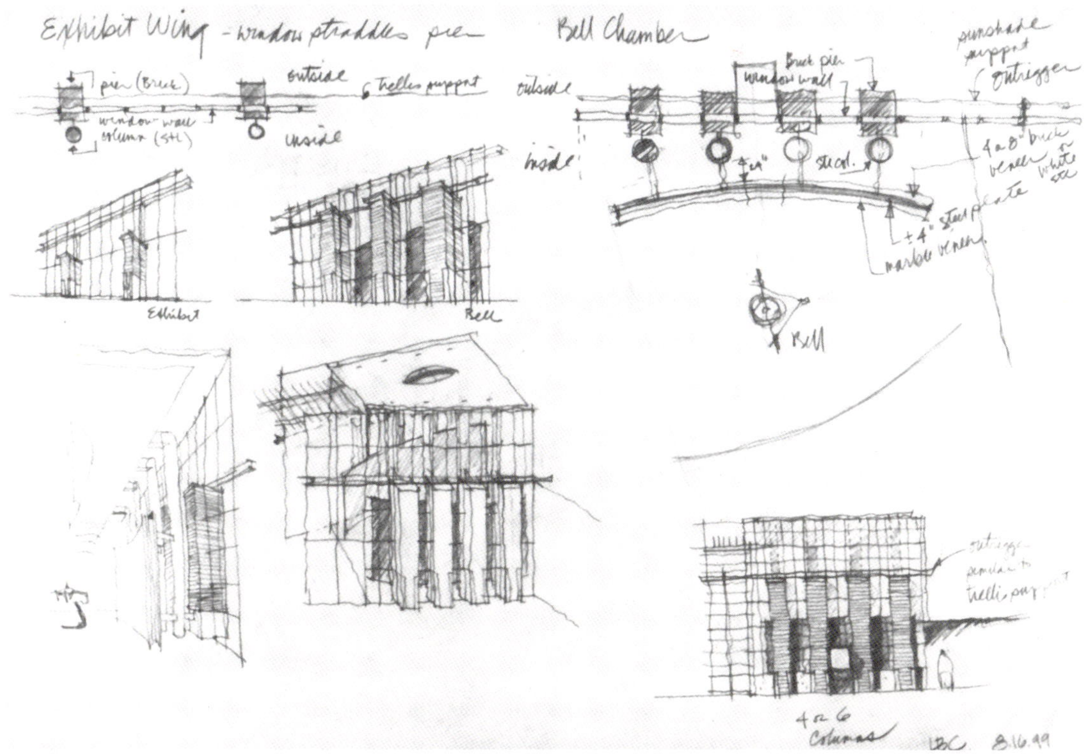

34

35

35 View of interior light baffles and roof   36, 37 Perspectives of Bell Chamber and Independence Hall

36

37

38

39

40

38 Bell Chamber sketch 39, 40 Exhibit sketches 41 Floor plan study

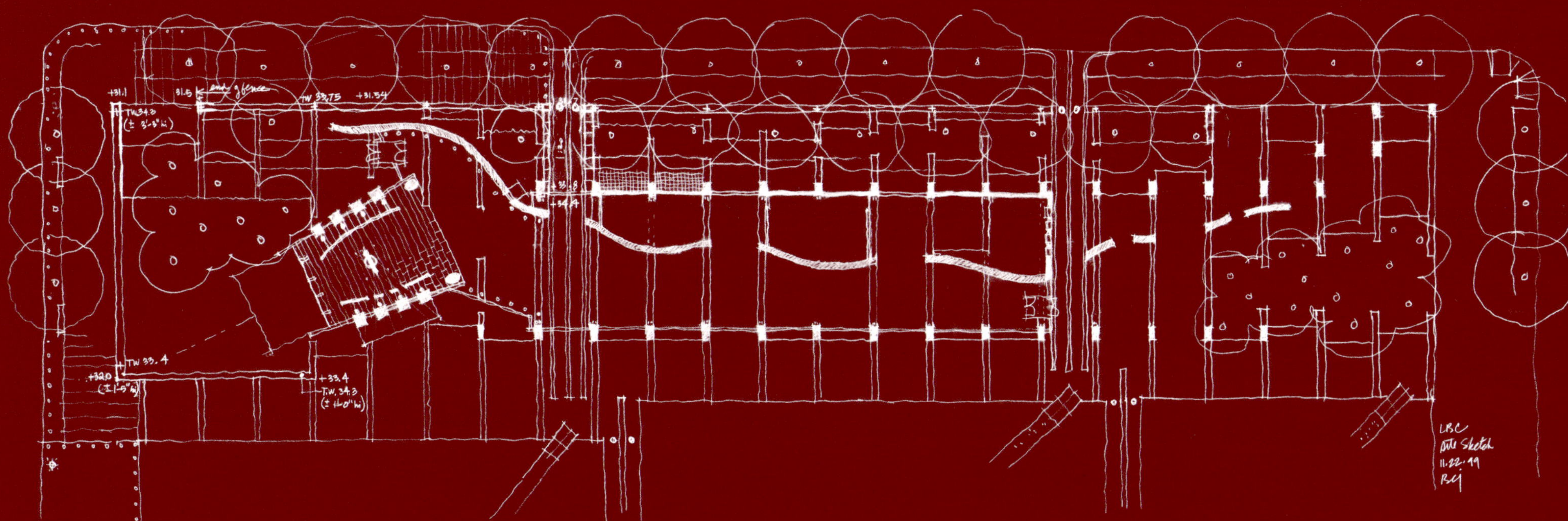

bell yoke trunnion
bell support
'99

Diagrams

44 Plan diagram showing structure 45, 46 Shadow plans of building

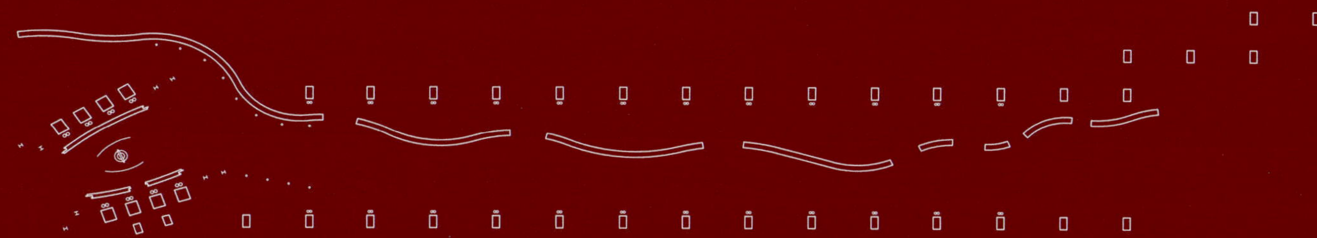

44

45

46

Presentation Drawings

47 Overall site plan

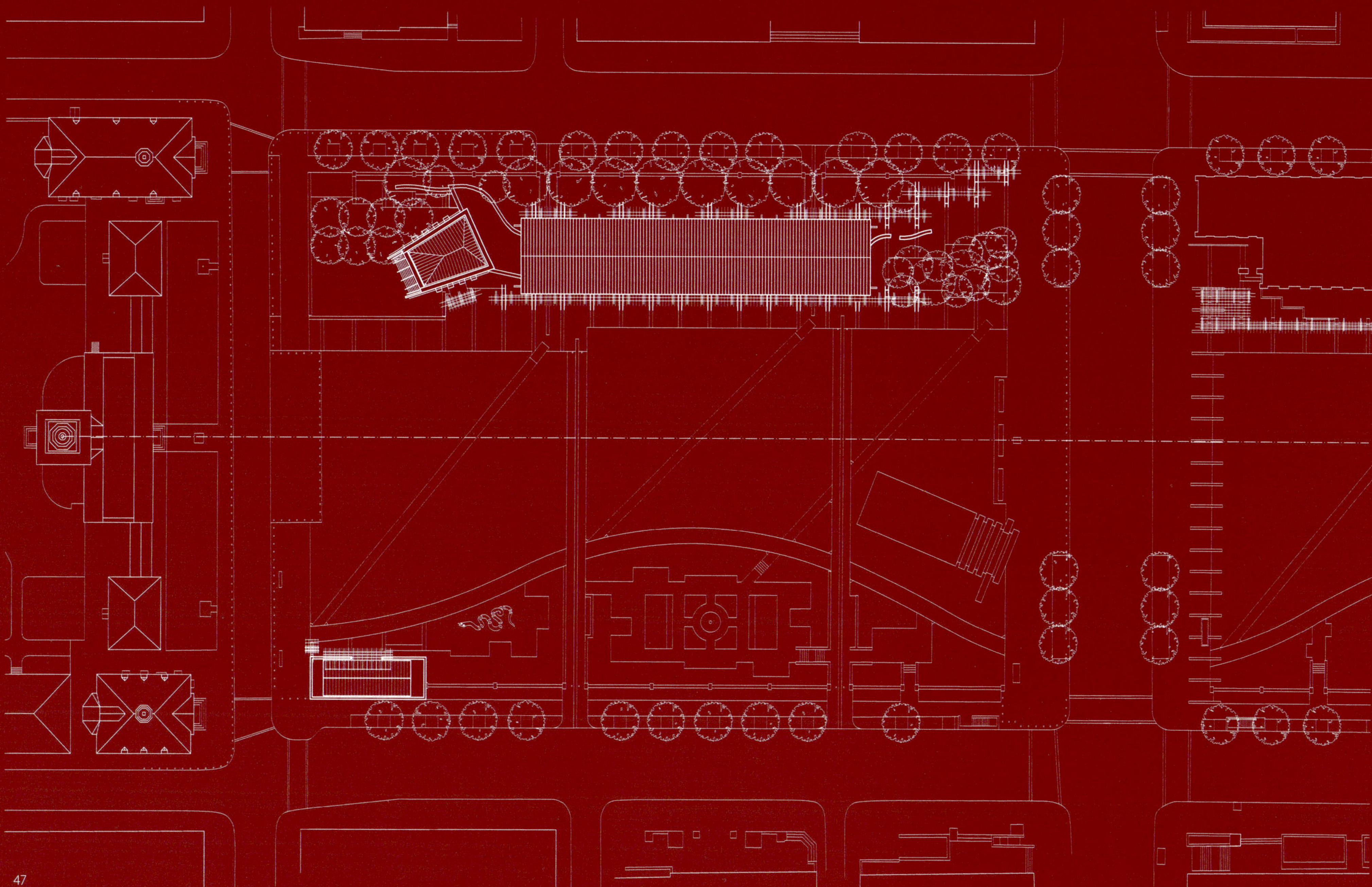

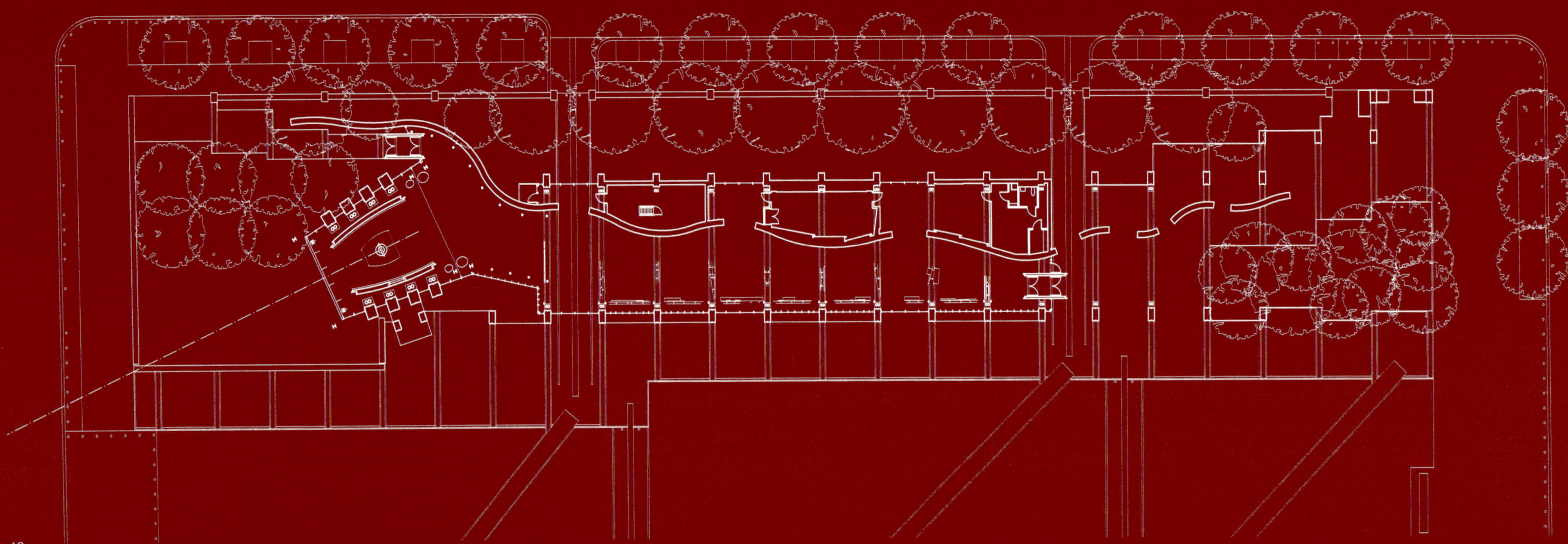

48 Building floor plan with site 49 Exploded axonometric

50

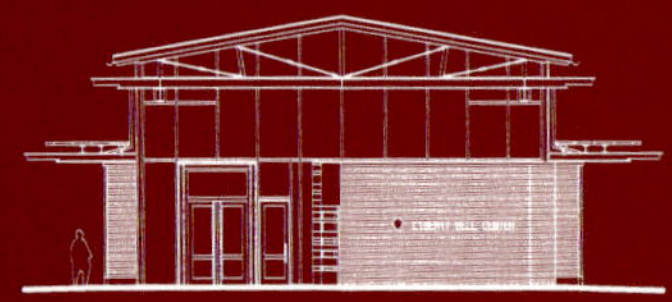

51

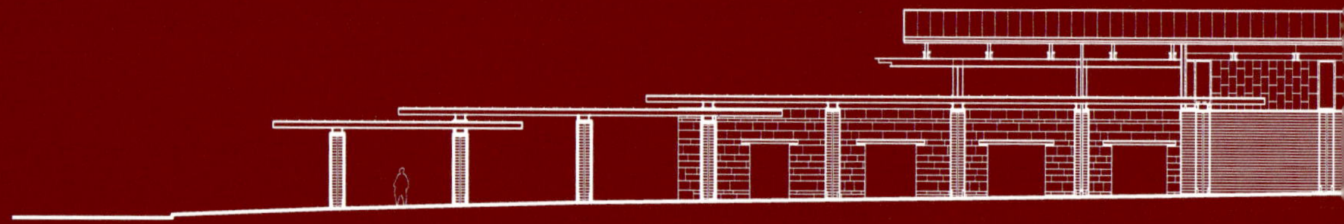

53

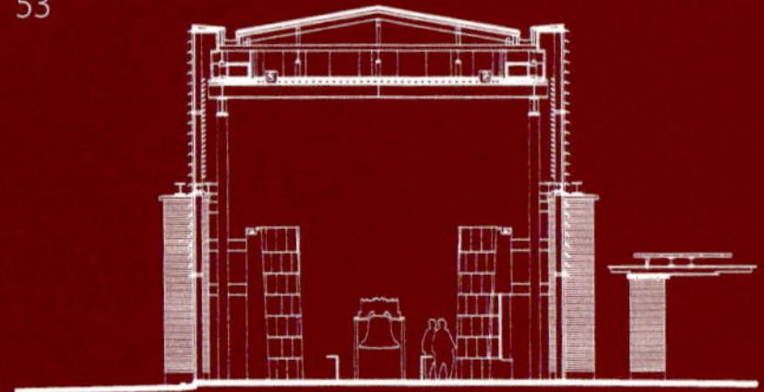

54

56

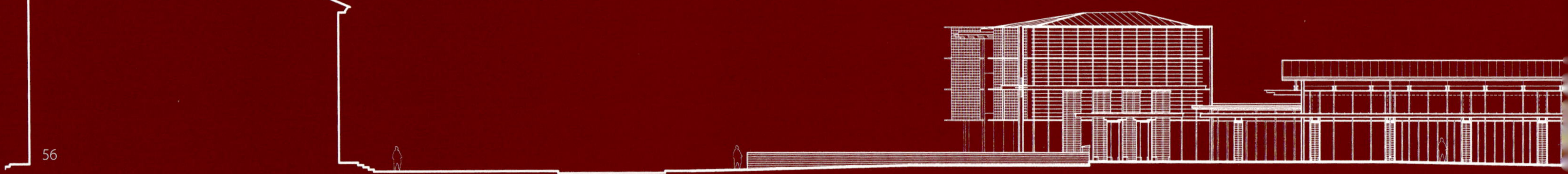

50 North elevation 51 West elevation 52 South elevation 53 Section through Bell Chamber facing north 54 Building section facing west 55 Section of exhibit hall facing south 56 East elevation with Independence Hall

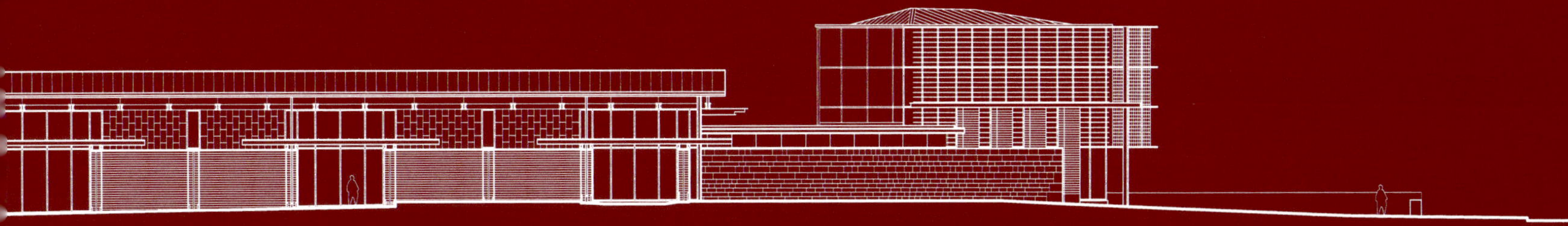

52

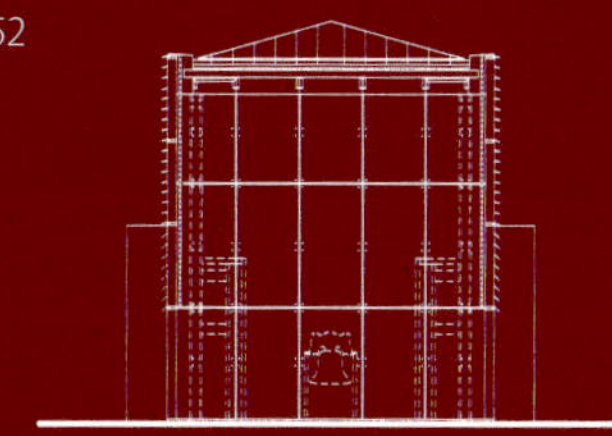

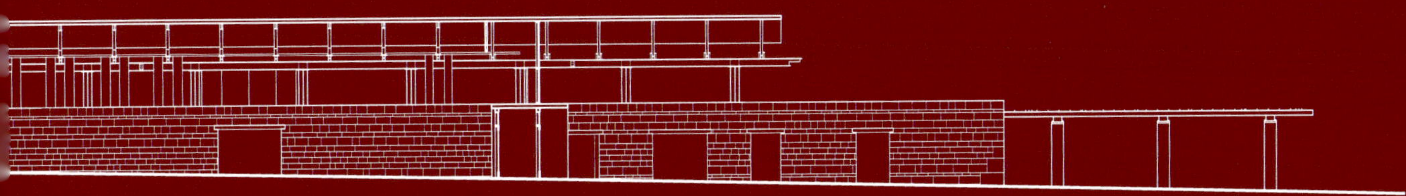

55

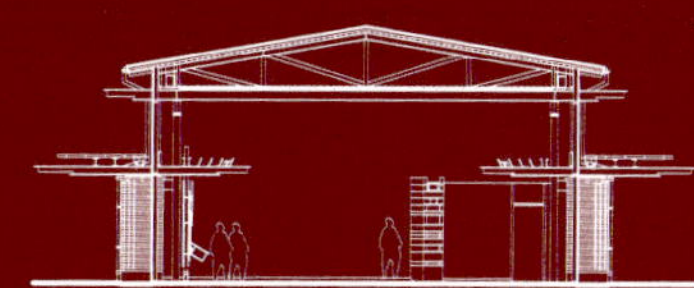

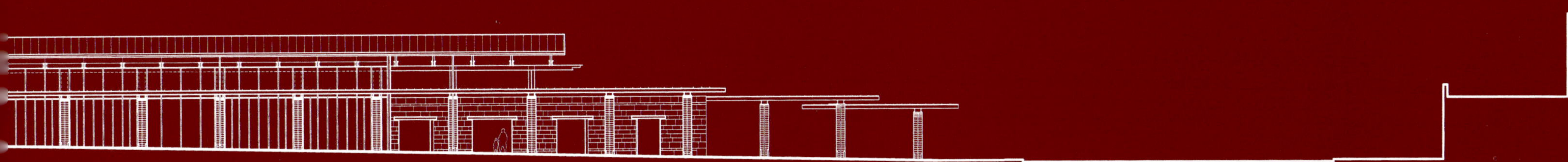

57

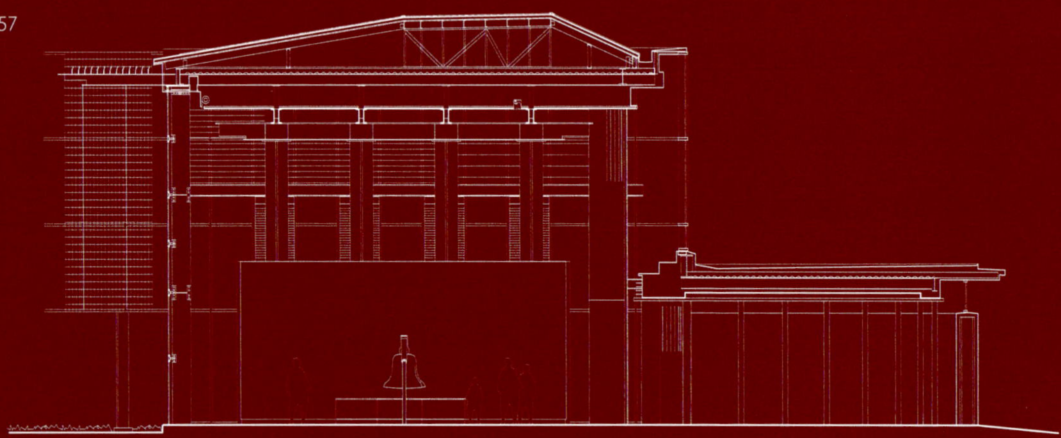

58

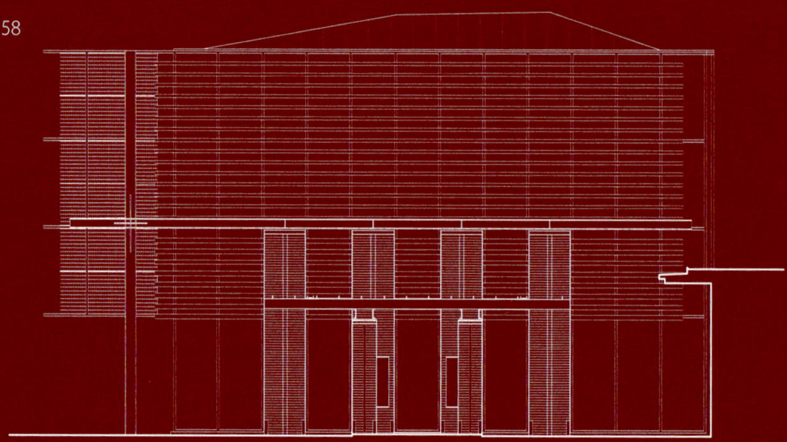

57 Section through Bell Chamber facing west 58 East elevation of Bell Chamber 59 Exploded axonometric of Bell Chamber

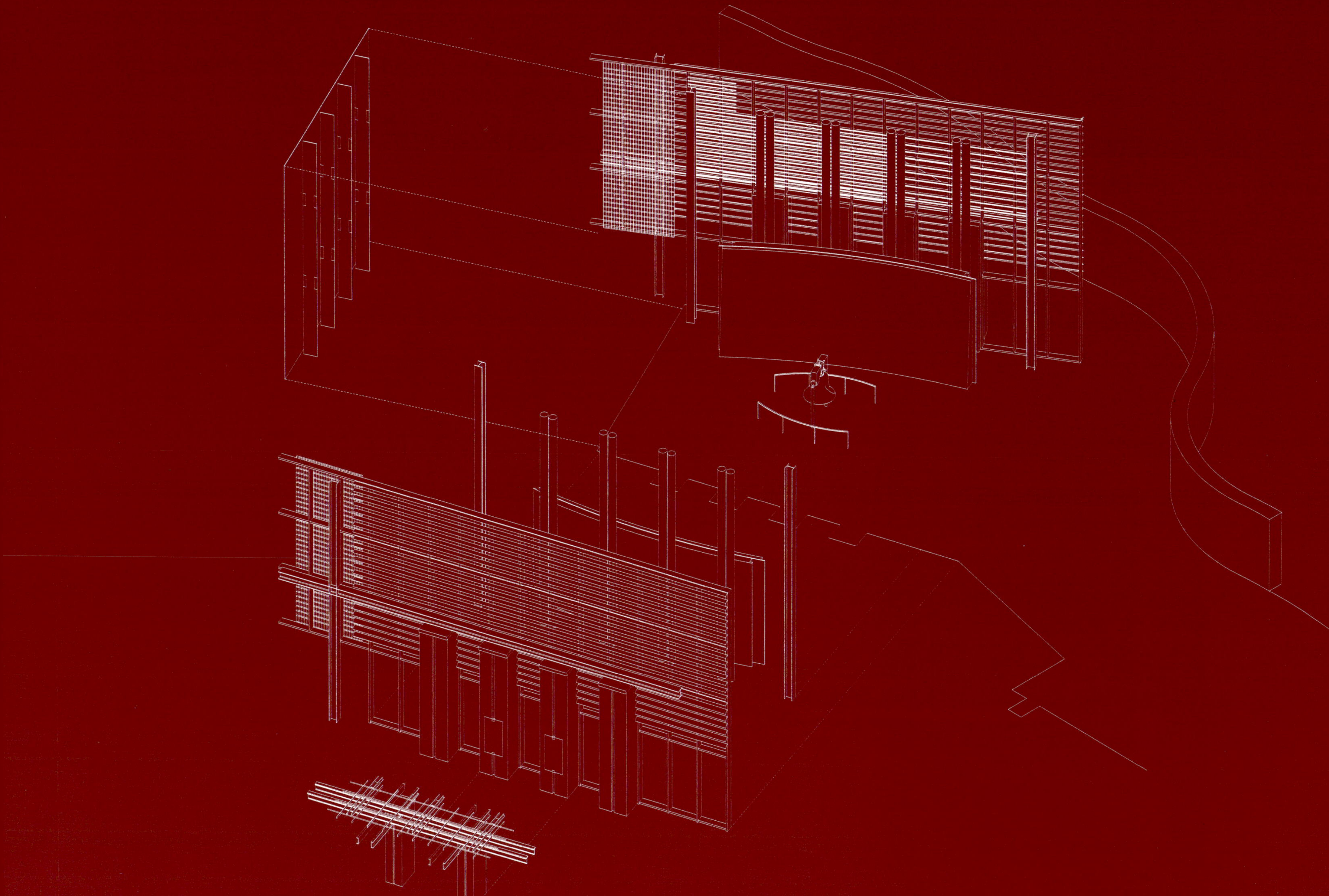

59

60 Section showing sight line from bell to Independence Hall tower 61 Computer-generated rendering of Bell Chamber at night

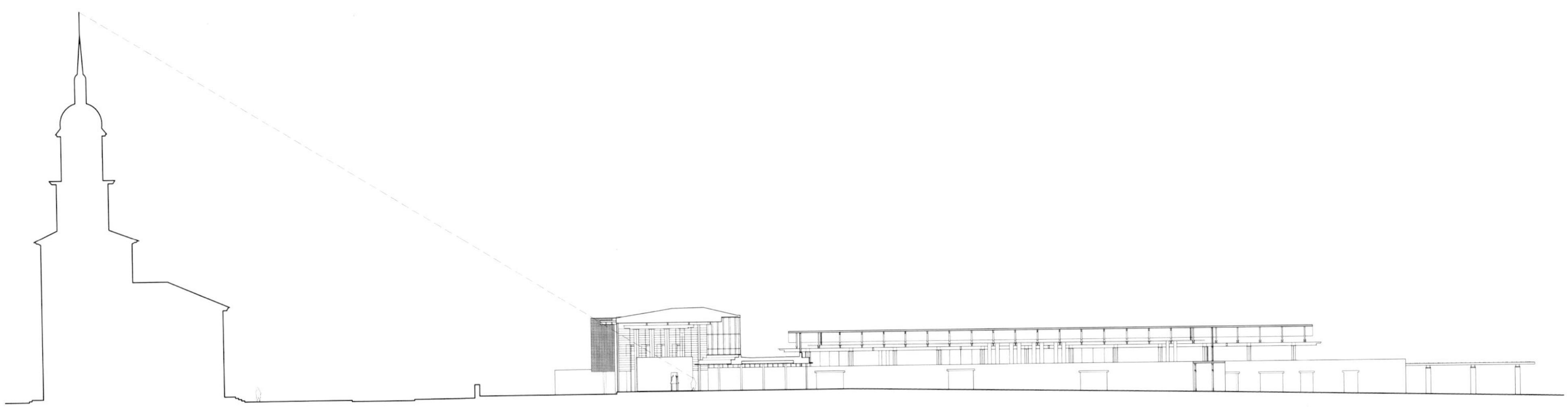

60

Construction Documents

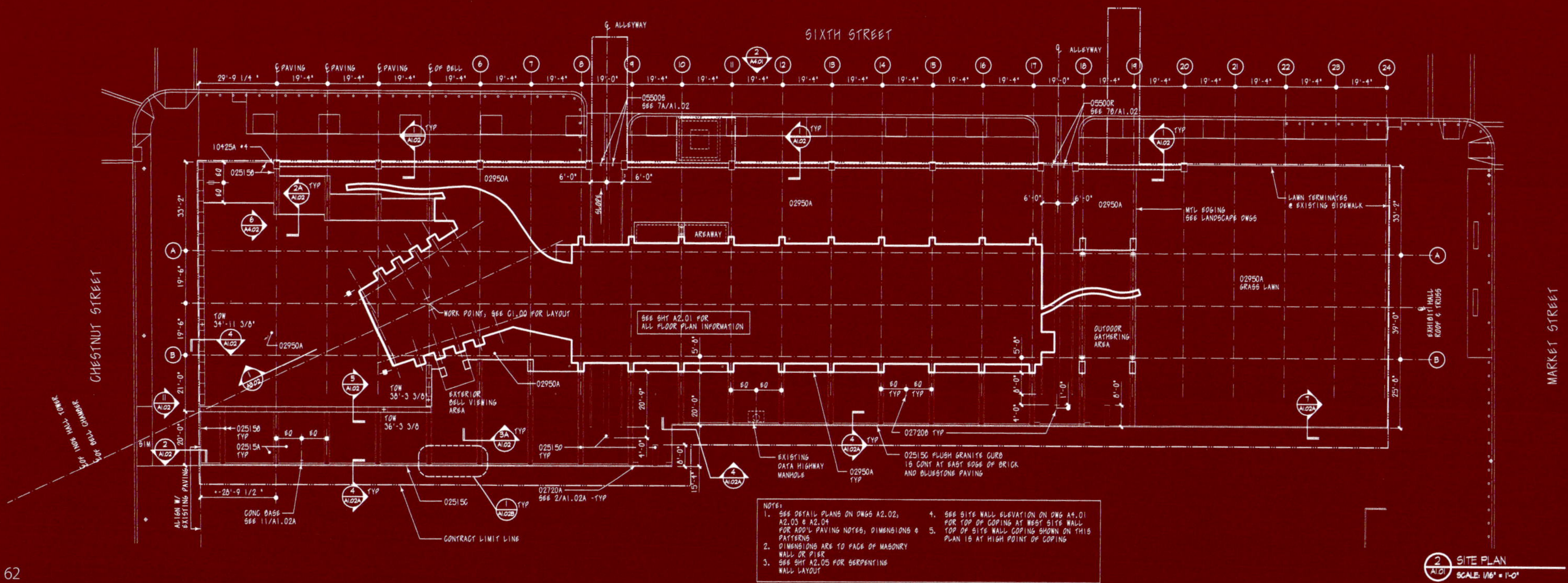
SIXTH STREET
CHESTNUT STREET
MARKET STREET
OUTDOOR GATHERING AREA
EXTERIOR BELL VIEWING AREA
SEE SHT A2.01 FOR ALL FLOOR PLAN INFORMATION
CONTRACT LIMIT LINE
2 SITE PLAN
SCALE: 1/16" = 1'-0"

62

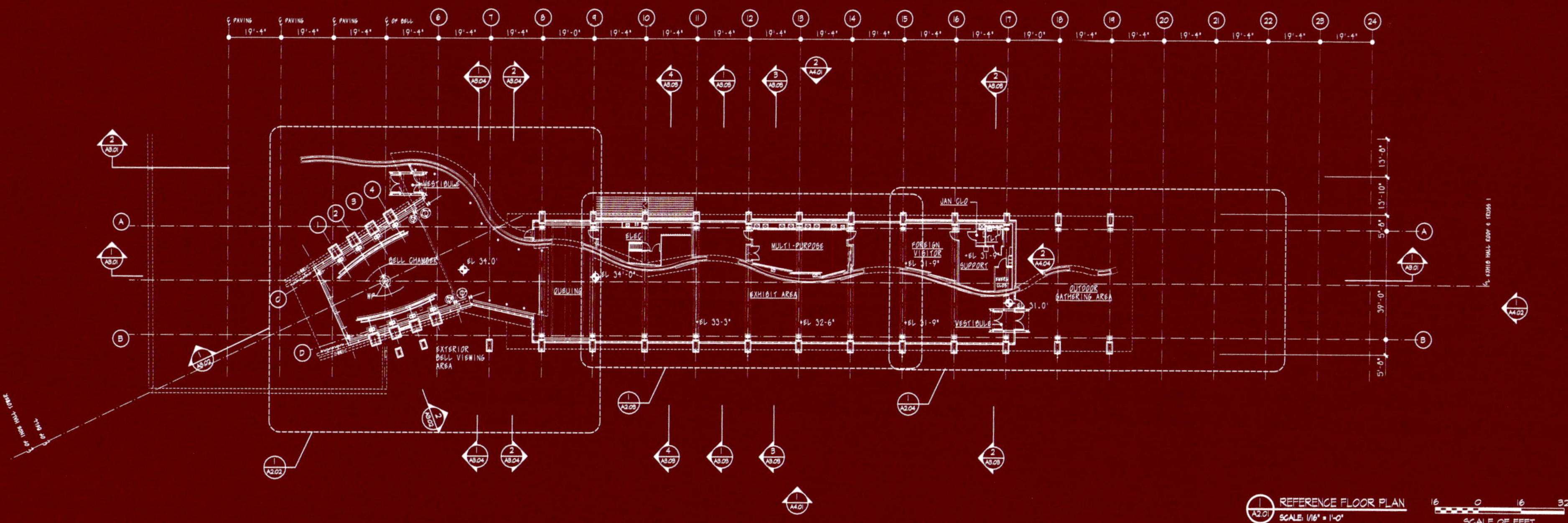
BELL CHAMBER
VESTIBULE
MULTI-PURPOSE
EXHIBIT AREA
FOREIGN VISITOR
SUPPORT
OUTDOOR GATHERING AREA
EXTERIOR BELL VIEWING AREA
1 REFERENCE FLOOR PLAN
SCALE: 1/16" = 1'-0"
SCALE OF FEET

63

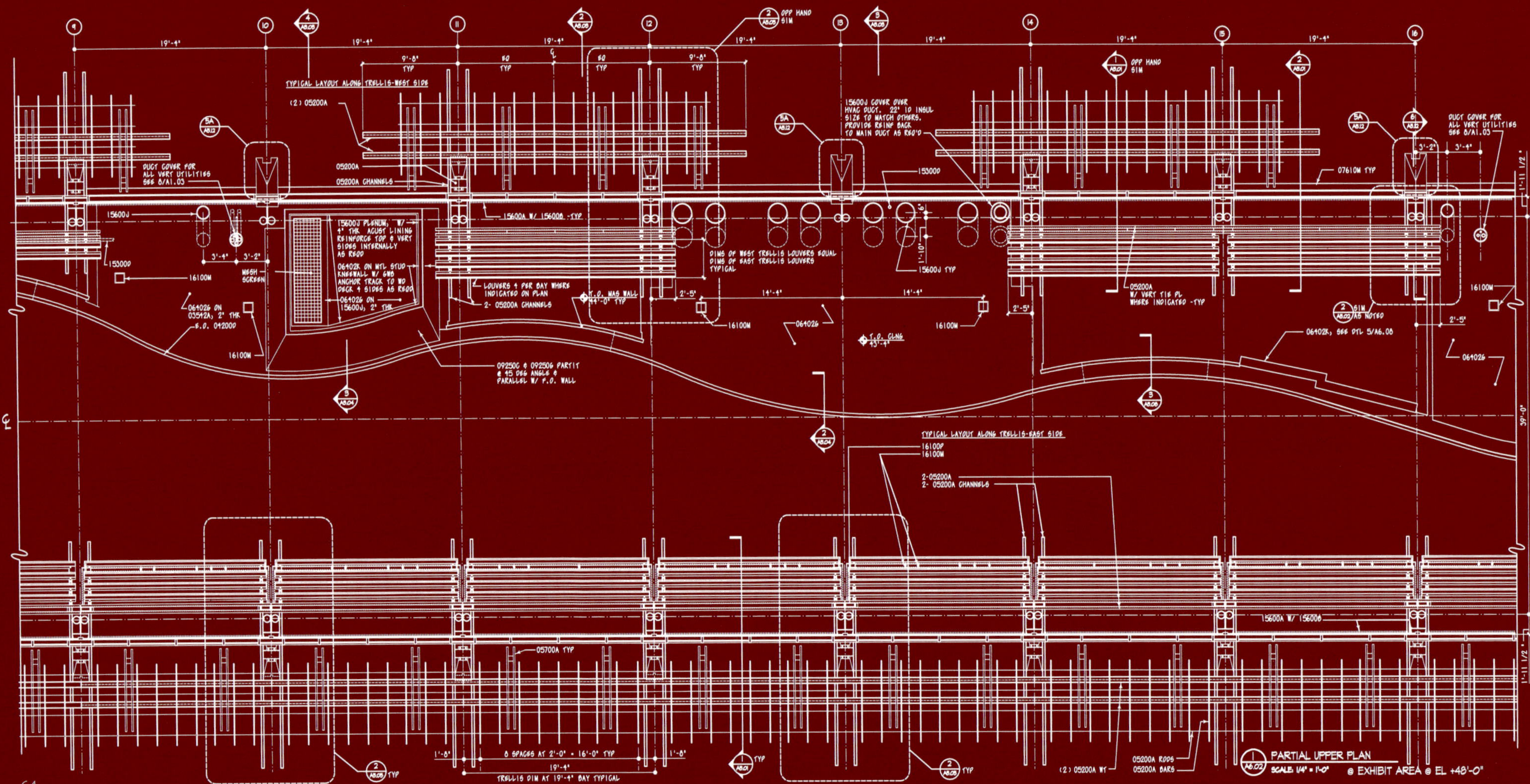
TYPICAL LAYOUT ALONG TRELLIS-WEST SIDE
TYPICAL LAYOUT ALONG TRELLIS-EAST SIDE
PARTIAL UPPER PLAN
SCALE: 1/4" = 1'-0"
@ EXHIBIT AREA @ EL +48'-0"

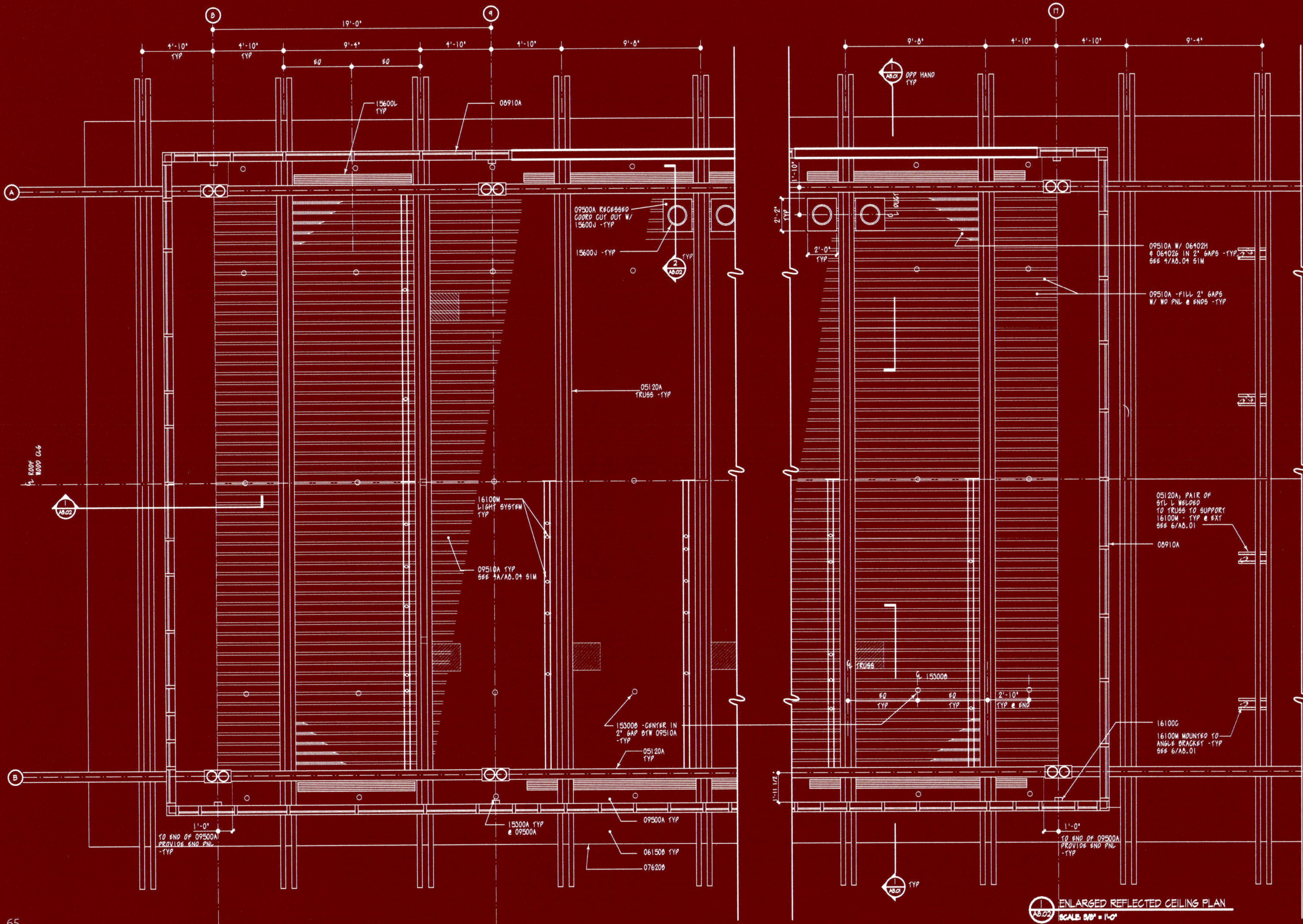
ENLARGED REFLECTED CEILING PLAN
SCALE: 3/8" = 1'-0"

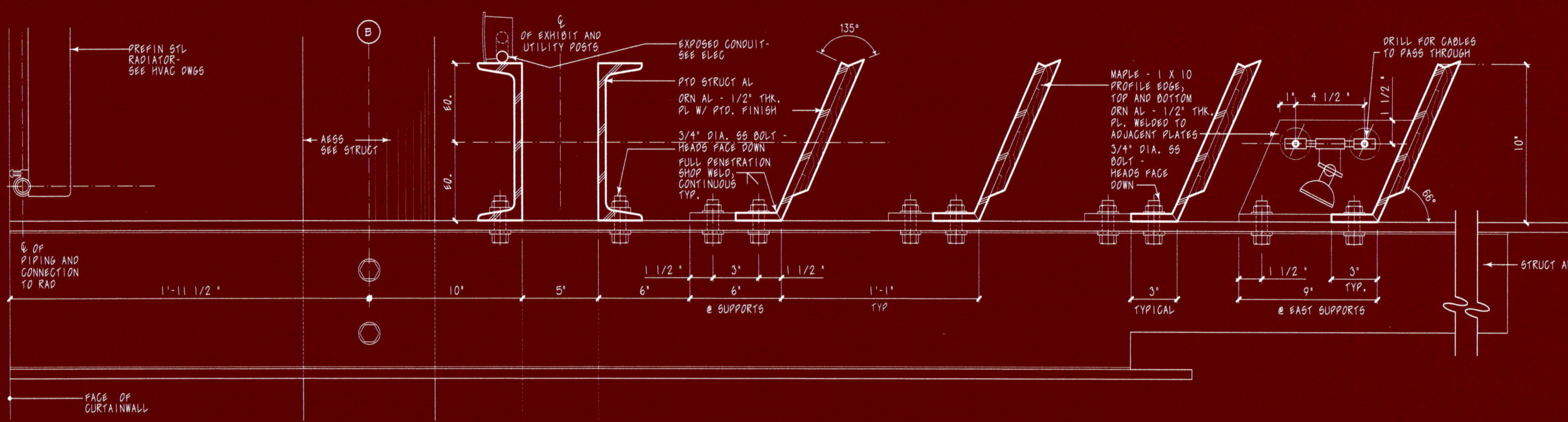

8/A6.09 SECTION THROUGH LIGHT BAFFLE @ EAST
SCALE: 3" = 1'-0"

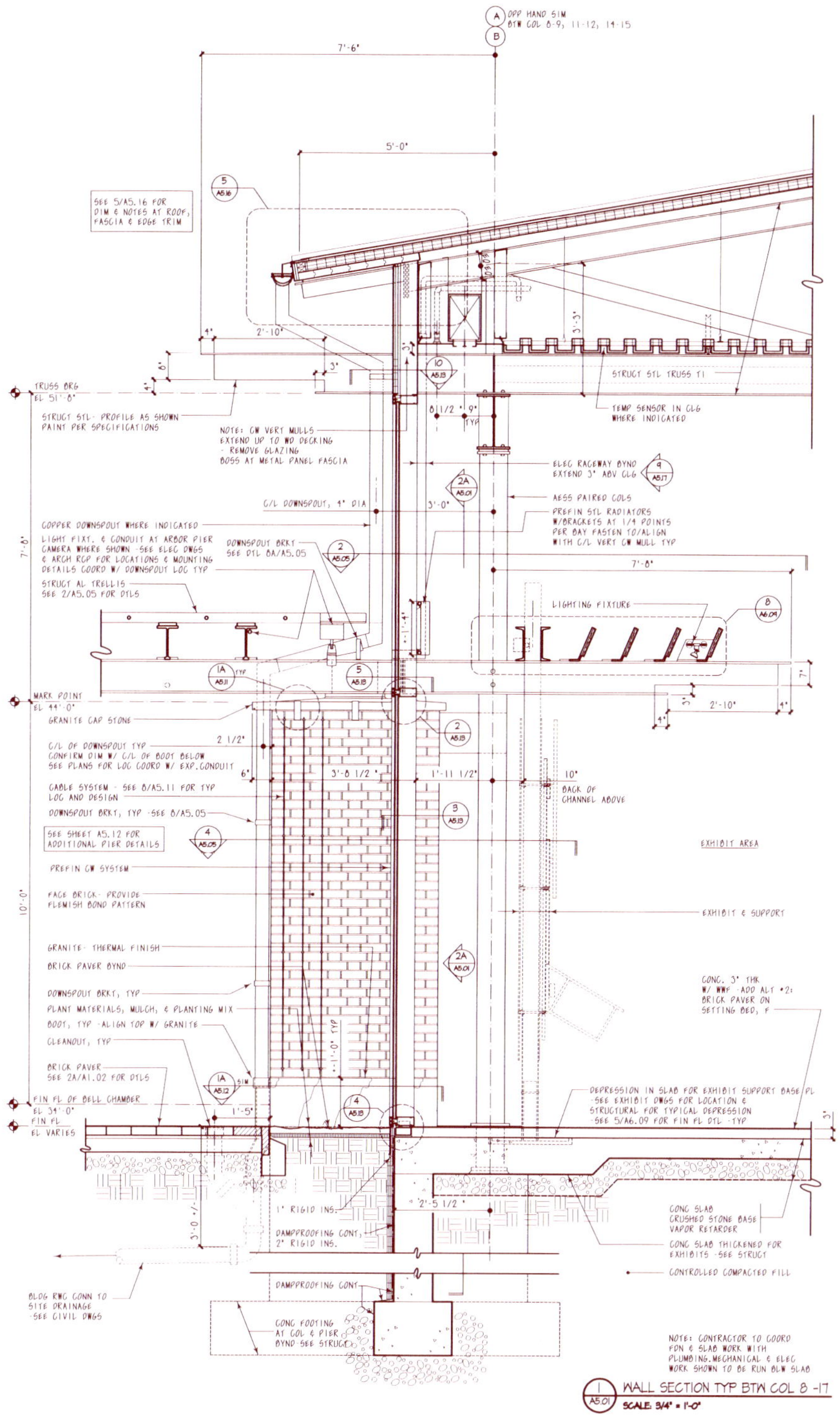
OPP HAND SIM BTW COL 8-9, 11-12, 14-15
7'-6"
5'-0"
SEE 5/A5.16 FOR DIM & NOTES AT ROOF, FASCIA & EDGE TRIM
TRUSS BRG EL 51'-0"
STRUCT STL PROFILE AS SHOWN PAINT PER SPECIFICATIONS
STRUCT STL TRUSS T1
TEMP SENSOR IN CLG WHERE INDICATED
ELEC RACEWAY BYND EXTEND 3" ABV CLG
AESS PAIRED COLS
C/L DOWNSPOUT, 4" DIA
COPPER DOWNSPOUT WHERE INDICATED
STRUCT AL TRELLIS SEE 2/A5.05 FOR DTLS
LIGHTING FIXTURE
MARK POINT EL 44'-0"
GRANITE CAP STONE
SEE SHEET A5.12 FOR ADDITIONAL PIER DETAILS
PREFIN CW SYSTEM
FACE BRICK- PROVIDE FLEMISH BOND PATTERN
GRANITE- THERMAL FINISH
BRICK PAVER BYND
DOWNSPOUT BRKT, TYP
PLANT MATERIALS, MULCH, & PLANTING MIX
CLEANOUT, TYP
BRICK PAVER SEE 2A/A1.02 FOR DTLS
FIN FL OF BELL CHAMBER EL 34'-0"
FIN FL EL VARIES
EXHIBIT AREA
EXHIBIT & SUPPORT
1" RIGID INS.
DAMPPROOFING CONT, 2" RIGID INS.
DAMPPROOFING CONT
CONC SLAB CRUSHED STONE BASE VAPOR RETARDER
CONC SLAB THICKENED FOR EXHIBITS SEE STRUCT
CONTROLLED COMPACTED FILL
BLDG RWC CONN TO SITE DRAINAGE SEE CIVIL DWGS
CONC FOOTING AT COL & PIER BYND SEE STRUCT
WALL SECTION TYP BTW COL 8-17
SCALE 3/4" = 1'-0"

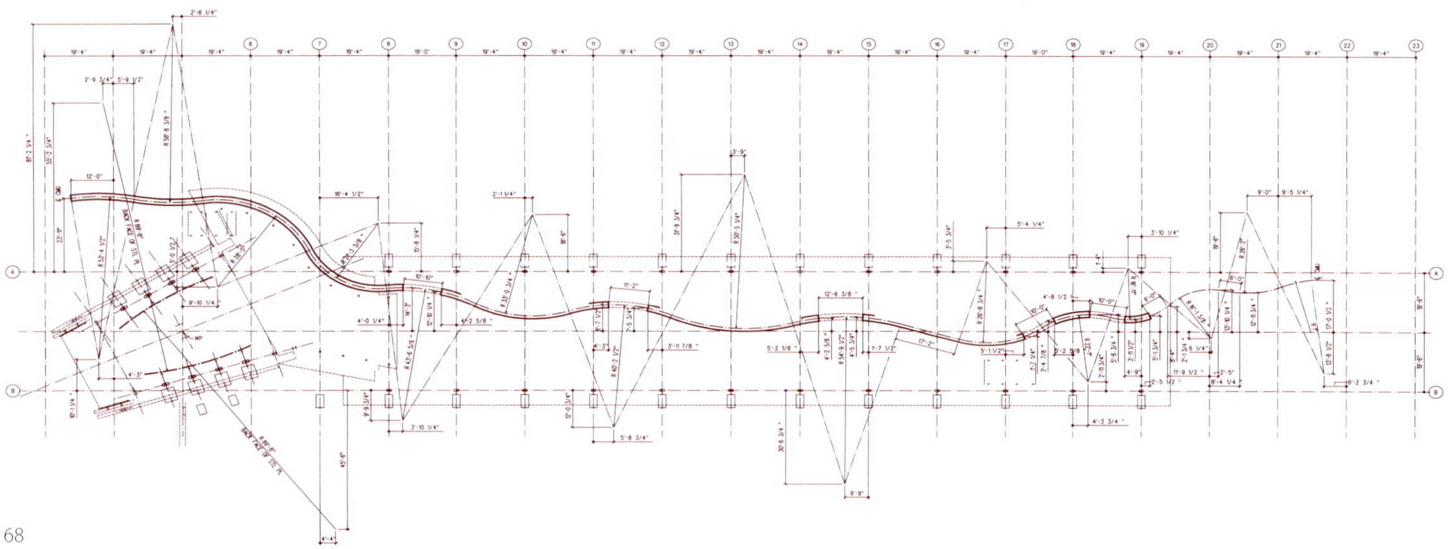

68

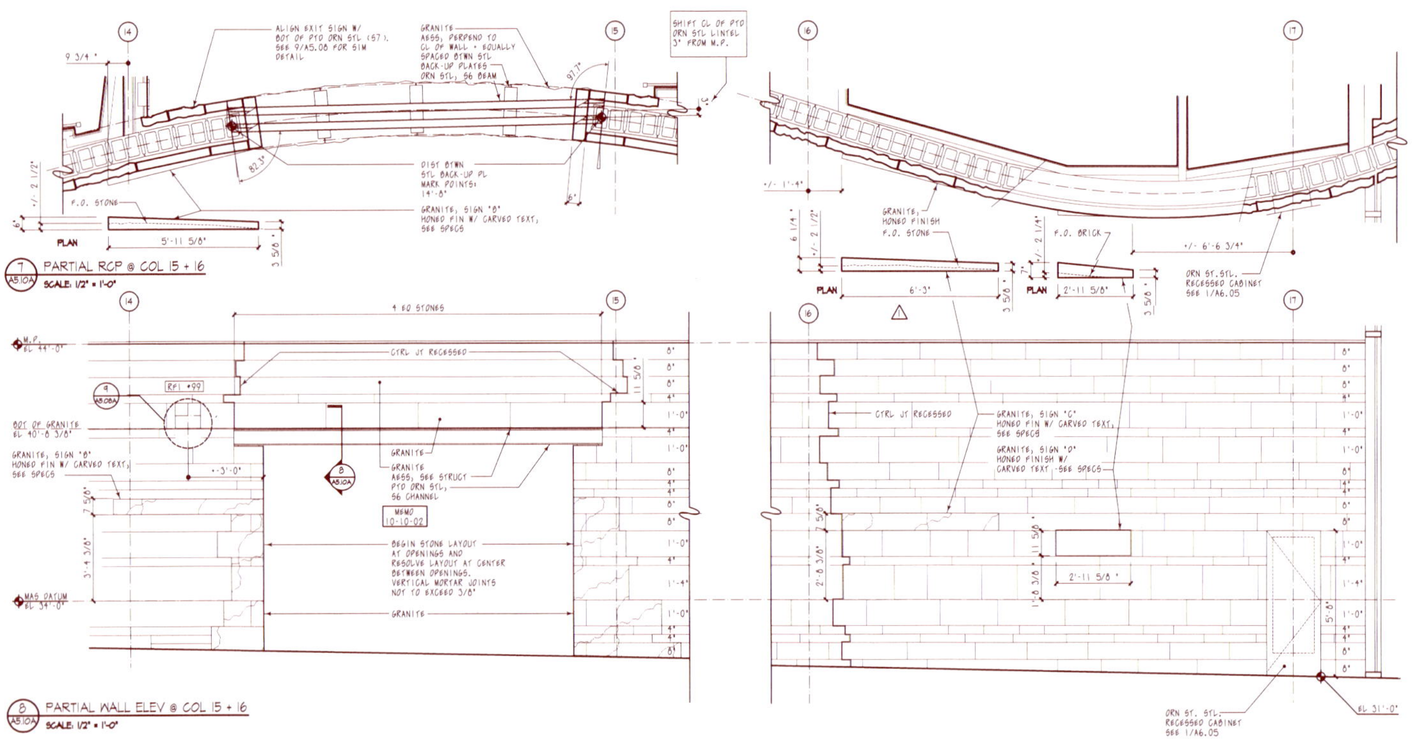
PARTIAL RCP @ COL 15 + 16
SCALE: 1/2" = 1'-0"
PARTIAL WALL ELEV @ COL 15 + 16
SCALE: 1/2" = 1'-0"

69

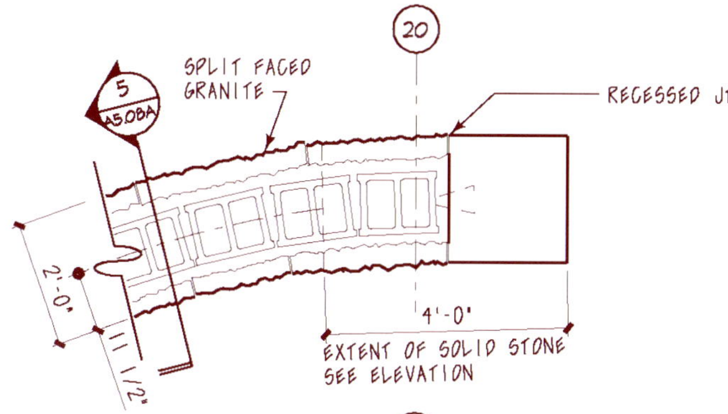

6 A5.09A PARTIAL WALL RCP @ COL 20

SCALE: 1/2" = 1'-0"

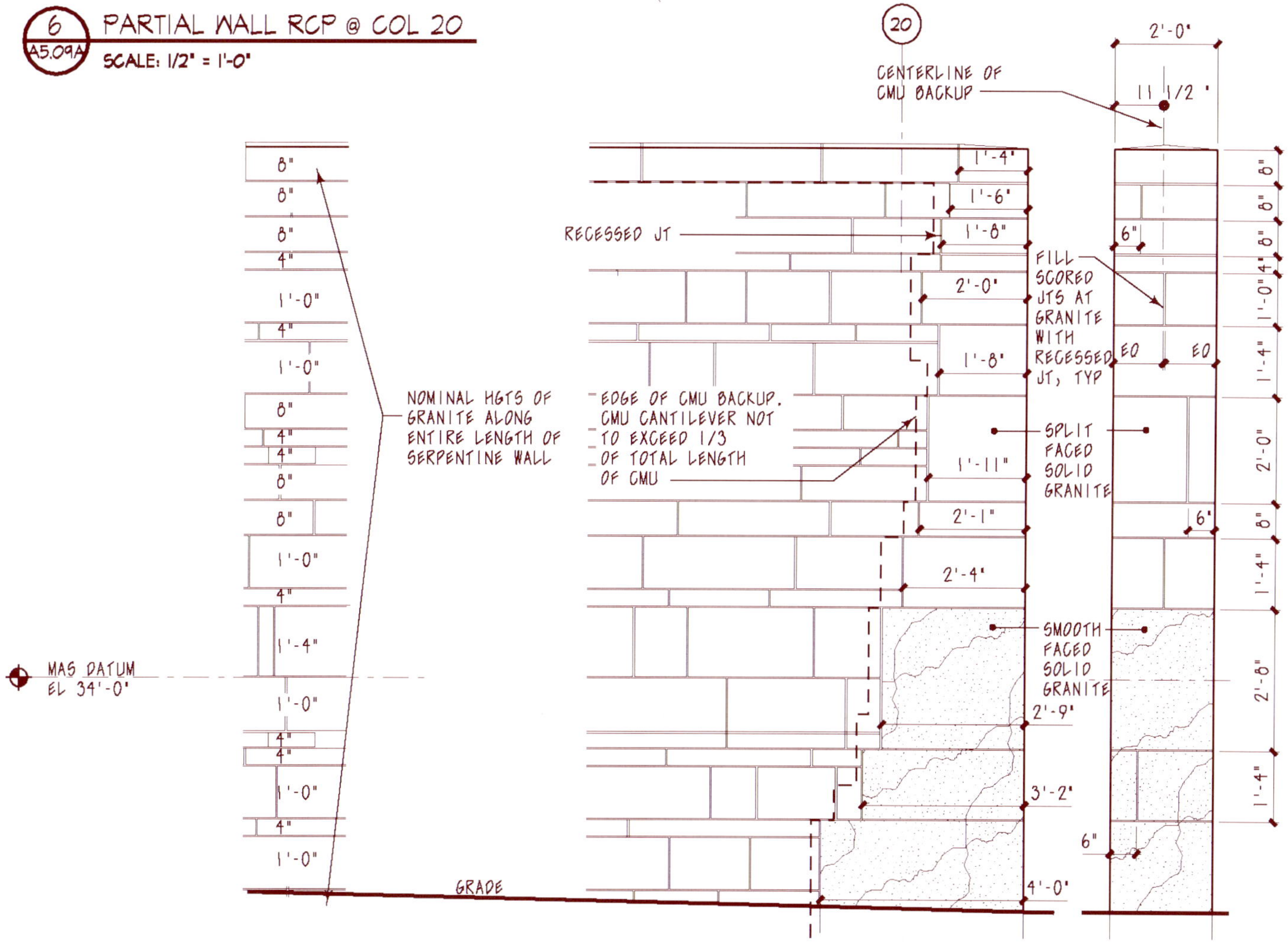

7 A5.09A PARTIAL WALL ELEVATION @ NORTH END

SCALE: 1/2" = 1'-0"

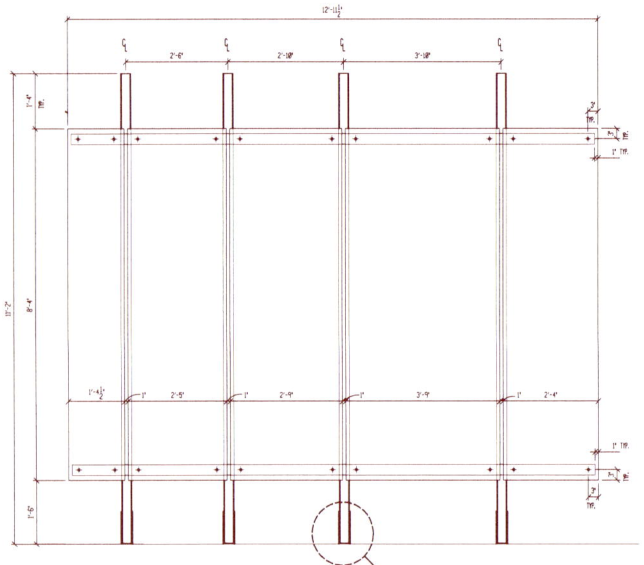

1 X10.2 UNIT #15 - NORTH ELEV.
ETCHED GLASS AND STRUCTURE
3/4"=1'-0"

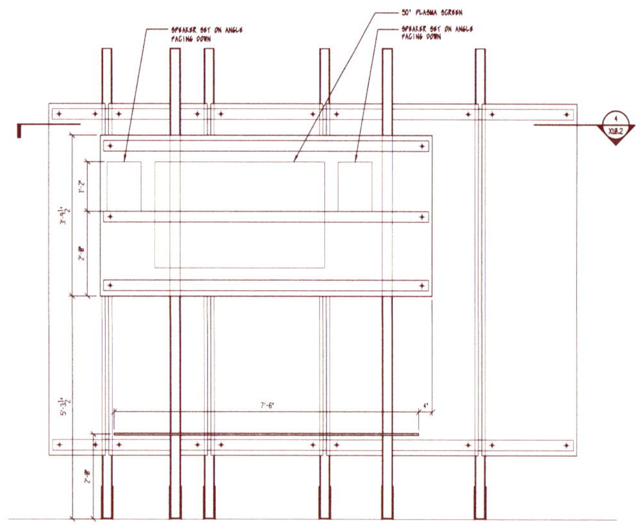

2 X10.2 UNIT #15 - NORTH ELEV.
VIDEO MONITOR STRUCTURE
3/4"=1'-0"

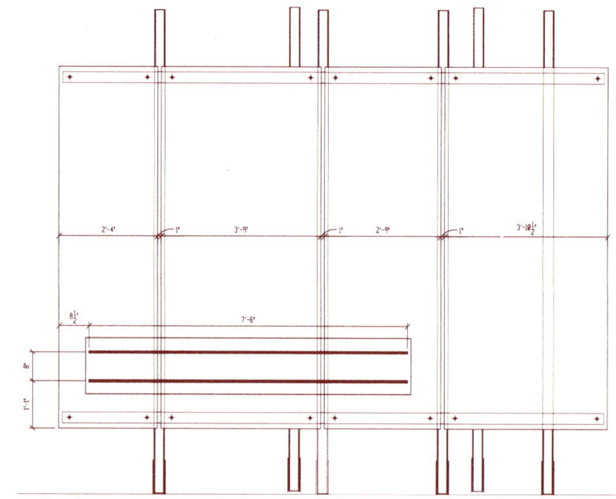

3 X10.2 UNIT #15 - SOUTH ELEV.
ETCHED GLASS AND STRUCTURE
3/4"=1'-0"

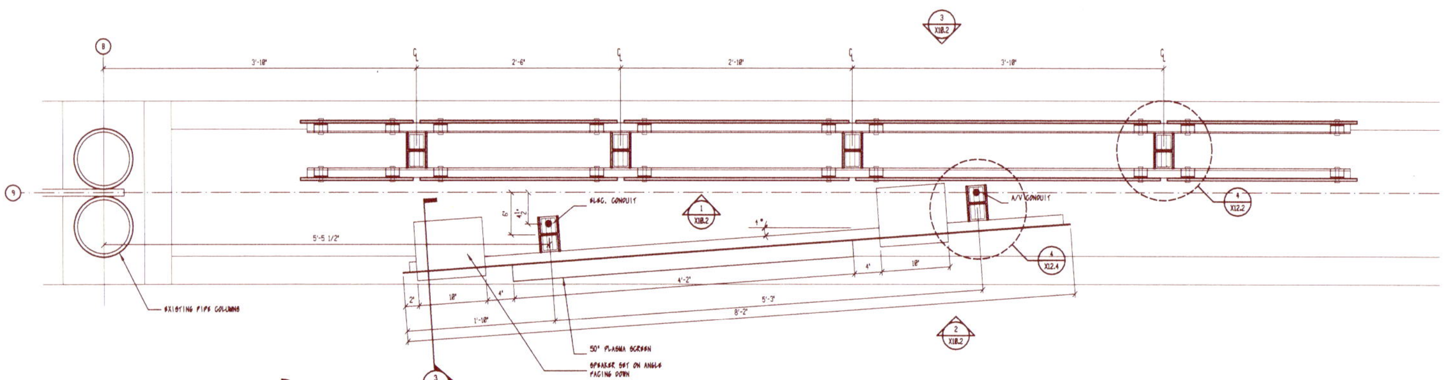

4 X10.2 UNIT #15 - PLAN
1 1/2"=1'-0"

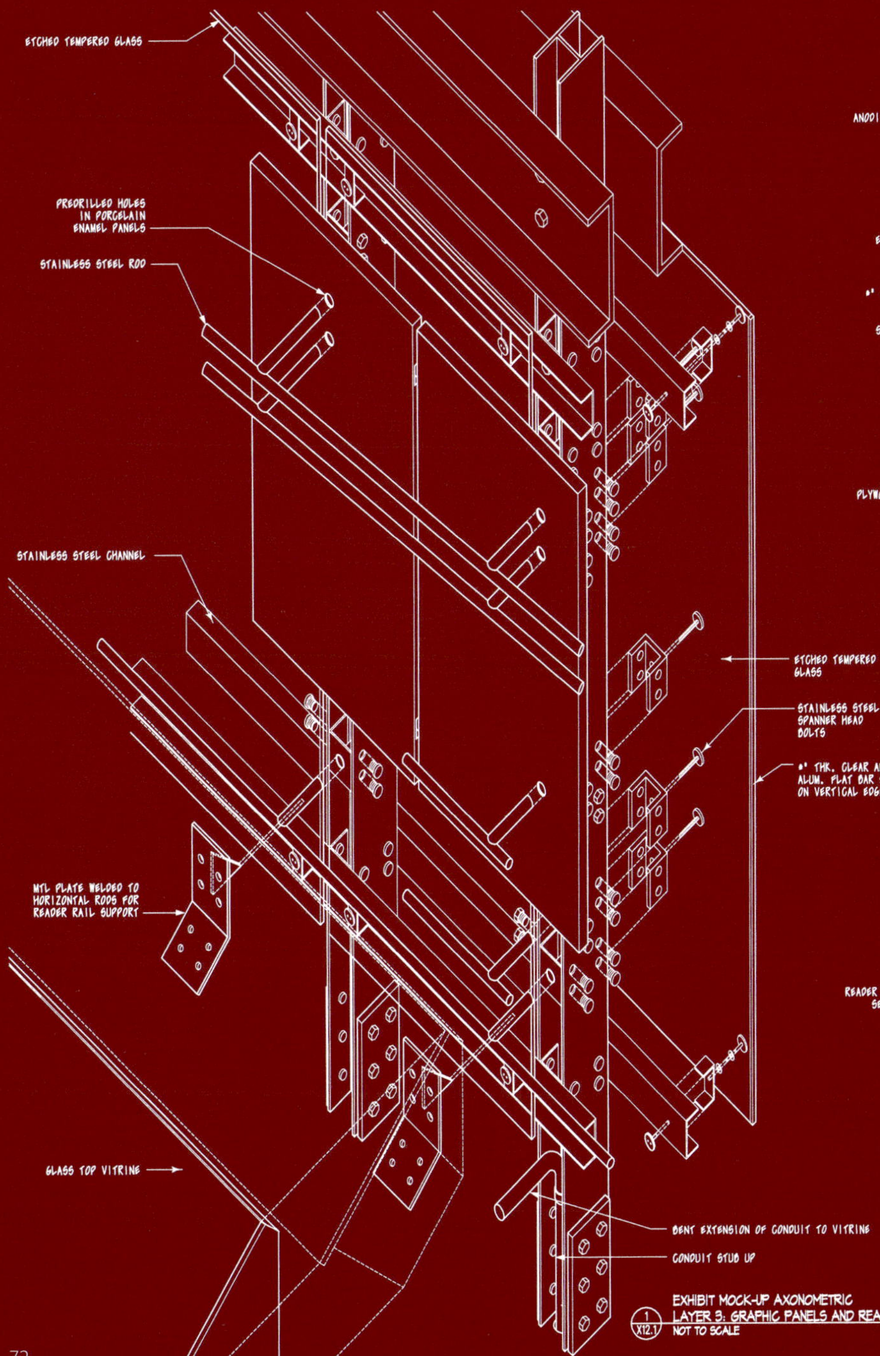

1 X12.1 EXHIBIT MOCK-UP AXONOMETRIC
LAYER 3: GRAPHIC PANELS AND READER RAIL
NOT TO SCALE

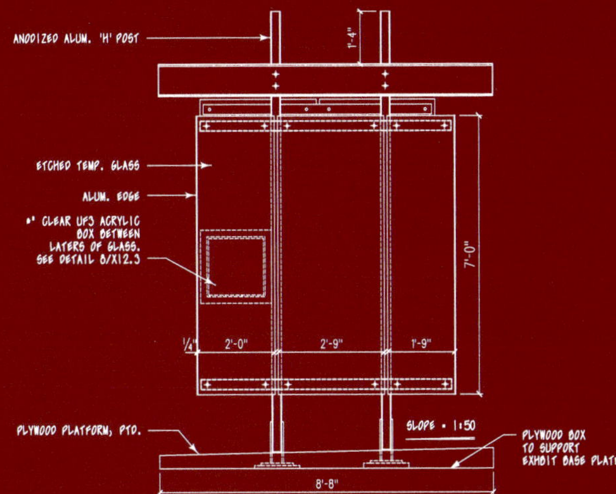

2 X12.1 EXHIBIT MOCK-UP UNIT
ETCHED GLASS AND STRUCTURE
3/4"=1'-0"

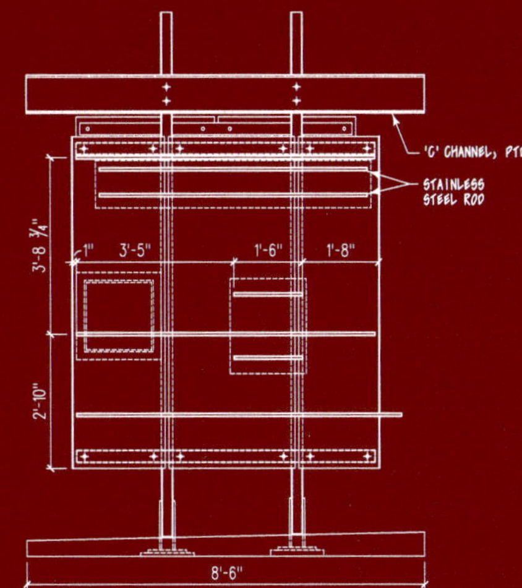

3 X12.1 EXHIBIT MOCK-UP UNIT
MTL ROD FRAMING FOR GRAPHIC PANELS
3/4"=1'-0"

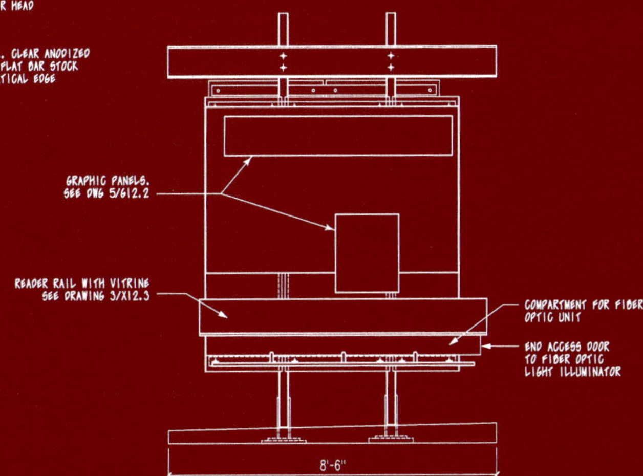

4 X12.1 EXHIBIT MOCK-UP UNIT
GRAPHIC PANELS AND READER RAIL
3/4"=1'-0"

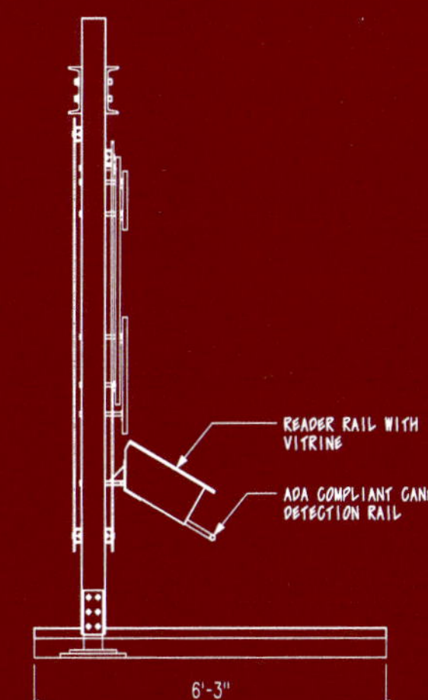

4 X12.1 EXHIBIT MOCK-UP UNIT
SIDE ELEVATION
3/4"=1'-0"

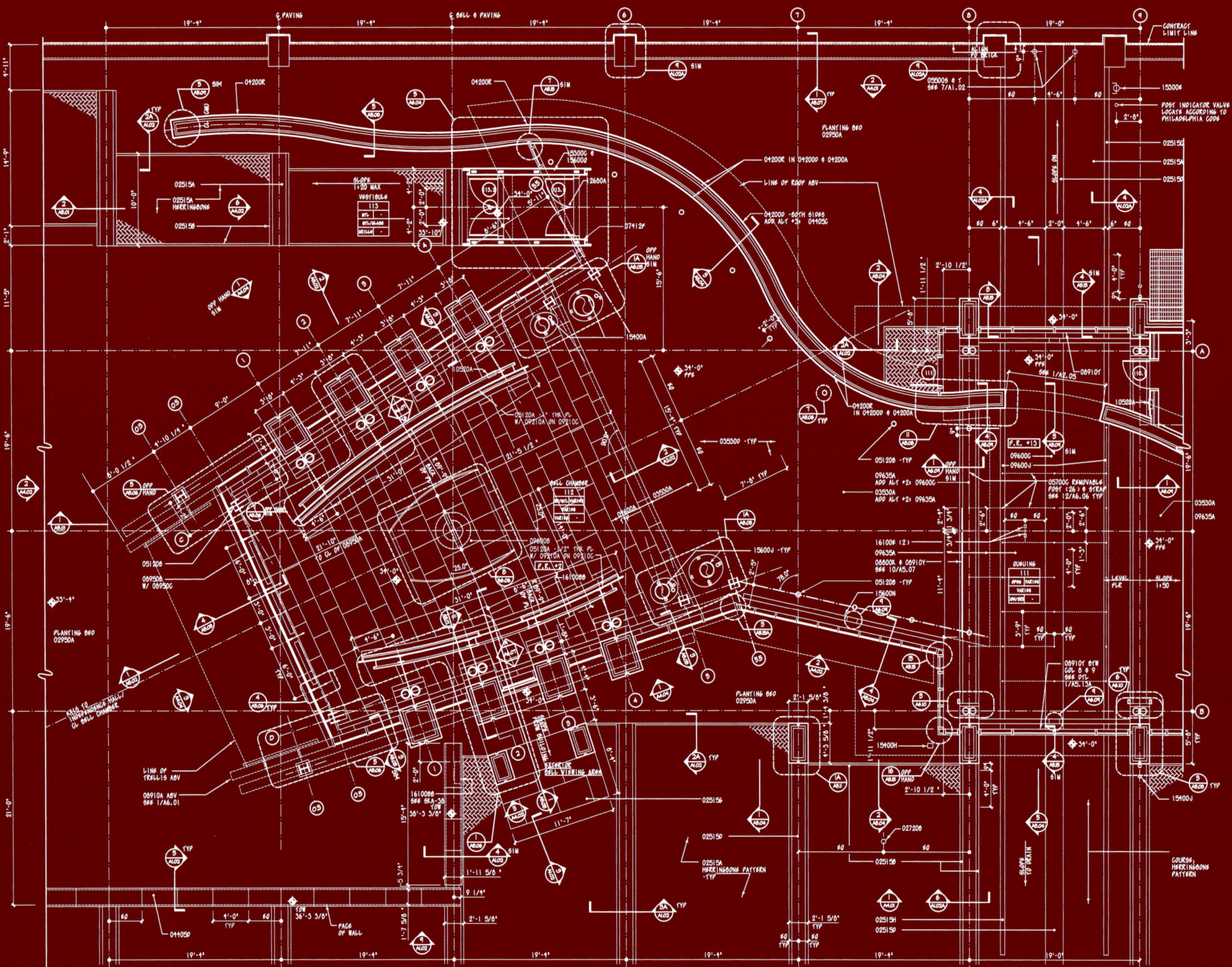

PARTIAL PLAN @ BELL CHAMBER
SCALE 1/4" = 1'-0"

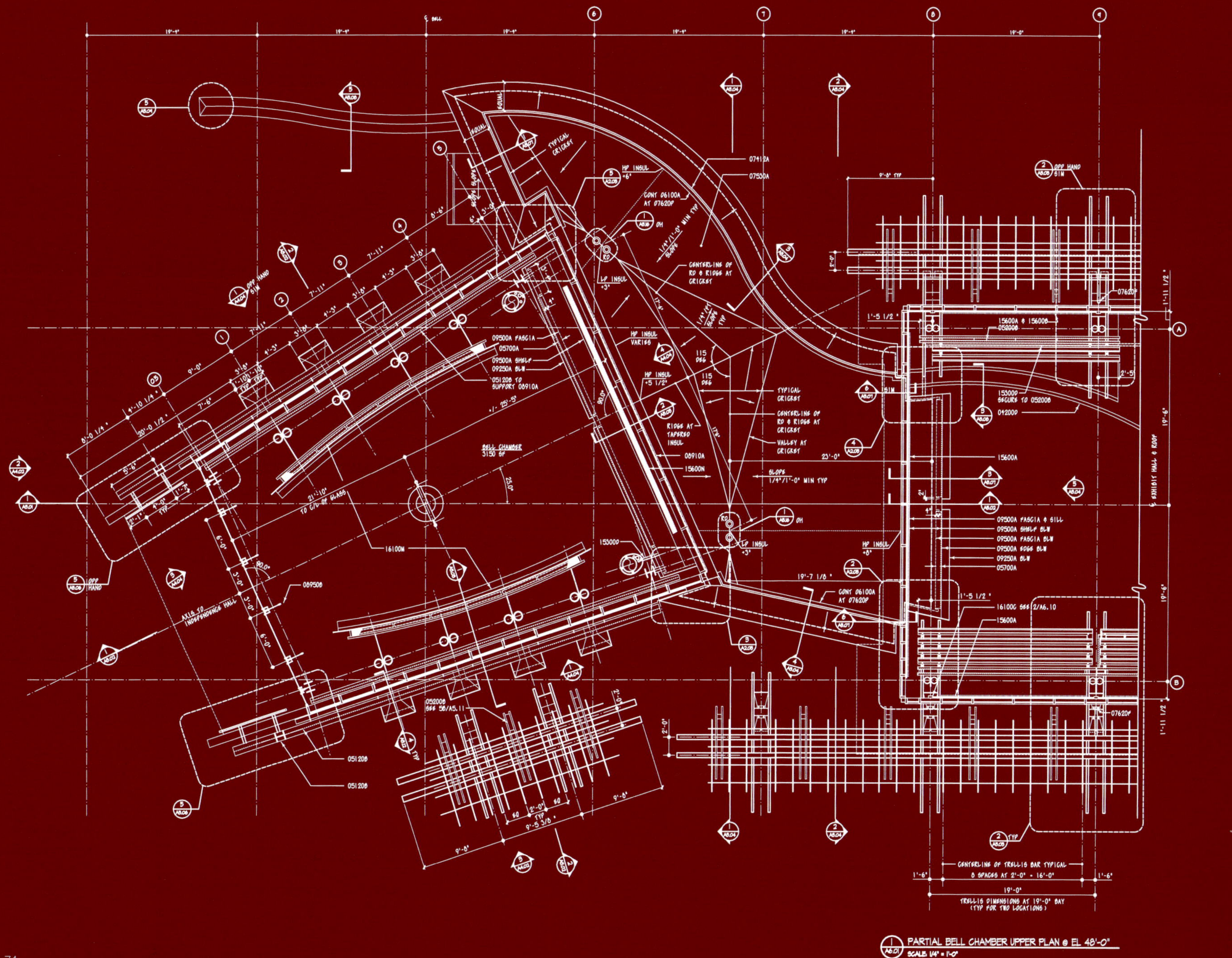
BELL CHAMBER
3150 SF
TYPICAL CRICKET
HP INSUL
LP INSUL
09500A FASCIA
05700A
09500A SHELF
09250A BLW
16100M
153000
08950B
051208
AXIS TO INDEPENDENCE HALL
CENTERLINE OF RD & RIDGE AT CRICKET
VALLEY AT CRICKET
RIDGES AT TAPERED INSUL
SLOPE 1/4"/1'-0" MIN TYP
15600A
15600N
08910A
042000
CONT 06100A AT 07620P
CENTERLINE OF TRELLIS BAR TYPICAL
8 SPACES AT 2'-0" = 16'-0"
TRELLIS DIMENSIONS AT 19'-0" BAY (TYP FOR TWO LOCATIONS)
EXHIBIT HALL & ROOF
PARTIAL BELL CHAMBER UPPER PLAN @ EL 48'-0"
SCALE: 1/4" = 1'-0"

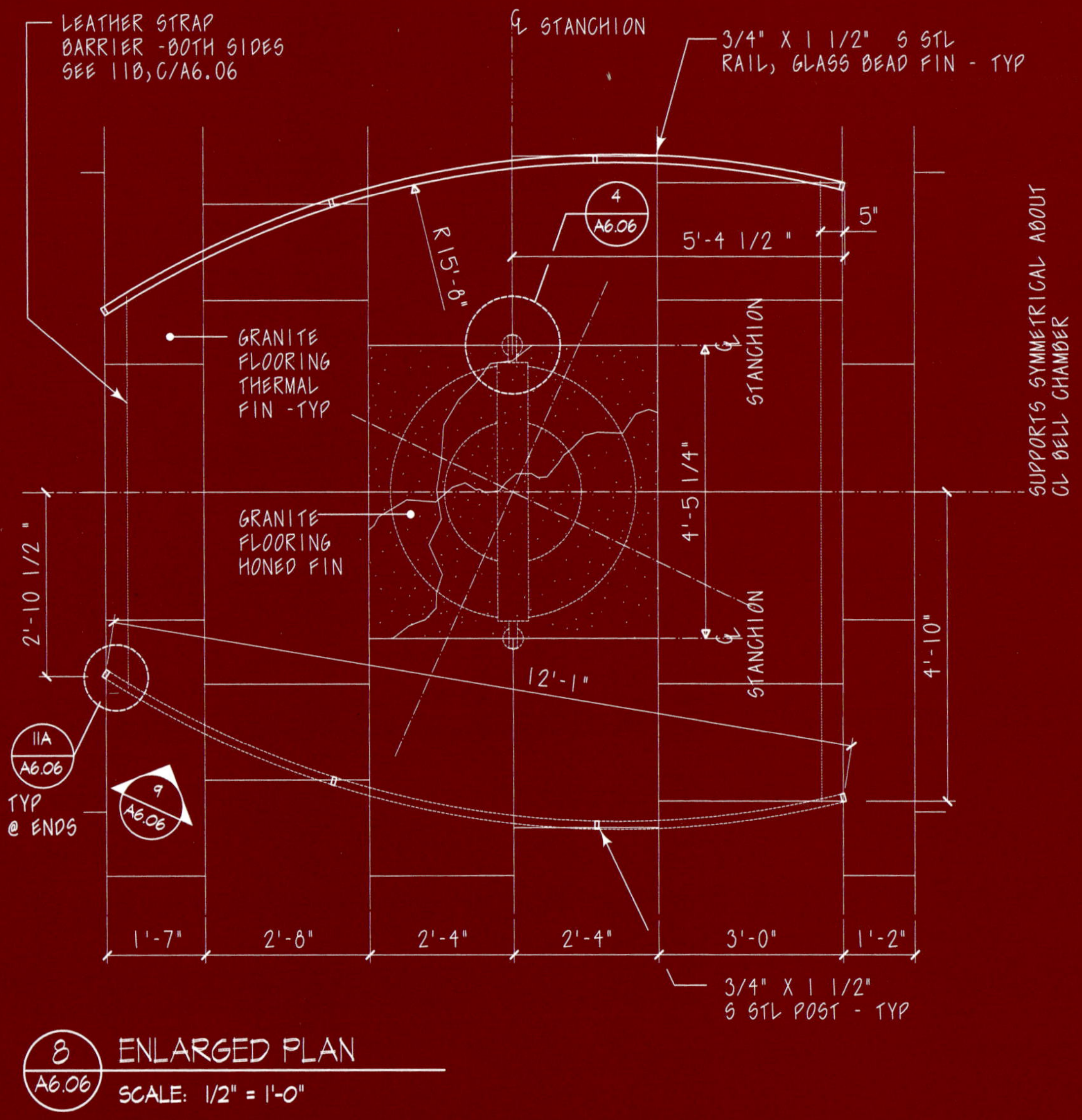
LEATHER STRAP
BARRIER -BOTH SIDES
SEE 11B,C/A6.06
℄ STANCHION
3/4" X 1 1/2" S STL
RAIL, GLASS BEAD FIN - TYP
4
A6.06
R15'-8"
5"
5'-4 1/2 "
GRANITE
FLOORING
THERMAL
FIN -TYP
℄ STANCHION
4'-5 1/4"
SUPPORTS SYMMETRICAL ABOUT
CL BELL CHAMBER
GRANITE
FLOORING
HONED FIN
2'-10 1/2 "
℄ STANCHION
12'-1"
4'-10"
11A
A6.06
9
A6.06
TYP
@ ENDS
1'-7"
2'-8"
2'-4"
2'-4"
3'-0"
1'-2"
3/4" X 1 1/2"
S STL POST - TYP
8
A6.06
ENLARGED PLAN
SCALE: 1/2" = 1'-0"

75 Plan detail of area around the Liberty Bell support 76, 77 Details of Bell Chamber railing 78-80 Details of bell support posts

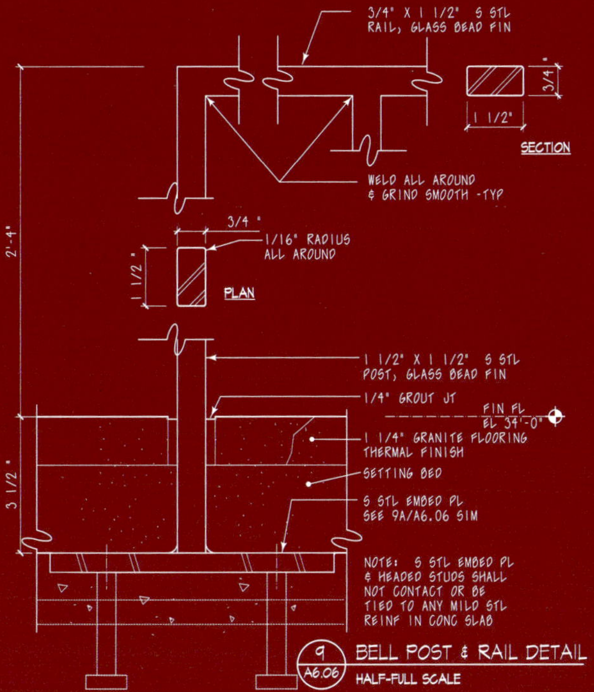

76

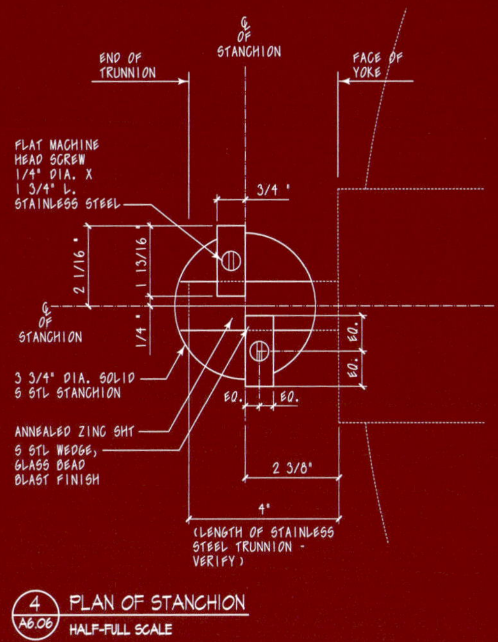

78

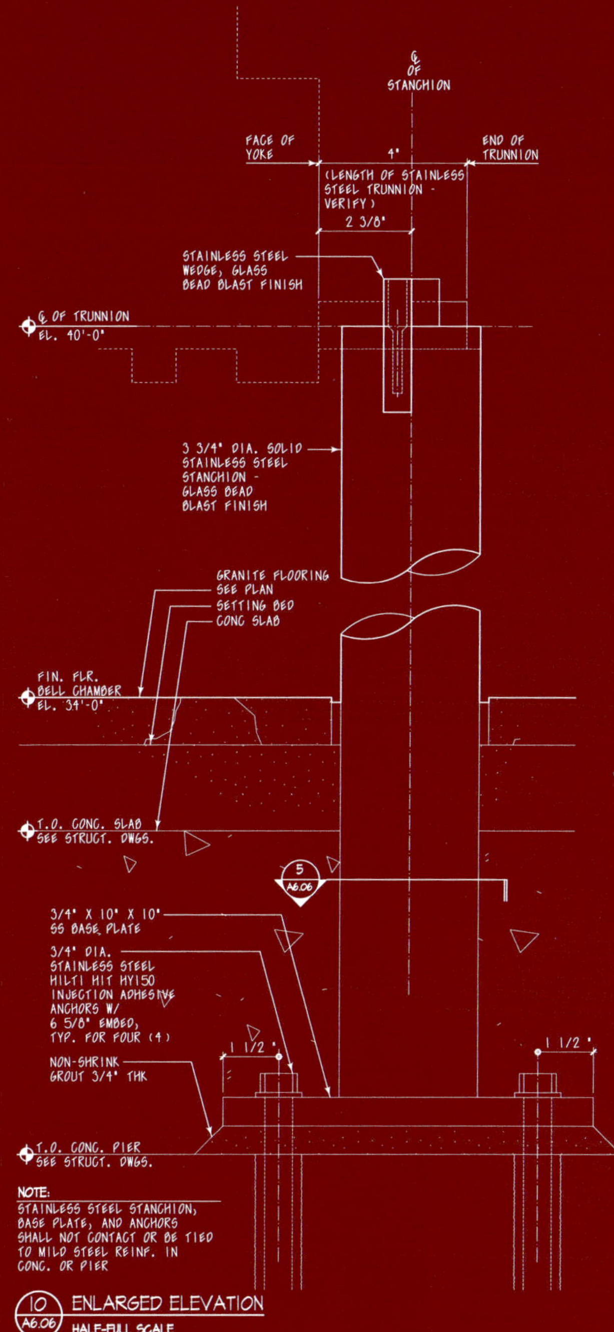

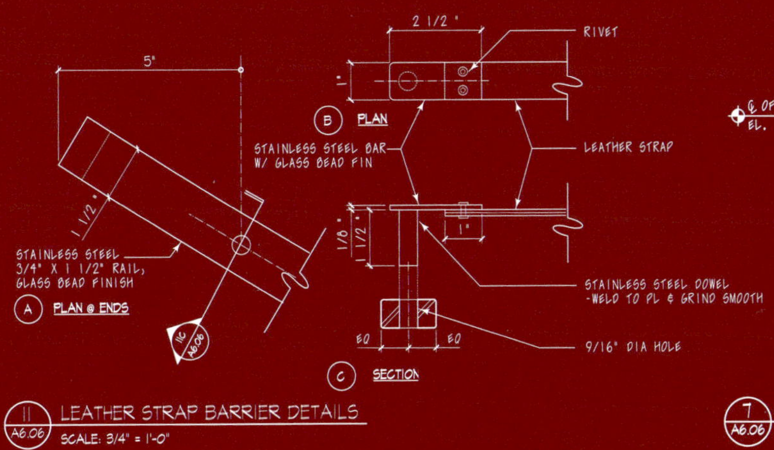

77

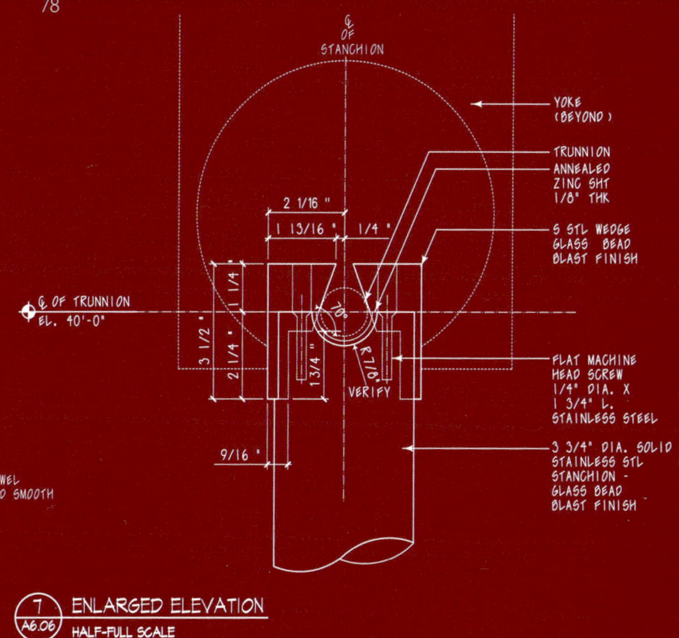

79

80

Ima

ges

Models
Construction
Exterior
Interior

1, 2 Views of design development phase model

1

2

3-6 Views of design development phase model

4

5

6

7

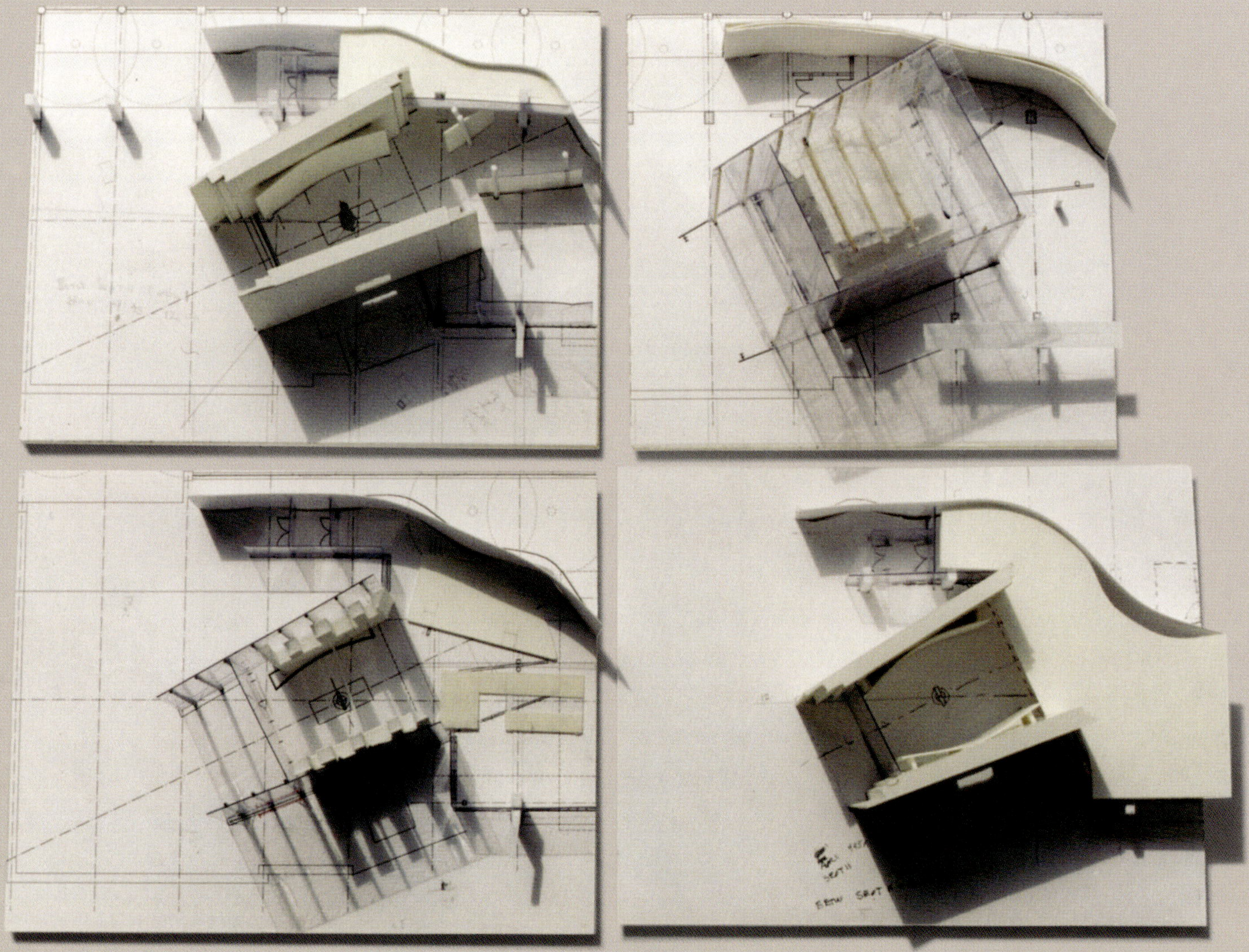

7 Schematic design phase study models of various Bell Chamber designs

8-17 Schematic design phase study models of Bell Chamber and exhibit hall roof design

21

22

18-21 Model of brick pier and trellis arborway 22 Design development phase model of building and exhibits 23-25 Top of bell support

23

24

25

Construction

	1	2
3	4	5
6	7	

1 Archaeological excavations prior to construction of LBC 03.01.02
2 Demolition of existing site walls 03.27.02
3 Excavation for mechanical room basement 04.24.02
4 Basement walls of mechanical room basement 05.22.02
5 Footings for the exhibit hall 06.05.02
6 Mechanical room basement facing north 07.03.02
7 Footings for the Bell Chamber 07.31.02

8	9	10
11	12	
13	14	15

8 View of exhibit hall facing south 08.14.02
9 Mechanical basement with holes for duct penetration 08.14.02
10 Formwork for concrete columns for Bell Chamber 08.25.02
11 Installation of underground ductwork 08.28.02
12 Bell Chamber foundations 08.28.02
13 Steel in the exhibit hall 09.04.02
14 Installation of double steel columns in exhibit hall 09.04.02
15 Erection of steel roof trusses over exhibit hall 09.05.02

16	17	18
19		20
21	22	23

16 Erection steel roof trusses over exhibit hall 09.05.02
17 Erection steel roof trusses over exhibit hall 09.05.02
18 Installation of elevated slab above mechanical room 09.11.02
19 Electric/data conduit installation prior to concrete pour 10.09.02
20 North end outdoor gathering area 10.23.02
21 Steel beams and wood roof at outdoor gathering area 10.23.02
22 Exhibit hall facing the Bell Chamber 10.23.02
23 Concrete columns at Bell Chamber 10.23.02

24	25	
26	27	28
29	30	31

24 Sample of wood acoustical ceiling panel 10.23.02
25 Steel roof trusses and wood roof eave 11.05.02
26 Base of double steel columns in exhibit hall 11.05.02
27 Steel columns and beam in Bell Chamber 11.05.02
28 Steel roof trusses at south end of exhibit hall 11.05.02
29 Bernard Cywinski reviewing steel roof trusses 11.05.02
30 Steel columns and beams in Bell Chamber 11.05.02
31 Exhibit hall – east elevation 11.05.02

32	33	34
35	36	37
38		39

32 Installation of steel in Bell Chamber 11.05.02
33 Bernard Cywinski, Kenneth Mitchell, Craig Hunt PM of Keating Construction Co. 11.05.02
34 Installation of Bell Chamber steel and wood roof 11.06.02
35 Exhibit hall facing south 11.12.02
36 Installation of stone serpentine wall 11.12.02
37 Bell Chamber steel 11.20.02
38 Bell Chamber steel 11.20.02
39 Installation of steel and CMU in transition area 11.20.02

	40	41
42	43	44
45	46	47

40 Installation of steel and CMU in transition area 11.20.02
41 Aerial view of Bell Chamber 11.26.02
42 Installation of copper roof over exhibit hall 11.26.02
43 Bell Chamber roof steel installation 12.04.02
44 Transition area roof installation 01.08.03
45 Sample of stone engraving and coloring 01.22.03
46 Bell Chamber 01.22.03
47 Alleyway opening through building 02.19.03

48		49
50	51	52
53	54	55

48 Aerial view of Bell Chamber and transition area 02.19.03
49 General view of construction site 03.05.03
50 West side of exhibit hall – installation of curtain wall framing 03.19.03
51 West side of Bell Chamber – installation of curtain wall framing 03.19.03
52 Wolfram Arendt reviewing progress of construction 03.19.03
53 Installation of wood acoustical ceiling 04.02.03
54 Kenneth Mitchell reviewing installation of brick paving 04.16.03
55 Kenneth Mitchell and Bernard Cywinski reviewing the full scale mock-up of one of the exhibit panels 04.25.03

56	57	58
59		60
61	62	63

56 Installation of CMU backup for exterior granite wall 05.14.03
57 Building exit 05.14.03
58 West side of building with lead-coated copper cladding installed 05.28.03
59 Primary structural elements for trellis installed 05.28.03
60 Jeff Lew reviewing construction of Bell Chamber 05.28.03
61 Installation of exhibit supports 05.28.03
62 Installation of brick flooring 05.28.03
63 Roof of Bell Chamber 05.28.03

64	65	66
	67	68
69	70	71

64 Installation of marble wall in Bell Chamber 06.06.03
65 Installation of glass in curtain wall of Bell Chamber 06.11.03
66 Steel connection details at outdoor gathering area 06.25.03
67 Trellis on east side of building 07.09.03
68 Installation of exhibit case support 07.23.03
69 Ceiling of the Bell Chamber 07.23.03
70 Installation of metal trim on a hot day 07.23.03
71 Installation of structural glass wall in Bell Chamber 08.05.03

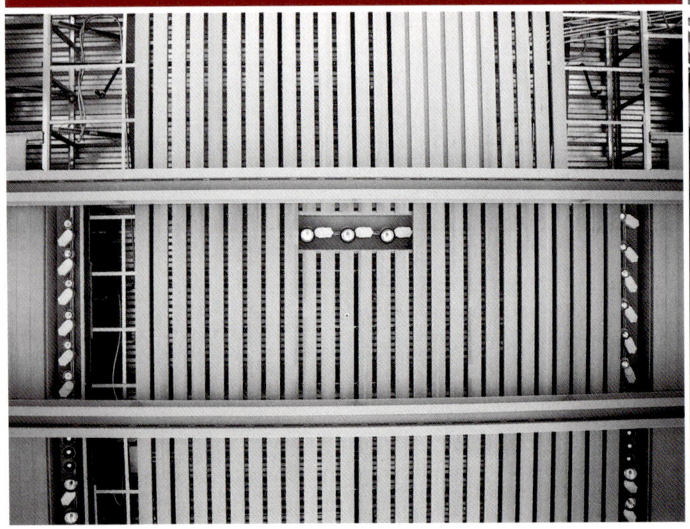

72	73	74
75	76	77
78		79

72 Installation of glass wall in Bell Chamber 08.05.03
73 Installation of glass wall in Bell Chamber 08.05.03
74 Installation of graphic exhibit panels 08.06.03
75 Front door handle detail 08.20.03
76 Jeff Lew reviewing installation of exhibit panels 08.20.03
77 Bell Chamber with stanchions protected 09.03.03
78 North elevation of building 10.01.03
79 Installation of the Liberty Bell in the Bell Chamber 10.09.03

Views from Independence Hall Tower

	1	2
3	4	
5	6	7

1 Basement excavation 05.08.02
2 Concrete basement walls 06.05.02
3 Concrete structure 08.14.02
4 Exhibit hall metal roof and Bell Chamber concrete columns 10.09.02
5 Exhibit hall wood roof deck and Bell Chamber steel 11.06.02
6 Exhibit hall copper roof and Bell Chamber roof 12.18.02
7 Transition area roof and exit enclosure 03.19.03

8 North-south walkway and Bell Chamber copper roof 05.14.03
9 Trellis and Bell Chamber light baffle steel 08.06.03
10 Bell Chamber south glass wall and exterior stone wall 09.10.03
11 Landscaping and site cleanup 09.17.03
12 Building open 11.25.03

Exterior

1 Aerial view of Liberty Bell Center and Independence Hall from the south 2 Aerial view of Liberty Bell Center from northeast

1

3

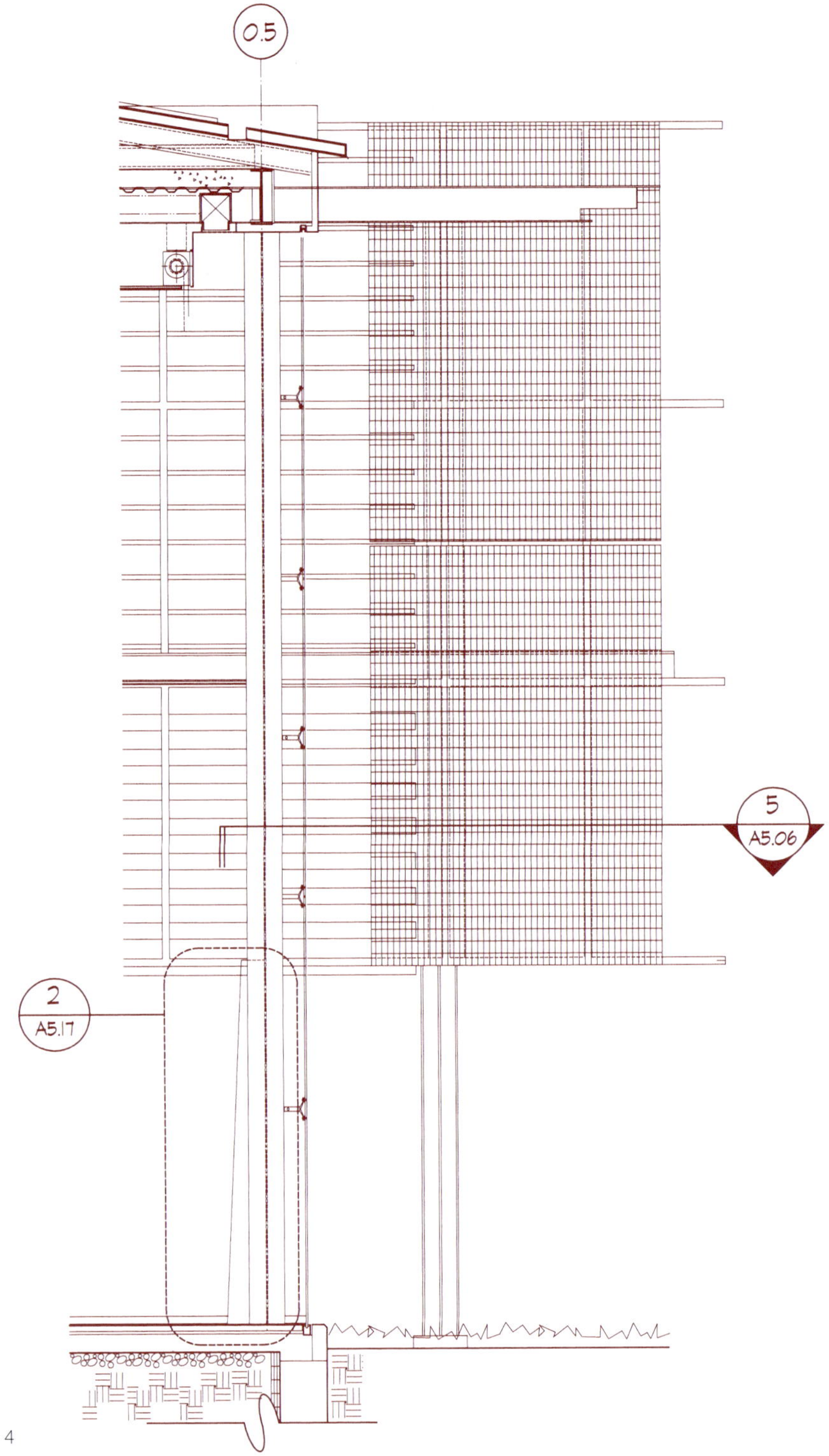

4

3 South end of the Bell Chamber 4 Construction drawing of south wall and light baffle of Bell Chamber 5 View of Liberty Bell Center from Independence Hall

6 Independence Hall and light baffles of Bell Chamber 7 Bell Chamber

6

8

8 Bell Chamber and east side of building 9 Bell Chamber at night

9

10

10 Bell Chamber at night   11, 12 Schematic design presentation drawings - east and west elevation

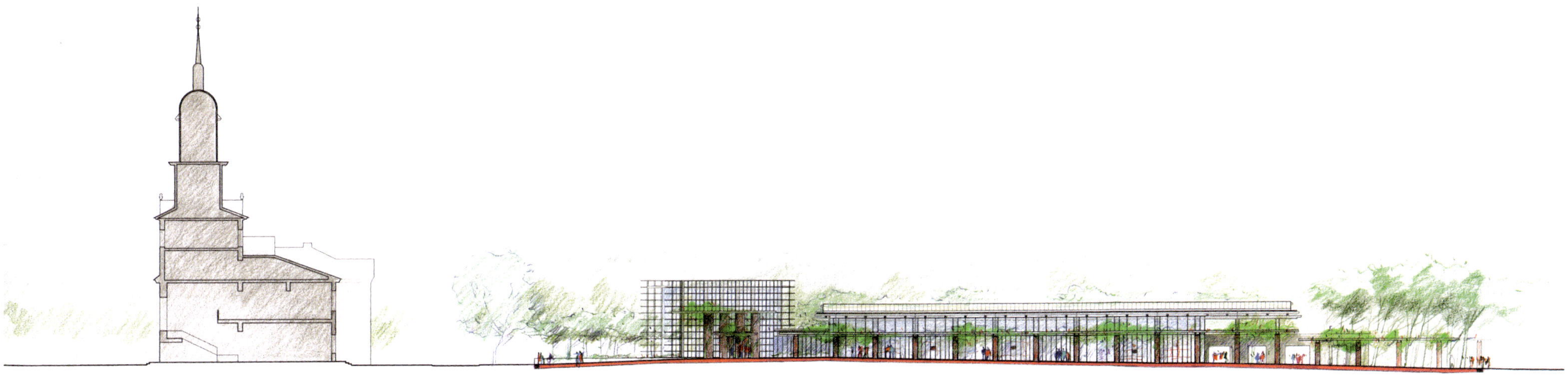

11

12

13

13, 14 Light baffle details on south end of Bell Chamber

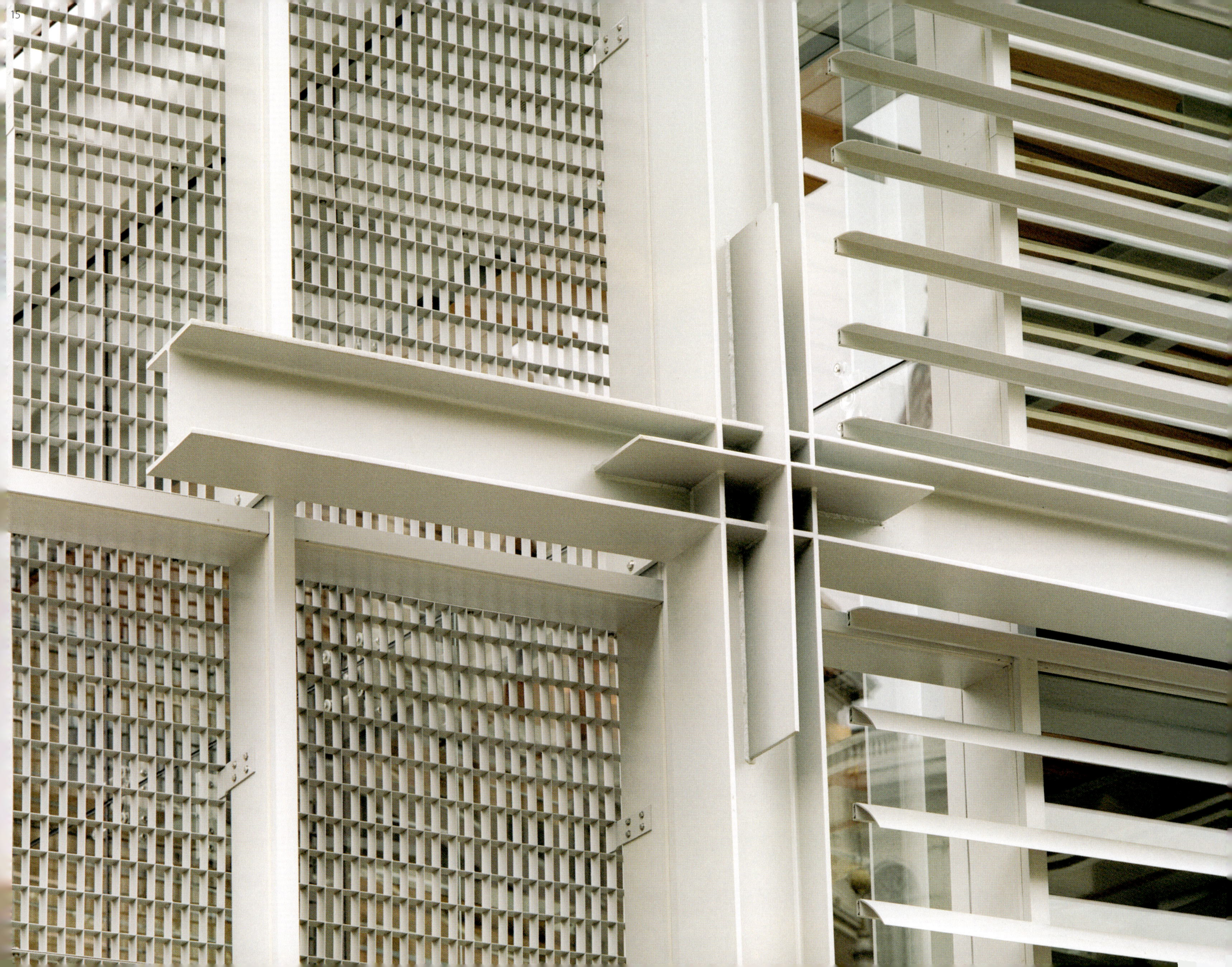

15 - 17 Exterior details of Bell Chamber

16

17

18 Exterior viewing window into Bell Chamber 19 Exterior details of Bell Chamber

20

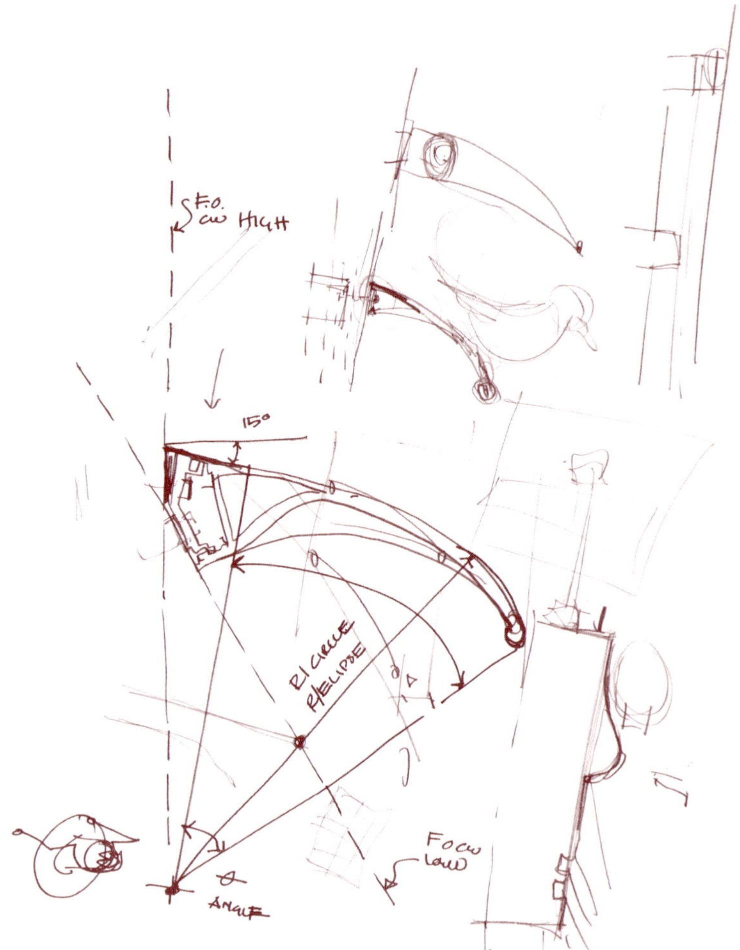

21

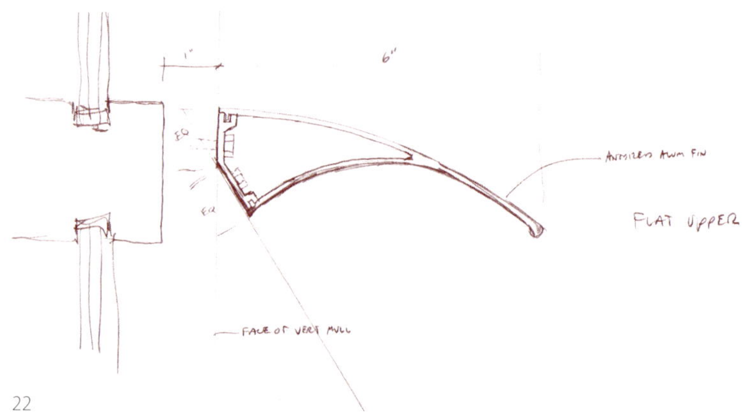

22

20 Exterior viewing window into the Bell Chamber 21, 22 Bell Chamber light baffle fin sketches 23 East elevation of Bell Chamber

23

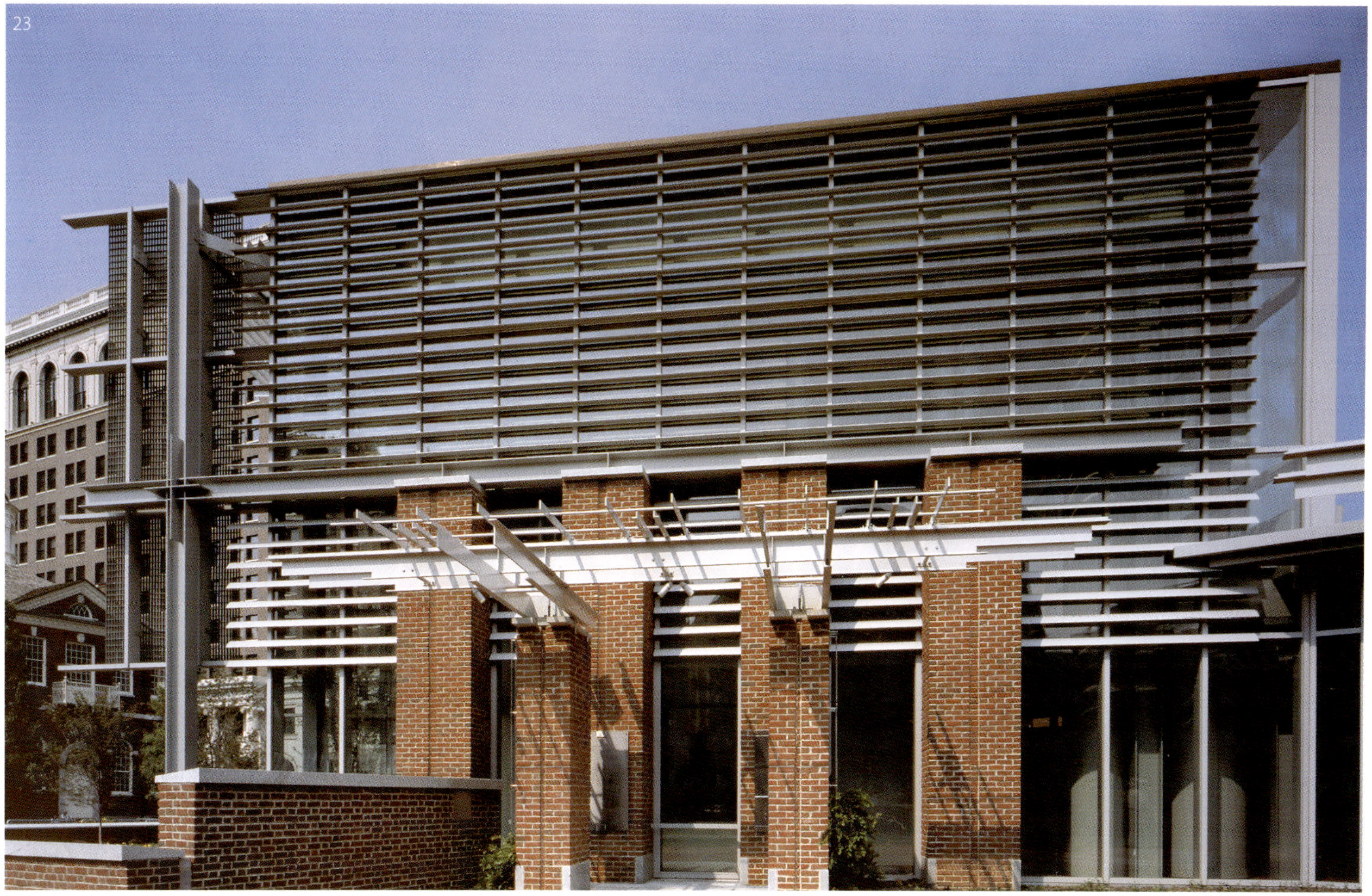

24

24 Northeast corner of Bell Chamber 25 East side of Bell Chamber

25

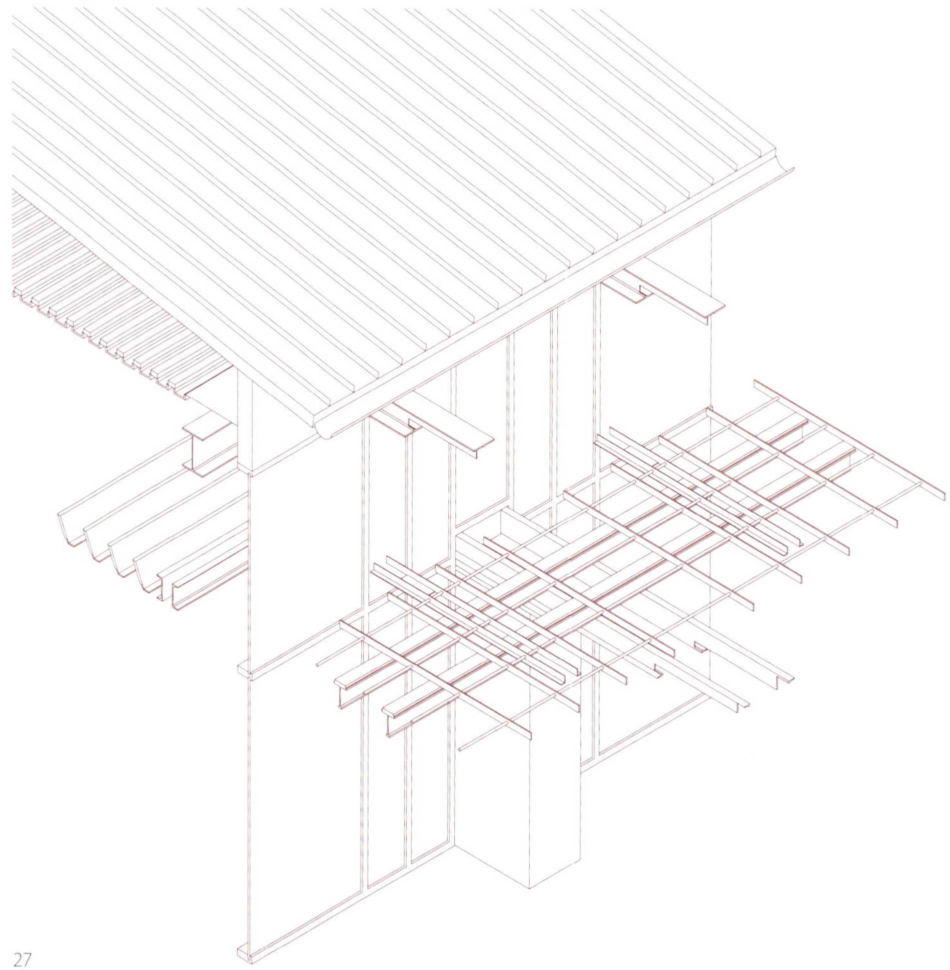

26 East side of exhibit hall facing north 27 Axonometric of exterior trellis and interior light baffles 28 East side of transition area and exhibit hall 29 Liberty Bell Center from the east end of the south alleyway

28

29

30 Bell Chamber 31 East wall of Bell Chamber 32 Wall section at east wall of exhibit hall 33 Alleyway passing through the building

30

31

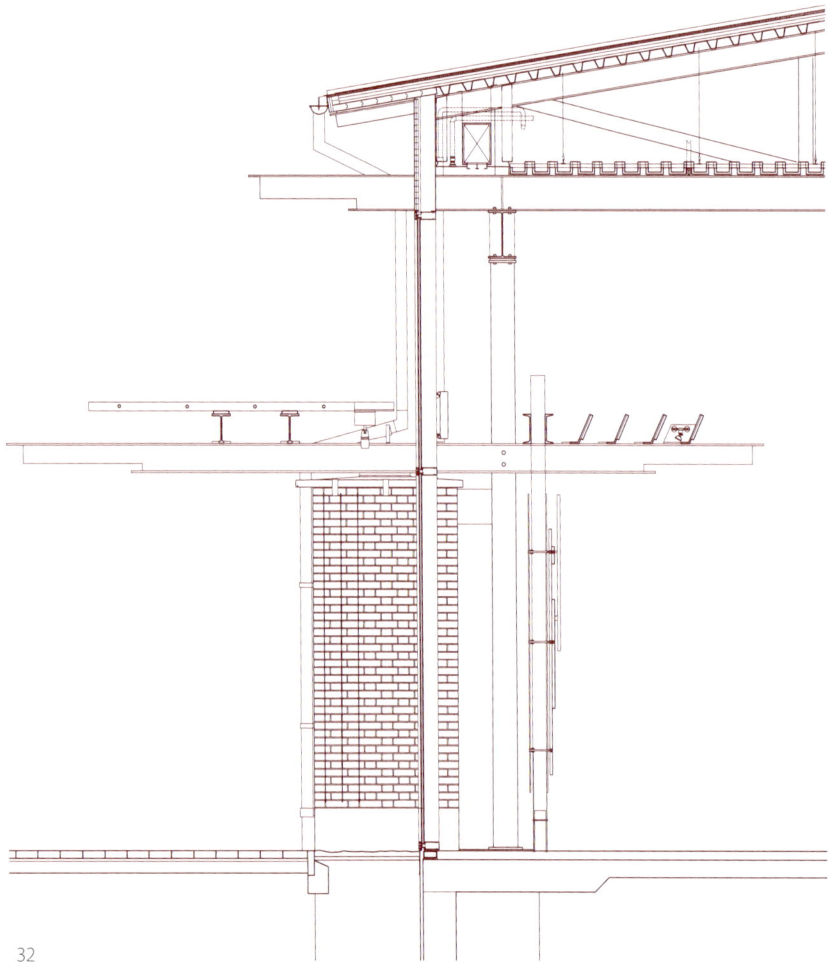

32

33

34 East side of building at night 35 Exploded axonometric of exterior trellis and interior light baffles 36–38 Elevations of exhibit hall

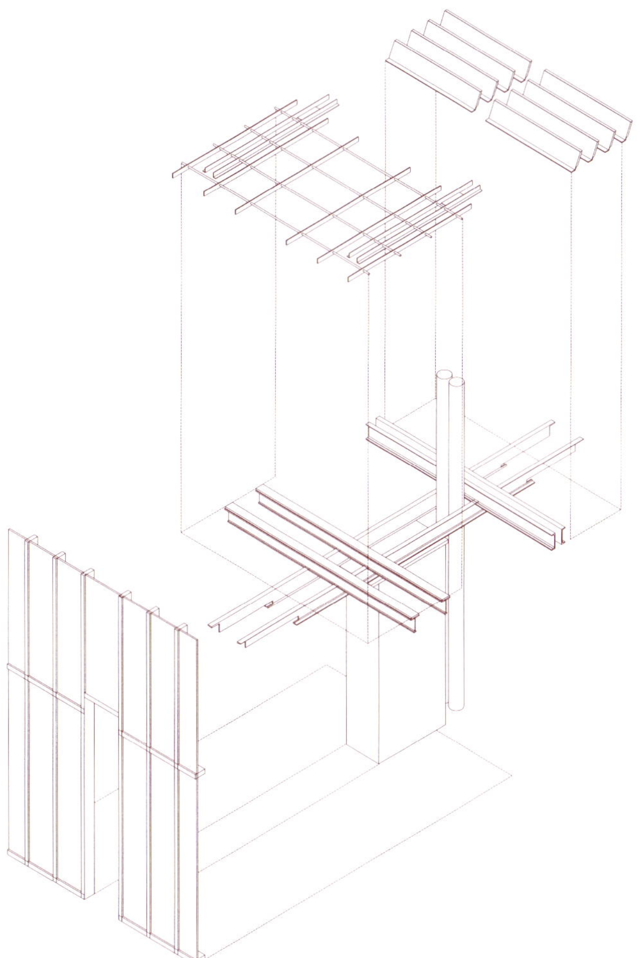

35

36

37

38

39, 40 Trellis along east side of building

41

42

41 Schematic design drawing - east elevation

42 View of Liberty Bell Center from Block Two

43 East side of exhibit hall

43

44 Detail of exhibit panel from exterior 45 Plan view of exterior trellis and interior light baffles 46 View from exterior into the exhibit hall 47 East side of exhibit hall

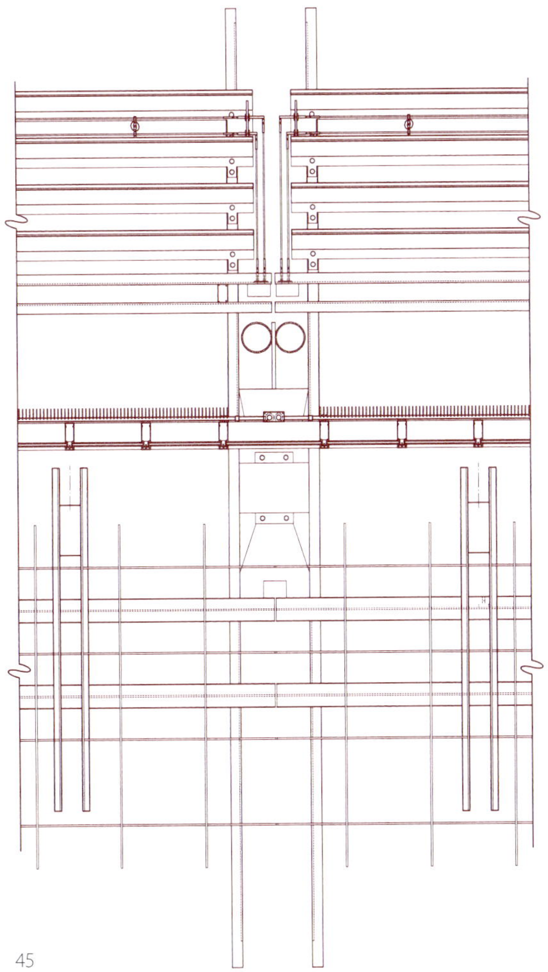

45

46

47

48 Outdoor gathering area 49 North (entry) end of building

48

BELL CENTER

LIBERTY BELL CENTER

50 North alleyway and outdoor gathering area 51 Building entrance

51

Interior

52 Building entrance from inside exhibit hall 53 Front door handles 54 Detail of door handles 55 Exhibit hall facing south

52

53

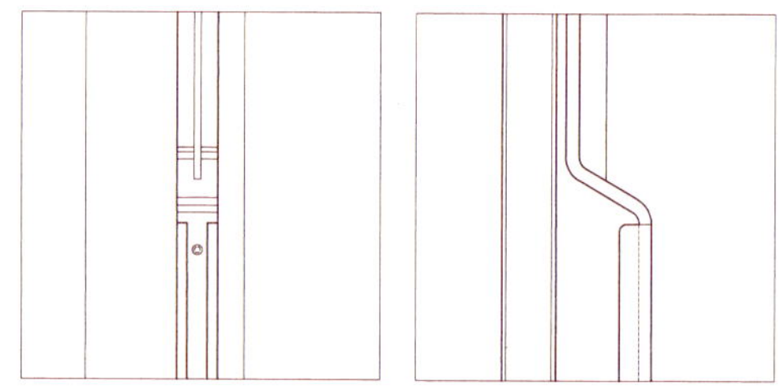

54

"Proclaim Liberty throughout all the Land
unto all the Inhabitants thereof"
Inscription on the Liberty Bell, from Leviticus XXV, v.10, The Bible
The Liberty Bell is a symbol of the American Revolution. It is a symbol of liberties gained and a reminder of liberties denied.
It is a relic of the nation's beginning.
It has inspired and challenged visitors, especially in times of crisis.
Its outline, familiar throughout the world, conveys the idea of the continuing expansion of liberty to new peoples and into new aspects of life.
Irreparably Cracked

56 Exhibit hall facing north   57 Exhibit hall facing south   58 Interactive exhibit panel

57

58

"This venerable relic of the Revolution…
irreparably cracked…"

59

59 Exhibit panels 60 Exhibit hall facing south

60

01 Exhibit panels 02 One bay of the exhibit hall

61

"The Bell rings and I must go
among the Grave ones, and talk Politiks."
"This venerable relic of the Revolution...
irreparably cracked..."

"In Penn's Fair City, calm and grave
Hangs the old Bell which rings no more
For Freedom sleeps on Freedom's Shore."

63

63 Exhibit hall viewed from foreign visitor area 64, 65 Views of the foreign visitor area

65

66 Engraved granite sign on serpentine wall 67 Serpentine wall 68 Serpentine wall detailing

66

67

69

70

71

73

74

75

76

77

The World's Symbol for

78 Exhibit hall facing north   79, 80 Exhibit hall facing south   81 Exhibit panel elevation

82 Elevation of exhibit panel 83 Plan of exhibit panel 84 One bay of the exhibit hall

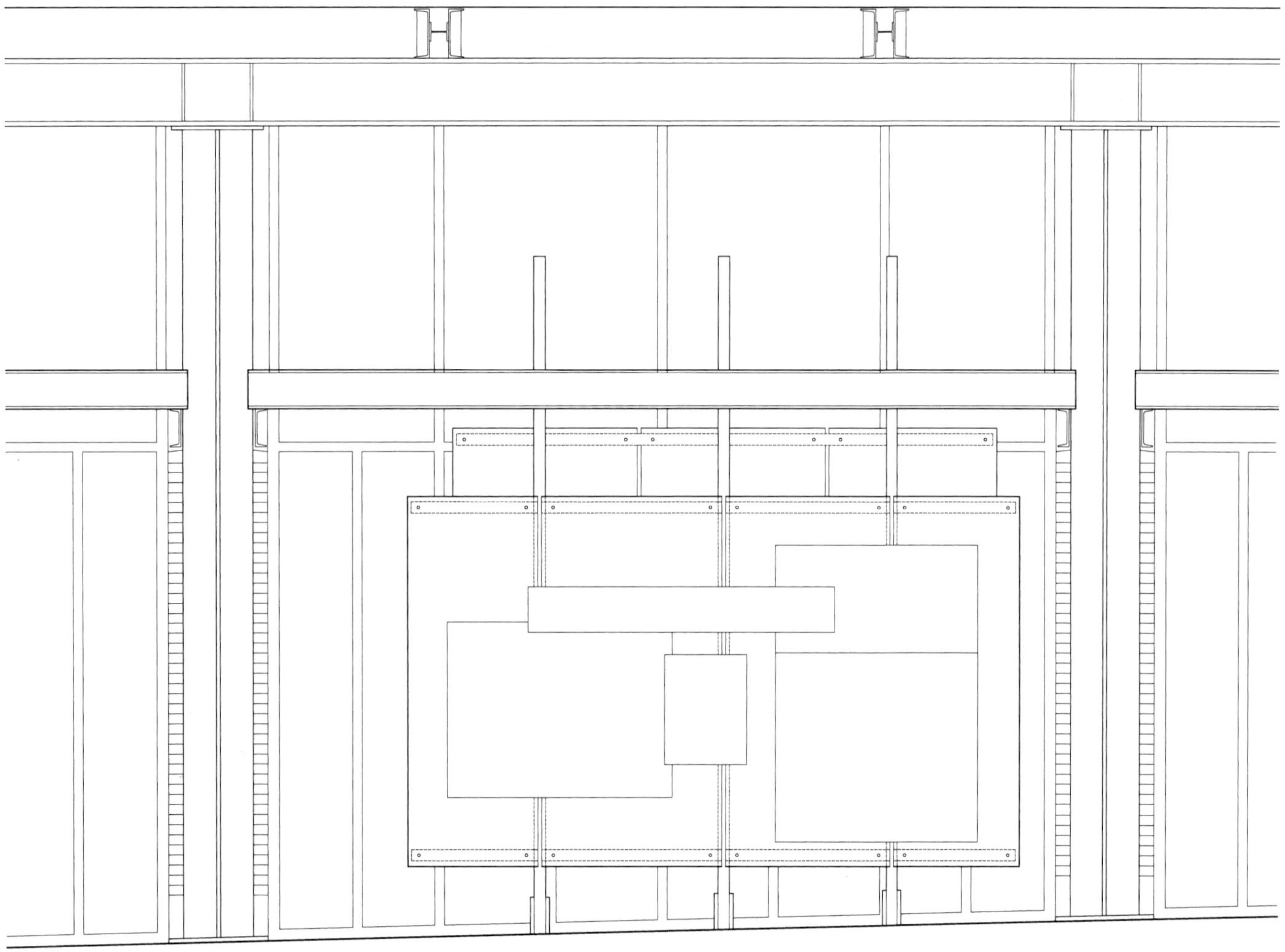

82

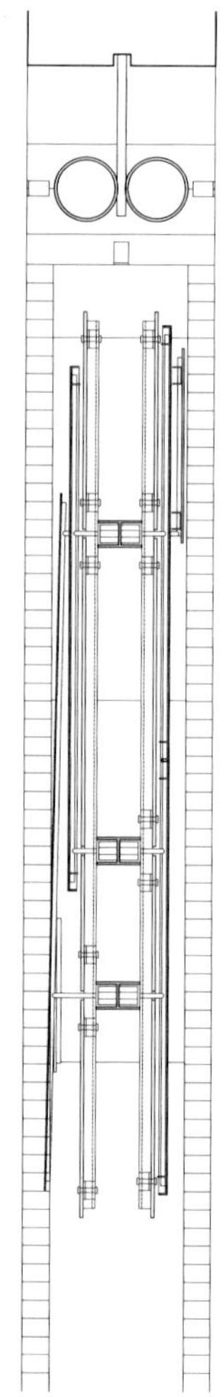

83

The Liberty Bell is "a very significant symbol for the entire democratic world."
Nelson Mandela, Philadelphia Inquirer, July 4, 1993.

85

85 Exhibit panels and armatures with light baffle above

86 Details of light baffles in exhibit hall

87 Light baffle, exhibit panels, and armatures 88 Light baffle and ceiling within exhibit hall 89 Exhibit panel details

88

89

90

90 View of brick piers and steel columns along east wall facing south 91 Plan detail at steel column/brick pier 92 Exhibit panels 93 Brick piers and steel columns along east wall facing north

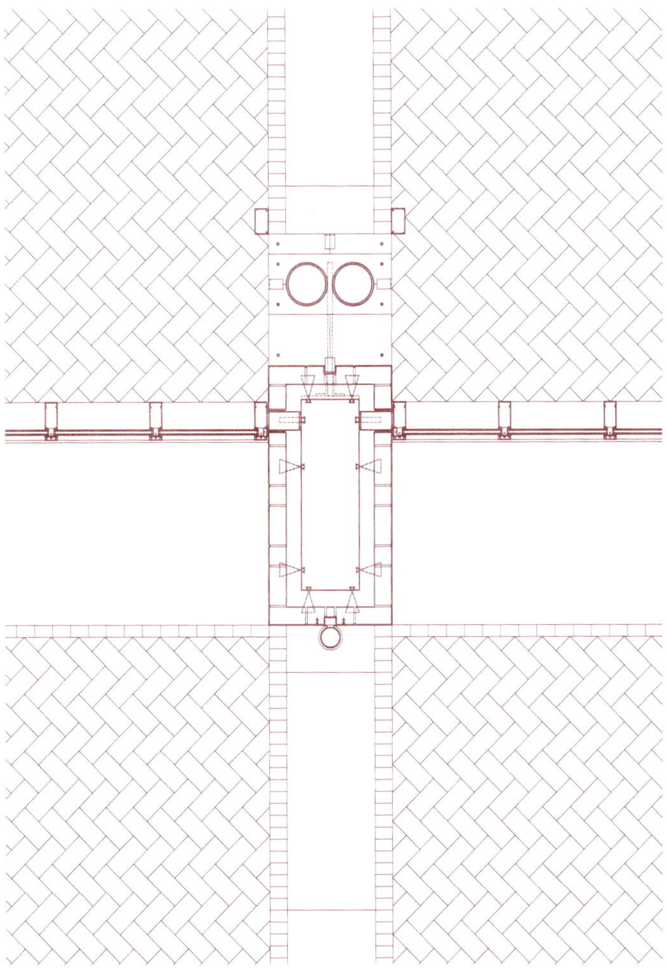
91

92

93

94 Detail of exhibit panel and glass curtain wall 95 View through glass curtain wall at entrance

95

96

97

96–98 Exhibit panel details

98

99, 100 Exhibit panel details

100

101 Exhibit hall facing north from transition area

102 Exhibit panels and cases

102

103 South wall of multi-purpose room   104 Serpentine wall and wood wall   105 Paving detail as alleyway passes through building   106 Alleyway passing through the building facing west

104

105

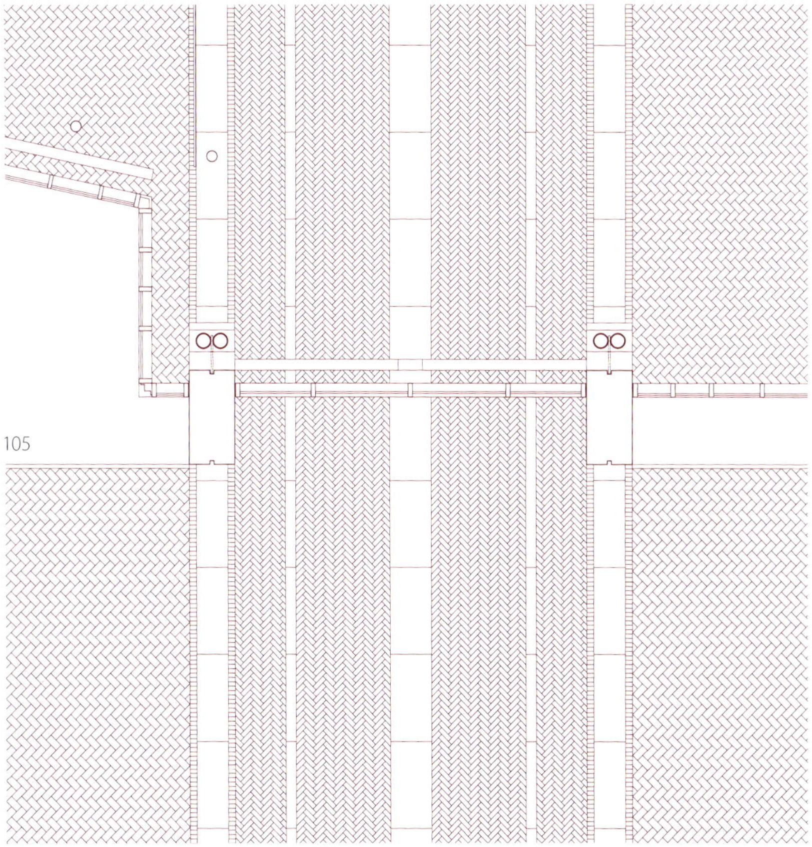

106

107 Transition area columns and wall 108 Exhibit hall from the transition area facing north

109 Translucent glass wall at transition area 110 – 113 Various interior views

114 Looking through gap in translucent glass wall

115 Transition area columns facing Bell Chamber

116 Bell Chamber 117 - 119 Views facing the Bell Chamber

117

118

119

120 Marble wall in Bell Chamber

121 Liberty Bell and bell support post

122 Bell Chamber

120

121

123

123 Bell Chamber facing Independence Hall 124 Reflected ceiling plan of Bell Chamber 125 Visitors examining the Liberty Bell

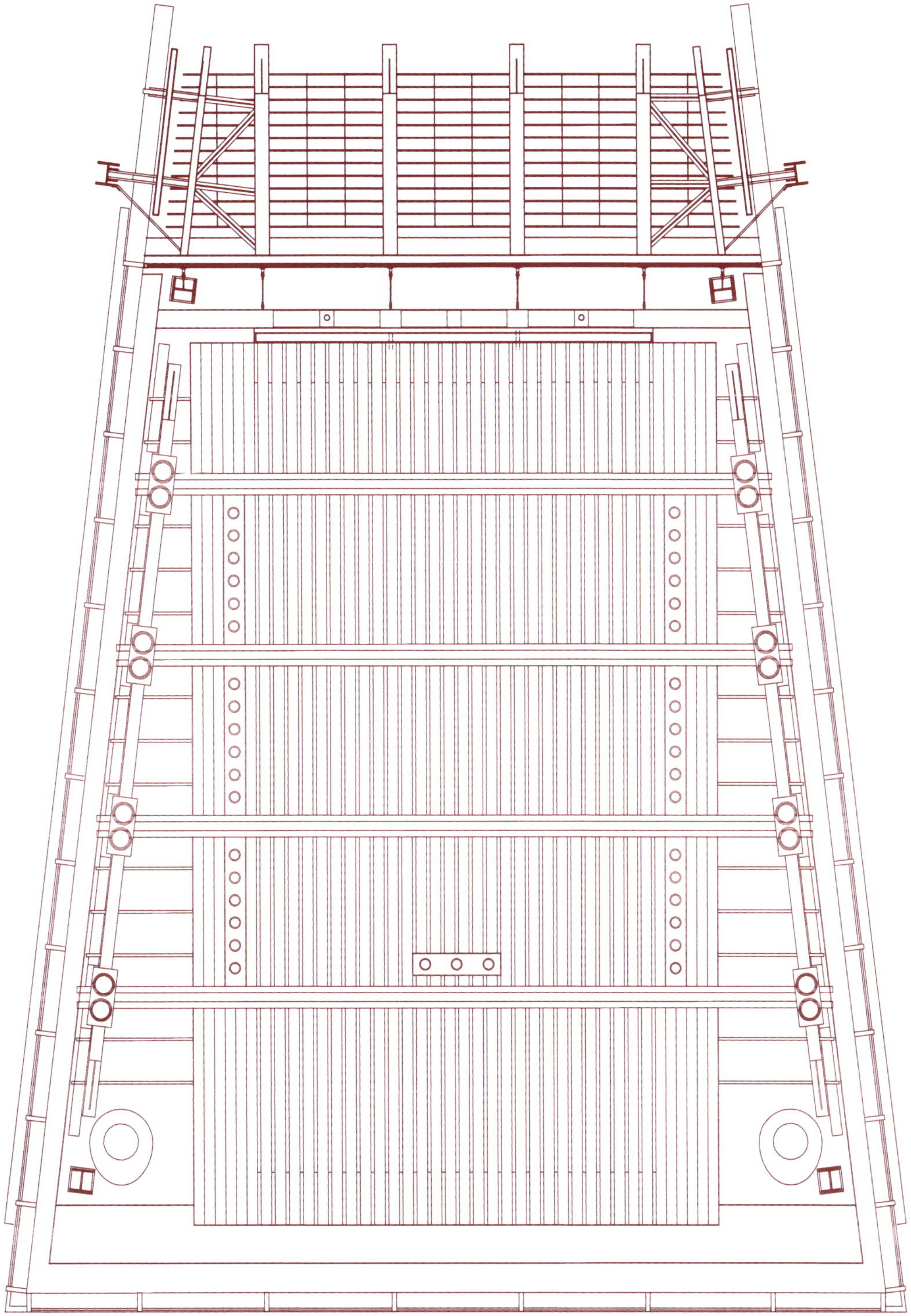

126

127

126 South glass wall of Bell Chamber 127 Ceiling of Bell Chamber 128 Light baffle fins in Bell Chamber 129 Bell Chamber

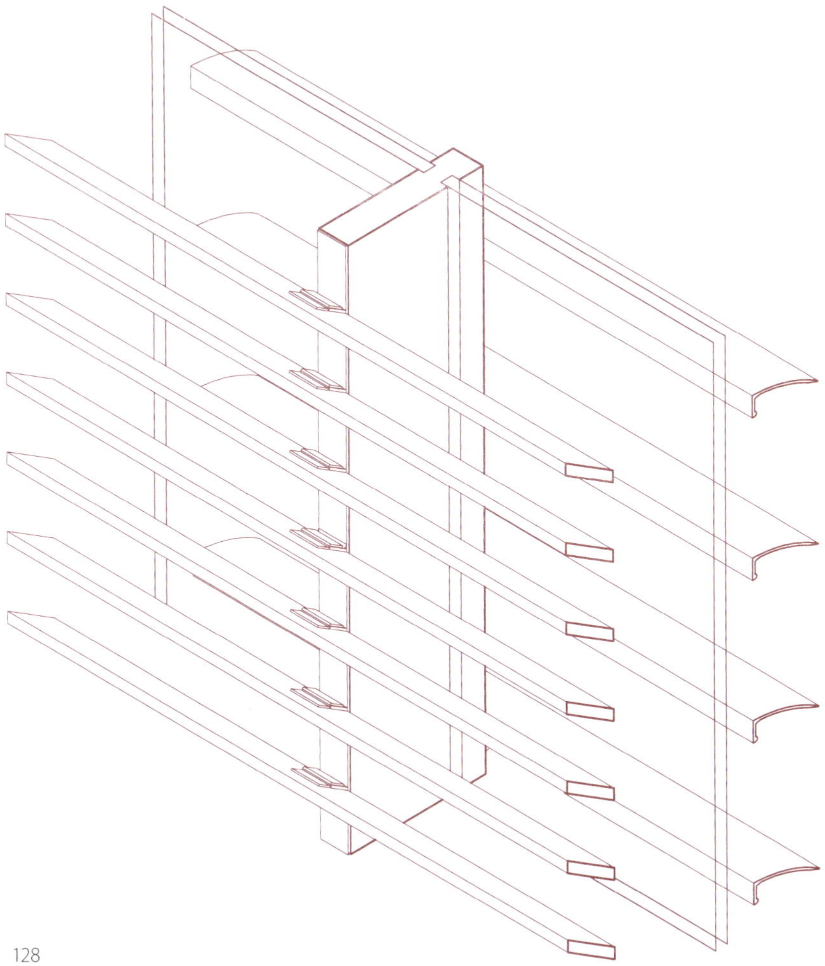
128

129

130

131

133

133, 134 Visitors in Bell Chamber

134

135, 136 Visitors in Bell Chamber

136

137

139

139 - 141 Details of south glass wall of Bell Chamber

142

142 Independence Hall and light baffles of Bell Chamber 143, 144 Visitors leaving Liberty Bell Center along serpentine wall

143

144

145

145 Building exit with Bell Chamber to the right

146 Partial west elevation of perimeter wall

147 Independence Hall beyond the Bell Chamber

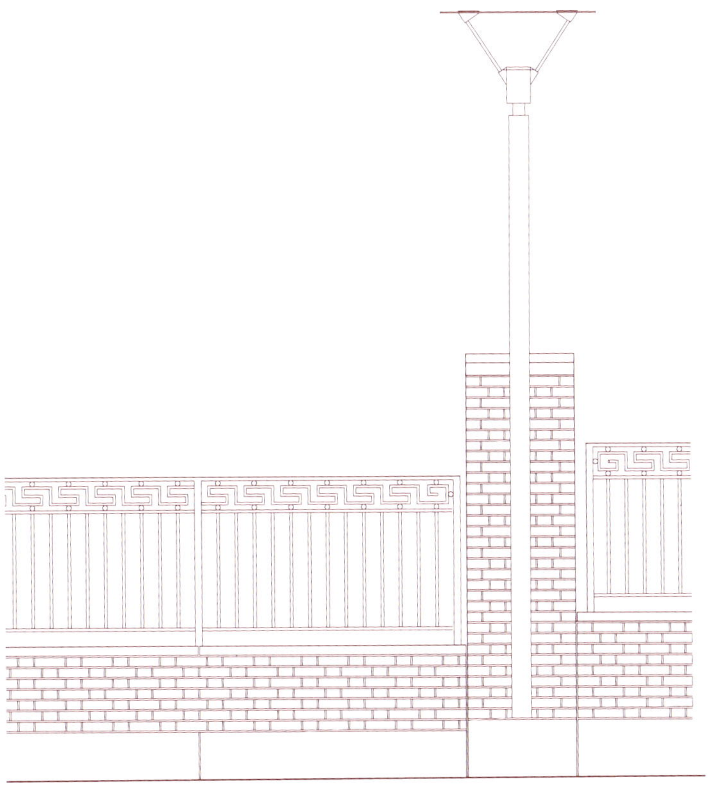

147

148, 149 Transition area roof and wall

150 Northwest corner of Bell Chamber

149

150

151 West side of Bell Chamber 152 Alleyway passing through the building 153 Shadows of trellis on west side of building

Appe

endix

Appendix

Project Data

Building Area	14,000 square feet
Date of Design	1998-2001
Date of Completion	October 2003
Owner	National Park Service Independence National Historical Park
Project Team	Bernard Cywinski, FAIA, Principal-in-Charge Kenneth Mitchell, AIA, Project Manager Jeff Lew, AIA, Project Architect Wolfram Arendt, RA Monica Barton, AIA Joseph Bridy, AIA Anthony Pregiato Erin Roark, RA
Project Managers	Hill International Incorporated
General Contractor	Daniel J. Keating Company
Exhibit Contractor	Maltbie Incorporated

Project Consultants

Acoustical Engineer	Robert A. Hansen Associates, Inc.
Blast Mitigation Design	Hinman Consulting Engineers, Inc.
Building Security	Applied Research Associates, Inc.
Civil Engineer	Barton & Martin Engineers
Electrical Engineer	BR+A Engineers, Inc.
Exhibit Design	Ueland Junker McCauley Nicholson
Landscape Architect	Olin Partnership
Lighting Design	Grenald Waldron Associates
Mechanical Engineer	BR+A Engineers, Inc.
Structural Engineer	CVM Engineers

Photography and Image Credits

Liberty Bell Center and its Double

1. Bohlin Cywinski Jackson, Liberty Bell Pavilion, 1999.
2. Peter Aaron/Esto, Interior view of the Bell Chamber.
3. Sebastiano Serlio (1474-1554), "Tragic Scene," *Architettura*, 1535-1551.
4. Giuseppe Galli-Bibiena (1696-1757), *Architettura, e prospettive*, 1740.
5. Bernard Cywinski, "Preliminary Sketch of Liberty Bell Center," October 24, 1998, Bohlin Cywinski Jackson.
6. Bernard Cywinski, "Sketch showing the influence of the street grid on plan of building," undated, Bohlin Cywinski Jackson.
7. Nic Lehoux Photography, Alleyway passing through the building.
8. Bernard Cywinski and Peter Bohlin, "Preliminary Sketches of Liberty Bell Chamber," undated, Bohlin Cywinski Jackson.
9. Bernard Cywinski, Liberty Bell, Independence Hall and Mr. el-Khoury.
10. Nic Lehoux Photography, Exterior view of Liberty Bell Center.
11. Peter Aaron/Esto, Interior stone wall detail.

What Becomes a Democracy's Monuments Most?

12. The Historical Society of Pennsylvania (HSP), "Portraiture of the City of Philadelphia," [Of 610 1683], Thomas Holmes.
13. Library of Congress, "This plan of the city of Philadelphia and its environs (shewing the improved parts) is dedicated to the mayor, aldermen, the citizens thereof, by their most obedient servant, John Hills, surveyor and draughtsmen, May 30, 1796. Engraved by John Cooke. Philadelphia, John Hills, 1797." LC Call Number: G3824.P5 1796. H Vault (G & M).
14. The Athenaeum of Philadelphia, Perspective, Paul Cret, Catalogue Number: CRET.001.001.
15. PM Photo & Computer Services, Pennsylvania Building, Court of States, 1939 New York World's Fair Photo Collection.
16. Temple University Libraries, Urban Archives, Philadelphia Pennsylvania. "Judge Edwin O. Lewis, president of Independence Hall Association & Edward M. Biddle, treasurer of the association, October 12, 1945." Reviewing a model of Independence Mall.
17. Independence Park Plan. Roy Larson, Source: Pamphlet "Independence Hall and Adjacent Buildings, A plan for their Preservation and the Improvement of their Surroundings (Philadelphia: Fairmount Park Association in collaboration with the Independence Hall Association, 1944).
18. Alois K. Strobl, Illustration from "Design of Cities" by Edmund Bacon, © 1967, 1974 by Edmund N. Bacon. Used by permission of Penguin, a division of Penguin Group (USA) Inc.
19. Louis I. Kahn, "Philadelphia City Planning: Traffic Studies, Philadelphia, PA". Unbuilt, 1951-53. © 1977 Louis I. Kahn Collection, University of Pennsylvania and Pennsylvania Historical and Museum Commission.
20. Mark Cohn, Photograph, "Benjamin Franklin Court," Reproduced with permission from Venturi, Scott Brown and Associates, Inc.
21. Bernard Cywinski, "Independence National Historical Park Master Plan, Concept Plan With Alleyways," 1997, Bohlin Cywinski Jackson.
22. Nic Lehoux Photography, Alleyway passing through building.
23. Bernard Cywinski, "Liberty Bell Center Exhibit Hall Sketch," January 12, 1999, Bohlin Cywinski Jackson.
24. Bernard Cywinski, "Influence of street grid on plan of the building," undated, Bohlin Cywinski Jackson.
25. Peter Aaron/Esto, Interior view of the Bell Chamber.

Giving Form to a Creation Story — The Remaking of Independence Mall

26. John Lewis Krimmel, "Election Scene, State House in Philadelphia," 1815. Courtesy, Winterthur Museum.
27. Independence Hall (mid 1900s). Reproduced with permission from Independence National Historical Park.
28. Independence Hall and Independence Mall (1970s). Reproduced with permission from Independence National Historical Park.
29. Independence Hall and Independence Mall, 1997. Reproduced with permission from Olin Partnership.
30. Olin Partnership, "Independence National Historical Park in the Context of the City of Philadelphia," undated. Reproduced with permission from Olin Partnership.
31. Edward Hicks, "Peaceable Kingdom," 1844-46. Courtesy, Abby Aldrich Rockefeller Folk Art Museum, Colonial Williamsburg Foundation.
32. Independence Hall, 1997. Reproduced with permission from Olin Partnership.
33. Bernard Cywinski, "Nolli Plan of Former Park," undated, Bohlin Cywinski Jackson.
34. Independence Hall Tower, 1998. Bohlin Cywinski Jackson.
35. Bernard Cywinski, "Independence National Historical Park Master Plan, Concept Plan With 100 Foot Grid," 1997, Bohlin Cywinski Jackson.
36. Bernard Cywinski, "Independence National Historical Park Master Plan, Concept Plan With Alleyways," 1997, Bohlin Cywinski Jackson.
37. Bernard Cywinski, "Independence National Historical Park Master Plan, Concept Plan With Circulation and Building Placement Diagrams," 1997, Bohlin Cywinski Jackson.
38. Restored Historic Philadelphia Alley, 1997. Reproduced with permission from Olin Partnership.
39. Bernard Cywinski, "Sketch of Brick Pier Arborway," June 1998, Bohlin Cywinski Jackson.
40. Bernard Cywinski, "Sketch of Brick Pier Arborway," July 4, 1998, Bohlin Cywinski Jackson.
41. Bernard Cywinski, "Sketch of Brick Pier Arborway," June 1998, Bohlin Cywinski Jackson.
42. Bernard Cywinski, "Sketch of Brick Pier Arborway," June 1998, Bohlin Cywinski Jackson.
43. Bernard Cywinski, "Sketch of Brick Pier Arborway," June 1998, Bohlin Cywinski Jackson.
44. Bernard Cywinski, "Sketch of Brick Pier Arborway," June 1998, Bohlin Cywinski Jackson.
45. Bernard Cywinski, "Independence National Historical Park Master Plan, Concept Plan With Building Block Diagrams," 1997, Bohlin Cywinski Jackson.
46. Bernard Cywinski, "Section Through Block 2 Parking Garage and Future Visitor Center," 1997, Bohlin Cywinski Jackson.
47. Bohlin Cywinski Jackson, drawing of Block 1 Building Placement Diagram, from "Independence National Historical Park, Independence Mall Master Plan and Design Guidelines," July 1998.
48. Bohlin Cywinski Jackson, drawing of Block 2 Building Placement Diagram, from "Independence National Historical Park, Independence Mall Master Plan and Design Guidelines," July 1998.
49. Bohlin Cywinski Jackson, drawing of Block 3 Building Placement Diagram, from "Independence National Historical Park, Independence Mall Master Plan and Design Guidelines," July 1998.

50. Olin Partnership, drawing of Independence Mall Master Plan, from "Independence National Historical Park, Independence Mall Master Plan and Design Guidelines," July 1998. Reproduced with permission from Olin Partnership.
51. Laurie Olin, View From the National Constitution Center Toward Independence Hall, from "Independence National Historical Park, Independence Mall Master Plan and Design Guidelines," July 1998. Reproduced with permission from Olin Partnership.
52. Olin Partnership, wireframe drawing from "Independence National Historical Park, Independence Mall Master Plan and Design Guidelines," July 1998. Reproduced with permission from Olin Partnership.
53. Laurie Olin, View of Block 2 Café on Independence Mall, from "Independence National Historical Park, Independence Mall Master Plan and Design Guidelines," July 1998. Reproduced with permission from Olin Partnership.
54. Laurie Olin, View From the New Visitor Center Toward Independence Hall, from "Independence National Historical Park, Independence Mall Master Plan and Design Guidelines," July 1998. Reproduced with permission from Olin Partnership.
55. Laurie Olin, View From Inside Future Liberty Bell Center, from "Independence National Historical Park, Independence Mall Master Plan and Design Guidelines," July 1998. Reproduced with permission from Olin Partnership.
56. Laurie Olin, View of Independence Mall From Independence Hall, from "Independence National Historical Park, Independence Mall Master Plan and Design Guidelines," July 1998. Reproduced with permission from Olin Partnership.
57. Bernard Cywinski, Laurie Olin, Henry Cobb, and Michael McKinnell, June 23, 1999. Reproduced with permission from Olin Partnership.
58. Master Plan Team Meeting, June 23, 1999. Reproduced with permission from Olin Partnership.
59. Master Plan Team Meeting, February 5, 1999. Reproduced with permission from Olin Partnership.
60. Master Plan Team Meeting, February 5, 1999. Reproduced with permission from Olin Partnership.
61. Master Plan Team Meeting, February 5, 1999. Reproduced with permission from Olin Partnership.
62. Revised Master Plan Drawing Based on Actual Designs for New Buildings. Reproduced with permission from Olin Partnership.

Liberty Bell Center: Architecture and Symbol

63. Bernard Cywinski and Laurie Olin, Sketch, January 28, 1999, Bohlin Cywinski Jackson.
64. Bernard Cywinski, "Architecture / Exhibit Interface," February 1, 1999, Bohlin Cywinski Jackson.
65. Cover, "General Management Plan," Independence National Historical Park.
66. Bernard Cywinski, "View Shed Comparison Sketch," undated, Bohlin Cywinski Jackson.
67. Bernard Cywinski, "Independence National Historical Park Master Plan, Concept Plan With Circulation and Building Placement Diagrams," 1997, Bohlin Cywinski Jackson.
68. Liberty Bell Pavilion by Mitchell/Giurgola Associates, 1976. Reproduced with permission from Independence National Historical Park.
69. Liberty Bell Close-up. Reproduced with permission from Independence National Historical Park.
70. Master Plan Detail of Block 1. Reproduced with permission from Olin Partnership.

71. Independence Hall, 1998. Reproduced with permission from Olin Partnership.
72. Bernard Cywinski, "Studies of the Bell Chamber," April 19, 1999, Bohlin Cywinski Jackson.
73. Olin Partnership, drawing of Independence Mall and City Plan. Reproduced with permission from Olin Partnership.
74. Restored Historic Philadelphia Alley, 1997. Reproduced with permission from Olin Partnership.
75. Bernard Cywinski, "Alleys Define Exhibit Space," undated, Bohlin Cywinski Jackson.
76. Bernard Cywinski, "Trellis and Brick Pier Study," November 16, 1998, Bohlin Cywinski Jackson.
77. Bernard Cywinski, "Trellis and Brick Pier Study," November 15, 1998, Bohlin Cywinski Jackson.
78. Bernard Cywinski, "Trellis and Brick Pier Study," June 1998, Bohlin Cywinski Jackson.
79. Jeffrey Totaro, Arborway model detail.
80. William Russell Birch, "New Market, in South Second Street," 1799. Courtesy of S. Robert Teitelman.
81. William Russell Birch, "High Street, From the Country Market-place Philadelphia," 1799. Courtesy of S. Robert Teitelman.
82. Bernard Cywinski, "Exhibit Hall Sketch," undated, Bohlin Cywinski Jackson.
83. Bernard Cywinski, "Mediums for Exhibit Story-Telling," undated, Bohlin Cywinski Jackson.
84. Bernard Cywinski, "Circulation Diagrams," January 15, 1999, Bohlin Cywinski Jackson.
85. Bernard Cywinski, "Plan Sketches," March 1, 1999, Bohlin Cywinski Jackson.
86. Peter Aaron/Esto, Interior stone wall detail.
87. Peter Aaron/Esto, Interior stone wall detail.
88. Bernard Cywinski, "Flow Diagram fast lane / slow lane," undated, Bohlin Cywinski Jackson.
89. Bohlin Cywinski Jackson, Independence Hall Corner Detail.
90. Bohlin Cywinski Jackson, Liberty Bell Center under construction, October 9, 2002.
91. Bernard Cywinski, Building section, Bohlin Cywinski Jackson.
92. Peter Aaron/Esto, Bell Chamber from the exterior.
93. Bernard Cywinski, "Exhibit Hall Sketch," undated, Bohlin Cywinski Jackson.
94. Bernard Cywinski, "Bell Chamber Sketch," undated, Bohlin Cywinski Jackson.
95. Bohlin Cywinski Jackson, Exploded axonometric drawing of Bell Chamber.
96. Bohlin Cywinski Jackson, Liberty Bell Center building section with sight line from Liberty Bell to the top of Independence Hall tower.
97. Nic Lehoux Photography, Visitors in the Bell Chamber.
98. Bernard Cywinski, "Bell Chamber Sketch," undated, Bohlin Cywinski Jackson.

Lines Section

All sketches, diagrams, presentation drawings, and construction documents by Bohlin Cywinski Jackson with the exception of the drawings on pages 114 and 115, which were prepared by Ueland Junker McCauley Nicholson.

Images Section

Peter Aaron/Esto
Exterior Image Numbers: 8 – 10, 15, 17 – 19, 34, 37, 38, 44, 49, 51
Interior Image Numbers: 52, 62 – 64, 66 – 68, 78 – 81, 84, 107, 108, 123, 137, 138, 145, 147

Bohlin Cywinski Jackson
Construction Image Numbers: 1 – 79
Views from Independence Hall tower: 1 – 12
Models Image Numbers: 7 – 17 (Erin Roark)
Exterior Image Number: 29 (W. Dan Haden III)

Nic Lehoux Photography
Exterior Image Numbers: 1 - 3, 5, 7, 16, 20, 23 – 26, 28, 30, 31, 33, 36, 39, 42, 43, 46 – 48, 50
Interior Image Numbers: 53, 55 – 61, 65, 69 – 77, 87 – 89, 92 – 96, 99 – 104, 106, 109 – 119, 125, 126, 129 – 136, 139, 140, 142 – 144, 148 – 153, last two photographs of section

Jeffrey Totaro
Models Image Numbers: 18 – 21, 23 – 25

Paul Warchol Photography
Exterior Image Numbers: 6, 13, 14, 40
Interior Image Numbers: 85, 86, 90, 97, 98, 120 – 122, 127, 141

Matt Wargo
Models Image Numbers: 1 – 6, 22

Model Makers
Frank Whittock & Associates, Inc.: Image Numbers 1-6
Bohlin Cywinski Jackson: Image Numbers 7-21 and 23-25 (W. Dan Haden III)

Bohlin Cywinski Jackson (Erin Roark) & Ueland Junker McCauley Nicholson: Image Number 22

General Illustrations

Cover photograph:	Paul Warchol Photography
Half title page:	Liberty Bell close-up. Reproduced with permission from Independence National Historical Park.
Title page:	Peter Aaron/Esto
Contents:	Paul Warchol Photography,
	Bell Section, *Diderot Encyclopedia: the Complete Illustrations, 1762-1777*, Harry N. Abrams, Inc., New York, 1978.
Acknowledgements:	Nic Lehoux Photography
Appendix:	Eastman Kodak Company, X-Ray of the Liberty Bell, October 30,1975. Reproduced with permission from Independence National Historical Park.
Back cover:	Peter Aaron/Esto

Firm Profile

Bohlin Cywinski Jackson was founded in 1965 in Wilkes-Barre, Pennsylvania by Peter Bohlin and Richard Powell. Today the principals are Peter Bohlin, Bernard Cywinski, Jon Jackson, Dan Haden, Frank Grauman, William Loose, Randy Reid, Russell Roberts, Karl Backus, and Gregory Mottola. Additional offices are located in Pittsburgh, Philadelphia, Seattle, and San Francisco.

The practice's work ranges in scale and circumstance from major university, public, and corporate buildings to private homes, large and small. Its architecture is alive to the subtleties of place, both man-made and natural; to the varied natures of people; to the sensibilities of individuals; to the character of institutions; and to the rich possibilities of materials and the means of construction.

Bohlin Cywinski Jackson has received eight national AIA Honor Awards and over 300 regional, national, and international awards for design. In 1994, the practice received the Architecture Firm Award from the American Institute of Architects. The firm's work is published regularly in professional journals and books around the world.

Bohlin Cywinski Jackson
Architecture Planning Interior Design

8 West Market Street, Suite 1200,
Wilkes-Barre, Pennsylvania 18701-1811
Telephone 570 825-8756
Facsimile 570 825-3744

307 Fourth Avenue, Suite 1300,
Pittsburgh, Pennsylvania 15222-2113
Telephone 412 765-3890
Facsimile 412 765-2209

123 South Broad Street, Suite 1370,
Philadelphia, Pennsylvania 19109-1080
Telephone 215 790-5900
Facsimile 215 790-5901

1932 First Avenue, Suite 916,
Seattle, Washington 98101-1052
Telephone 206 256-0862
Facsimile 206 256-0864

49 Geary Street, Suite 300,
San Francisco, California 94108-5729
Telephone 415 989-2100
Facsimile 415 989-2101

www.bcj.com

Book Credits

Book Concept Oscar Riera Ojeda (oscar@oro-editions.com)

Project Coordination Kenneth D. Mitchell, AIA (kmitchell@bcj.com)

Copy Editing N. D. Koster (nd@ndkoster.com)

Graphic Design Oscar Riera Ojeda, Pablo Mandel GDC (pablo@circularstudio.com)

Project Assistance Michael F. Conner (mconner@bcj.com), Irene C. Martin (imartin@bcj.com), Sterling Alexander (salexander@bcj.com)

Photo Research Kenneth D. Mitchell, AIA, Rodolphe el-Khoury, Marika Simms (massim@bcj.com)

Foreign Editions Sales Gordon Goff (gordon@oroeditions.com)

Production Oscar Riera Ojeda, Gordon Goff

Color Separation and Printing ORO *editions* HK

Case Saifu custom died in Japan from Toyo cloth with dutch boards

End Paper Sheets 140 gsm wood-free from NPI, Tokyo

Text 157 gsm Japanese White A matt art paper. An off-line gloss spot varnish was applied to all photographs

Oscar Riera Ojeda is an editor and designer based both in Philadelphia and New York. Born in Buenos Aires, Argentina in 1966, he moved to the United States in 1990. Since that time, he has completed over 100 books, assembling a body of work with publishing houses such as ORO *editions*, Birkhäuser, Byggförlaget, The Monacelli Press, Gustavo Gili, Thames & Hudson, Rizzoli, Whitney Library of Design, Taschen, Page One, Images, Rockport, and Kliczkowski. Oscar Riera Ojeda is the creator of a number of architectural book series, including *Ten Houses*, *Contemporary World Architects*, *The New American House* and *The New American Apartment*, *Architecture in Detail*, as well as *Building Monograph*.

Oscar Riera Ojeda & Associates
Architecture Art Design
143 South 2nd Street, Suite 208
Philadelphia, PA, 19106-3039
Telephone 215 238-1333
Facsimile 215 238-1103
www.oro-associates.com

Copyright

ORO *editions*
Gordon Goff & Oscar Riera Ojeda
Publishers

West Coast
PO Box 150338,
San Rafael, CA 94915
t: 415 456-0789
f: 415 457-3650

East Coast
143 South 2nd Street, Suite 208
Philadelphia, PA 19106-3039
t: 215 238-1333
f: 215 238-1103

www.oroeditions.com
info@oroeditions.com

Library of Congress Catalog
Card Number
ISBN: 0-9746800-4-4
Liberty Bell Center edited by Rodolphe el-Khoury
Printed in China by ORO *editions* HK

Distributed in North America by:
D.A.P / Distributed Art Publishers
155 Sixth Avenue , 2nd Floor
New York, NY 10013
t: 212 627 1999
f: 212 627 9484